our current times, much of the ïnking on how to deal with social ¡sues is dominated by "modern ïlitarians"— the cost accountants, ïentific managers, and M.B.A.s who ïerpret human affairs with supply-ïd-demand logic and balance-sheet ïecision. *American Dilemmas* chal-ïnges this market-processes mindset, ; well as the way in which many of ïose in power study social issues.

As Jonathan H. Turner and David ïusick point out, sociology itself ïallenges the notion that humans re rational and that the broader ïcial world is ruled by market forces. ïere, they analyze how a number of ïcial concerns became critical prob-ïms and why they persist. The book ïrst addresses the structural and ïultural contradictions in advanced ïapitalistic societies, our own in ïarticular. From there the authors ïxplore other vital national and ïlobal topics: the tension between ïemocracy and governance, and ïetween social control and freedom; changes in the American family; education in a credentialed society; wealth and poverty in America; racial, ethnic, and sexual antagonism; problems of urbanization; America's position in the world political and economic order; and ecology and the survival of the human species.

Turner and Musick stress that not only are there no simple or easy solutions to these problems, but often there are no solutions at all. This they attribute to society's demand for "practical solutions"—answers that won't cost money or take too much time, won't change established ways, and won't offend anyone. Solving one set of problems would either create new difficulties or aggravate old ones. And that, the authors contend, is a trade-off most people wouldn't accept.

An original, sophisticated book that delves into complex social issues rather than glossing over them, *American Dilemmas* is a challenging text perfect for graduate or upper-level undergraduate courses.

Jonathan H. Turner is Professor of Sociology at the University of California, Riverside. He is the author of more than a dozen books in sociology, including *Societal Stratification: A Theoretical Analysis,* published by Columbia University Press.

David Musick is Associate Professor of Sociology at the University of Northern Colorado. He is coauthor (with Jonathan H. Turner and Royce Singleton, Jr.) of *Oppression: A Socio-History of Black/White Relations.*

American Dilemmas

American Dilemmas

A SOCIOLOGICAL INTERPRETATION
OF ENDURING SOCIAL ISSUES

**Jonathan H. Turner
and David Musick**

**Columbia University Press
New York   1985**

91-1855

Columbia University Press
New York   Guildford, Surrey
Copyright © 1985 Columbia University Press
All rights reserved
Printed in the United States of America

Library of Congress Cataloging in Publication Data

Turner, Jonathan H.
  American dilemmas.

  Bibliography: p.
  Includes index.
  1. United States—Social conditions—1980–
I. Musick, David. II. Title.
HN59.2.T87   1985   306'.0973   84-11397
ISBN 0-231-05956-6 (alk. paper)
ISBN 0-231-05957-4 (pbk.)

To Patricia, Donna, Jon, and Marie—
our children who, now that they are adults,
will have to confront these dilemmas for
themselves.

Contents

Preface

W̲e live in conservative times. We have watched the resurrection of "rational man" in a marketeering world of "supply and demand." Our problems have, once again, been dumped at the feet of Adam Smith. And the modern utilitarians—the cost accountants, scientific managers, budget analysts, Masters of Business Administration—currently dominate our thinking about how to deal with social issues.

This book is intended to challenge the way social issues and problems are analyzed by many of those in power. Indeed, all of sociology challenges the view that humans are rational and that the broader social world is governed by market processes. The general thrust of our analysis is that both the definition and the substance of social issues are lodged in cultural and social forces. This thrust draws from and builds upon the senior author's earlier works, *Social Problems in America* and *American Society: Problems of Structure;* and like these works, it stresses that there are no simple or easy solutions to problems. In fact, there are often no solutions, because most people would not accept the trade-off between dealing with one problem and activating new ones, or aggravating other long-standing problems.

Our goal then is to document, sociologically, how and why many social issues come to pose a dilemma. To address a problematic issue almost always involves trade-offs. The public, politicians, and decision-makers seek "practical solutions" to problems—which is their way of demanding that a solution to a problem not step on the toes of vested interests, not change established ways, not cost money, not take too much time, not offend anyone, and so on. Sociologists cannot promise these things because they are rarely possible. As a result, we are rarely asked to address social issues, because we tell powerful and important people, as well as the public, what they do not want to hear. Sociological analyses often appear "radical" because they see problematic conditions as the result of enduring and contradictory social and cultural forces and because we inevitably must conclude that to eliminate a problem requires major changes in social organization.

That is why we write books like this one. We have little else to do with our analyses. But perhaps, if sociologists keep presenting the message, it will get through. It is to this end that we dedicate these pages.

Jonathan H. Turner
Laguna Beach, California

David Musick
Greeley, Colorado

Acknowledgments

We wish to thank the Academic Senate of the University of California at Riverside for financial support of this project. The senior author also wishes to thank the Senate for its generous support on many other writing projects over the last fifteen years.

We are grateful for the support provided by the Graduate School, University of Northern Colorado. The excellent work of Karen Mitchell at Columbia University Press made this a better book.

American Dilemmas

Chapter 1

The Cultural
and Organizational Basis
of Human Dilemmas

Dilemmas in Human Affairs

Human society is a mixed blessing. Without society, we cannot live and prosper; with it we are constrained and restricted, and at times, abused, exploited, and annihilated. This contradiction between social organization and the individual is the underlying theme for much literature, art, and philosophy. And it is at the core of what makes sociology an interesting enterprise. Indeed, all early sociologists pondered this issue, wondering how to create patterns of social organization that promoted individual fulfillment and gratification. Though they had little else in common, Auguste Comte, Herbert Spencer, Karl Marx, Max Weber, and Emile Durkheim[1]—sociology's first family, as it were—all saw existing social arrangements as seriously flawed and all sought to develop new arrangements which, depending on the scholar, lessened such states as anomie, alienation, exploitation, inequality, restrictions on personal liberties, dehumanization, and other ills propagated on individuals by the society of the time.

Some, such as Max Weber, were pessimistic about the prospects for the individual, who was seen as trapped in the "iron cage"[2] of rational-legal, bureaucratic authority. Others, like Karl Marx,[3] were, to be blunt, overoptimistic in believing that a new stage in history had arrived in which the dynamics of power, inequality, alienation, and exploitation could be suspended with communism. Still others, such as Emile Durkheim,[4] were worried and concerned, advocating without complete confidence a program for increasing people's sense of involvement in and commitment to complex social orders. While these scholars and their intellectual successors typically overstated their case, they all have given us great insight into how societies operate and how *properties of social organization* produce certain effects on individuals.

It is in this tradition that we are writing this book, but unlike our intellectual forefathers and many of our contemporaries, we will hypothesize no "solution" to the ills of society. Indeed, one of our themes is that there are no ultimate solutions. We need not retreat into a depressing existentialism to make this point; rather, it follows from some very simple considerations. First, what is a social ill, pathology, or problem is a matter of social definition. And people carry with them different world views, orientations, and perspectives, and hence, define conditions differently. For example, what is, a deplorable state of affairs to a Marxist is often highly desirable to an embattled capitalist or "captain of industry." Second, societies are complex wholes revealing webs of connections. Making a conscious effort to resolve one problem often aggravates others, creates new ones, or rekindles forgotten ones. For instance, pursuing strict enforcement of drug and gambling prohibitions has created vast illegal marketplaces which has led to the emergence, expansion, and growing power of organized crime. Third, complex social structures often reveal contradictory dynamics. That is, they operate with built-in contradictions that create tensions, conflicts, and changes which are defined by some as a "problem." For example, a capitalist economic system is founded upon relatively free and competitive markets in which profit-seeking economic units compete for shares of the market. Such a system, as Marx was the first to appreciate fully,[5] is self-transforming because as some profit-making units "win" in the competition with others, they are in a position to monopolize the market, to reduce competition, and to set prices. The "solution" to this inevitable dynamic of capitalism is for government to enter the once-free market and regulate it—a situation which contradicts the initial form of capitalism and represents a problem for those who want to return to unbridled laissez-faire.

Thus, in trying to examine social controversies in any society, we are confronted with cultural conflicts over what is problematic. Complex social structures reveal so many interconnections and contradictory dynamics that solutions inevitably become defined as problems by some. In attempting to define and deal with social problems, then, we are typically placed between the horns of a dilemma.

The existence of "dilemmas" is, itself, problematic for Americans. We like to believe that there is *a* solution to a problem. With just a little bit of Yankee knowhow, the problem can be eliminated. But as Americans are becoming more aware, the natural world is not so easily subdued to our will. The use of pesticides to resolve insect problems in agriculture and in community health programs has had the ironical result of intensifying the problem by creating superbugs which are resistant to the pesticides. And it has resulted in widespread disruption of ecological balances, creating a new complex of serious problems. The social world is no more readily brought to its knees by social technologies—despite the guarded optimism of an Emile Durkheim, the frantic optimism of a Karl Marx, or the naïve assertions of contemporary politicians, moral entrepreneurs, social commentators, and ordinary citizens. Matters which are seen as problems by some—inflation, governmental growth, economic stagnation, consumer manipulation, high divorce rates, the plight of the elderly, racial conflict, worker alienation, overcrowding, pollution, rising crime, falling test scores for students, world economic competition, corrupt and ineffective politicians, poverty, privilege, and so on—are increasingly seen to defy easy solutions. Our goal in this book is to indicate why this is so.

The Dynamics of Societal Organization

We must begin to analyze American dilemmas by presenting an overarching view of how a complex industrial society operates. For it is in the operative dynamics of the society that the dilemmas of most concern to Americans reside. From our viewpoint, a society can be conceptualized in terms of its cultural and structural processes. Cultural processes concern the ways in which symbols are organized into values, beliefs, and normative systems that guide people's cognitive and emotional orientations to their environment.[6] Structural processes concern the units of organization that circumscribe where people live and how they behave. Obviously, there is a great deal of interplay between cultural and structural processes, but there are good reasons for recognizing their distinctive qualities. We can appreciate these reasons by reviewing their characteristics in more detail.

Cultural Dynamics

Much of what occurs in a society involves people in concrete settings who confront each other and negotiate their respective courses of conduct.[7] These micro social processes do not, however, occur in a cultural vacuum. People carry with them "orientations" that provide general guidelines for how they see, define, and act in situations. These orientations are complexes of symbols, the most important of which from a sociological viewpoint are (1) values and (2) beliefs.

Value Systems. Values denote people's basic assumptions about good and bad, appropriate and inappropriate.[8]

They are highly abstract in that they are guidelines that are used in many diverse settings. For example, as we will see shortly, Americans value "achievement," which means that in virtually all social situations it is appropriate to strive to do well and to be successful.

When people in a society hold similar values, then they reveal a high degree of consensus over basic premises about what people *should* and *ought* to do. When people's values evidence a consistency and do not contradict each other, then they constitute an integrated system of moral directives. In most societies, and certainly in large and complex ones, consensus is far from perfect; different people operating in varying regions, occupations, social classes, and other structural locations often disagree over some basic values. If disagreements are sufficiently great, then cultural conflict prevails and considerable turmoil is likely to ensue in the society. Moreover, rarely are values completely consistent; there are usually contradictions in what people feel should and ought to be. For example, Americans value individualism, or the appropriateness of "being one's own person," and at the same time we value conformity, or the appropriateness of "getting along" and "fitting in." These moral directives often come into conflict, forcing Americans to deal with a basic contradiction in values.

Figure 1.1 provides one way to visualize these dimensions of values. Societies that evidence high levels of consistency among values and high degrees of consensus among their members over these values would be represented in the upper right corner as culturally integrated. Only relatively small, stable, and isolated societies reveal this pattern; no large-scale industrial system approaches high degrees of integration. Societies where there is low agreement over appropriate values but high degrees of consistency on the respective values of different subpopulations or subcultures are likely to reveal high rates of conflict as people holding different systems of values clash. Societies revealing this extreme, as represented in the upper left portion of figure 1.1, either break apart or evidence massive repression as one moral community uses its power to impose its will on others. A society that reveals high

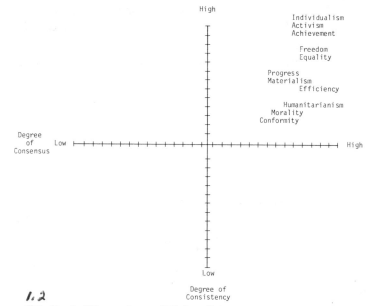

Figure 1.1 Basic Dimensions of Value Systems

consensus over contradictory values, as is represented in the lower right portion of the diagram, places its members in constant cognitive turmoil. And a society with low consensus and consistency is not likely to endure very long, since there is no common morality binding its members together. At times, of course, coercive power can be used to maintain order, but as Edmund Burke noted, "no society is ruled which must be perpetually conquered."

For most societies that endure, value systems must be somewhere in the upper right sector of figure 1.1. There must be at least moderate consensus and consistency in the components of a value system. In American society, we would argue that there are fairly high degrees of consensus over basic values, and only moderate consistency. Thus, many of the definitions of a social problem in America stem not so much from people disagreeing over basic values as from the differential application of varying and somewhat contradictory values. Thus, our cultural dilemmas are often subtle. For example, when confronted with poverty, some emphasize individualism, people's obligation to "make their own way" and "take the consequences of their acts," whereas others invoke equally agreed-upon values of humanitarianism and people's obligation "to help those less fortunate than themselves." Many of the arguments over the "problem of poverty" invoke differing values over which there is widespread agreement. Moreover, as we will come to appreciate, the social structural arrangements—for example, the American welfare system—reflect the contradiction in these values over which there is high consensus.

Belief Systems. For any concrete social setting people hold a series of cognitions. These cognitions tend to be organized into two types of system:[9] (1) evaluative beliefs, which are people's cognitions about what *should* and *ought* to exist in a situation; and (2) empirical beliefs, which are people's cognitions about what *actually does exist* in a situation.

Evaluative beliefs tend to reflect the way in which abstract cultural values are applied to a concrete situation— work, family, politics, recreation, community, school, and other major spheres of activity in a society. Empirical beliefs are greatly influenced by evaluative beliefs, and as a result, people's beliefs about what does exist are often highly inaccurate. For example, working Americans hold the evaluative belief that people should work for their income; and this evaluation causes a distorted perception of welfare recipients as "lazy," "not trying to find work." In actual fact, these perceptions are inaccurate, but the power of evaluative beliefs to distort people's perceptions of reality is great.

One of the principal dynamics in a society revolves around how values as they influence evaluative beliefs operate to distort empirical beliefs. The process of defining what is problematic and what should be done about a problem is greatly circumscribed by inaccurate beliefs. Thus, programs to deal with a problem can simply pander to inaccurate prejudices of decision-makers and the general population, or they can address the problem more realistically and thereby confront a powerful obstacle in people's biased beliefs. In either case, discovering the sources of a problem and developing an approach that confronts the realities become difficult.

These complications are compounded by the fact that in terms of the dimensions presented in figure 1.1, there is much less consensus in beliefs than in values. In complex societies where people perform many diverse roles, individuals' experiences vary widely,[10] and as a result, the formation of empirical beliefs often lowers consensus, even though agreed-upon evaluative beliefs and values may set limits on the formation of conflicting empirical beliefs. Conversely, people's unique experiences as they influence empirical beliefs lower the degree of consensus over evaluative beliefs, although to a lesser degree. For as individuals apply core values to concrete settings, their beliefs as to how things are do have some influence on their beliefs as to how things should be, so that their application of values to situations reveals less consensus than would be the case if everyone had similar experiences. For example, someone who works full time for a high wage will have experiences that differ from those of another person who is sporadically unemployed. Even though they may share the same general values, their empirical beliefs, as shaped by their respective work experience, will decrease their agreement over evaluative beliefs about work and welfare.

These same dynamics operate to lower the consistency within and between empirical and evaluative beliefs. Empirical beliefs are often highly contradictory, since people's actual experiences can be codified into a set of cognitions that can contradict their own more evaluative beliefs (since the latter are greatly influenced by less easily altered core values). Moreover, empirical beliefs that are codified from real-life experiences will often conflict with other empirical beliefs that are formulated more by reference to values and evaluative beliefs than to real experience. For example, a layed-off automobile worker who is collecting unemployment insurance can often hold anti-welfare beliefs about "those lazy welfare cheaters who, if they really wanted to, could find work," because his evaluative beliefs operate to distort his perceptions about "others out there" who are different from those layed off through "no fault of their own." Thus, people in any complex society live with contradictions in their beliefs. They mentally segregate those that are inconsistent and invoke them in ways that minimize their contradictory nature. Yet, when the population of individuals holding contradictory beliefs is our focus, these inconsistencies become more evident. For people have different ways of resolving cognitive contradictions, and as a result, public opinion on most social issues can be highly divided.

As is evident, then, cultural forces greatly complicate the analysis of social ills. They define these ills, but often in a contradictory manner. They also limit political options in dealing with a problem, again in frequently inconsistent and contradictory ways. Cultural values and beliefs thus become very much a part of social issues. In light of the multiple points of dissension and inconsistency in values, evaluative beliefs, and empirical beliefs, it is not surprising that many social issues become enduring dilemmas.

Structural Dynamics

When examining a society as a whole, we can visualize a number of organizing processes, that is, processes that organize the behaviors and interactions of individuals and groupings of individuals: (1) institutional processes, (2) community processes, (3) stratifying processes, (4) ecological processes, and (5) intersocietal processes. Such organizational patterns are, of course, greatly circumscribed by values and beliefs; reciprocally, they operate to generate new values and beliefs as well as to sustain old cultural symbols. It is in the actual operation of social institutions, community structures, social strata, ecological adaptations, and international relations that America's most enduring dilemmas emerge. Of course, cultural values and beliefs denote these dilemmas, often in contradictory ways. Moreover, they can also be substantively part of these dilemmas in that organizational processes are guided by values and beliefs. Yet, since the actual events that pose dilemmas are implicated in the organizational processes of a society, we should review these in more detail.

Institutional Processes.[11] In all societies, there are certain established and patterned ways of conducting crucial activities: production, socialization, coordination, control, anxiety reduction, and other critical tasks essential to the viability of the society. *Social institutions* cohere around related congeries of these crucial tasks. Economies are the patterns by which activities pertaining to gathering resources, producing usable goods, and distributing goods and services are organized. Government is the way power is organized to coordinate and control the distribution of human and material resources. Kinship is the way sexual relations, birth, and child rearing are organized. Education is the procedure for instilling critical knowledge and skills necessary to play certain roles. Law is the organization of rules and enforcement procedures for controlling deviance and for facilitating exchanges among social units. Religion is the way ritual activities toward, and beliefs about, the sacred and supernatural are organized.

In small societies with low levels of production (hunters and gatherers, for example), these institutional processes are organized within kinship units and small bands of families. But as production increases and as the size of a population grows, institutional processes are organized in separate structures. Thus, in industrial systems, economic, familial, governmental, legal, and religious activities take place for the most part, within distinct structures, separated in time and space. This differentiation of basic institutions increases problems of coordination among them, as we will come to see, but it is essential as the scope of society increases. Moreover, internal problems within each institution increase, partly as a result of conflicts and contradictions in relations with other institutions and partly as a consequence of their own internal contradictions.

Community Processes. To live and sustain themselves, humans must occupy space. Community processes are those which affect the way a population settles and organizes itself in geographical space.[12] The critical features of any community are the size of its population, the characteristics of this population, the degree of dispersion or concentration of the population, the modes of economic activity used by the population, the modes of communication among members of a population, the means for transporting the population, the procedures for making political decisions in the population, the levels of inequality among members of a population, and the way members of one community connect (articulate) with those of another.

Modern communities present a complex set of dynamics because of their size, coupled with the changing base of economic production and political organization. Moreover, they are often at the center of volatile social issues because it is in the communities that people live, work, engage in recreation, and undertake other institutional activities. Community is, in a sense, their most immediate and tangible experience; thus, it is often at the center of beliefs about "what is wrong" and "what is right" in a society.

Stratifying Processes. In all societies, scarce and valued resources—wealth, power, and prestige—are distributed unequally.[13] As the level of economic production escalates and as the mobilization of political power becomes a key mechanism of social control and coordination, the dynamics of a society increasingly revolve around issues of inequality. Who gets what? Is the distribution of resources fair? What can be done to maintain or change patterns of inequality? These are some of the most central questions in a complex society, and in a modern society the conflicts that ensue as parties vie for increased shares of valued resources become one of its most conspicuous features.

Inequality in distribution of resources creates social classes. People who receive a given level of wealth, power, and prestige typically converge in their beliefs and behavioral tendencies; and as a result, any complex society reveals a number of distinctive classes in terms of their shares of resources and associated lifestyles. Often, ethnic and racial criteria are used to place people in a given social class—a situation that adds yet another source of volatility to class relations.

In all societies, age and sex are also bases for distributing resources unequally. Such inequality revolves around differences in material wealth, power, and honor given to the sexes or to different age levels. These types of inequalities do not create distinctive social classes, since age and sex differences cut across existing classes. As a consequence, those who are in a favored social class but in an unfavored sex or age category have their class position to compensate for what is usually a loss of prestige due to their age or sex. In contrast, those in an unfavored class position and a devalued sex or age category must endure extra indignities. Thus, in most societies, social class processes are compounded by ethnic, racial, sexual, and age inequalities.[14] It is little wonder that many of the most controversial issues in contemporary societies revolve around one or all of these intersecting bases of inequality.

Ecological Processes. All societies exist in a natural environment of other life forms, mineral configurations, and crucial cycles and flows necessary for the maintenance of both the organic and the inorganic properties of the environment.[15] In very simple societies, the organization of the society itself is greatly influenced by processes in the natural environment. However, as productive processes escalate and as ever larger populations are organized in expanding communities, ecological processes are dramatically altered by forms of social structure as well as by the values and beliefs that legitimate these structures. Expanded production increases the need for stock resources, such as minerals and petroleum; and as a result, many are depleted in a region. In turn, expanded production leads to increased consumption, which results in large-scale discharge of toxic residues—heat, sludge, sewage, chemicals, etc.—into the environment. With industrial production, these discharges disrupt the natural flows and cycles critical in maintaining renewable resources—the air, water, and soil.

Thus, as industrial production and consumption disrupt ecological processes, industrial societies find themselves in a position of disrupting the very processes upon which life, and hence human society, depends. The extent to which this situation exists becomes one of the most debated issues in many contemporary societies. Dealing with the problem as defined by some involves dramatic alterations in cultural values and beliefs as well as in the institutional, community, and stratifying processes by which people organize their daily lives. Inevitably, proposed alterations of such magnitude will be resisted and become an arena of controversy.

Intersocietal Processes. The internal dynamics of a society are greatly influenced by its relations with other societies. If there are no relations with another society, this fact influences institutional, community, stratifying, and ecological processes. More typically, of course, societies have relations with each other, and the nature and forms of the interrelation become crucial. War is one of the most prevalent forms, and its existence and aftermath profoundly influence internal societal processes. Political domination without war, but with implied threats of coercion, similarly alters the internal dynamics of both superordinate and subordinate parties. Political alliances of equals or unequals also alter internal processes of those in the alliance. Economic exchanges, intersocietal migrations, cultural diffusion and borrowing, economic exploitation, and other forms of relations similarly affect in different ways internal societal processes.

It should not be surprising, therefore, that subjects like "international relations," "trade wars," "cold wars," "economic partnerships," "multinational cartels," "colonialism," "economic sanctions," "tariff restrictions," "immigration policies," and other issues dealing with intersocietal relations are centers of controversy. For these processes influence not only a "nation's standing" in a "world community," but also the internal functioning of the society.

The Dynamics and Dilemmas of American Society

In the chapters to follow, we will focus on some of America's most enduring social issues. These issues are defined by dominant cultural values and beliefs; and their dynamics inhere in key institutions, stratification processes, community patterns, ecological processes, and intersocietal relations. The pivotal social issues represent dilemmas because they are defined in terms of inconsistent and contradictory values and beliefs; and they are sustained by social structures to which some Americans have strong commitments. "Resolving" an issue is, in most cases, unrealistic, although it is possible to analyze the reasons for the definition of a social problem and its sociocultural causes. Such is the task of this book.

To facilitate our objectives, and as a way of introducing the topics, we should review some of the core values which shape our definitions of problems, and then outline in a general way the structural processes to be examined in each chapter.

Core Values in America

As we discussed earlier, values are highly abstract, general standards among members of a society for assessing appropriate and inappropriate conduct in most social settings. Not all values are seen as relevant to each social setting, but almost all interaction in society is guided by a small number of core values. The list offered here, of course, is a simplification of the complex value processes occurring in people's minds.[16] But as we will see, this simplifying activity is necessary if we are to understand American culture and its full impact on enduring social issues.

Activism. Americans value—that is, they think proper— taking a manipulative stance toward the world around them. They consider it desirable to master situations in the most rational and efficient manner possible. It would be impossible to understand Americans or American society without appreciating the extent to which this value is embedded in our emotions and thoughts. Thus, as we will come to appreciate more fully, much of the negative reaction of Americans to "laziness," "idleness," and "loafing" can only be appreciated when it is recognized that such activities are being judged by the value of activism.

Achievement. Americans value doing well and excelling as well as winning in competition. Much activity is evaluated by Americans in terms of how much effort people make to overcome obstacles in the pursuit of goals; the more efforts are oriented toward success, the more desirable are those efforts. Achievement and success are truly dominant orientations; it is considered important and proper to strive for success in virtually all spheres.

Efficiency. Americans value doing things in a rational and efficient manner. Waste of time, energy, and materials in "getting something done" is considered inappropriate, despite the fact that such waste is common. But Americans devote a great deal of emotional energy to worrying about waste, corruption, inefficiency, and similar topics—signaling the extent to which they hold this value.

Materialism. Americans value accumulating material possessions. In many ways we believe that the spoils should go to the victors in "life's competition," since those who display material goods have been the most "active" and "efficient" in their lives. Unless we appreciated the extent to which materialism is a part of the American consciousness, we could not understand people's efforts to have "the good life" of recreational vehicles, homes in suburbia, and all the other material symbols of success in America. Most Americans desire ever-increasing accumulations of material things, and while they may become concerned with displaying material well-being "tastefully," they nevertheless consider it appropriate

to acquire and display their achievements through possessions.

Progress. Americans also think it appropriate that human efforts be directed toward improving existing conditions. In many ways we maintain that our efforts to be active, to achieve, and to acquire material possessions will
improve both the individual and society. That is, both will
progress. It is only recently that this value has been challenged by the recognition that progress, as it has traditionally been defined (economic growth and increased wages, for
example), does not always lead to a better environment. Yet,
this recognition is not so much a rejection of the appropriateness of "progressive" actions but an indictment that present
actions have not led to the *real* progress of a clean environment, worker satisfaction, and personal contentment. Progress is a dominant value in America, and despite varying definitions of what progress is, most Americans feel that it is
appropriate and necessary.

Freedom. Americans value "freedom" from external
controls and constraints. To be free from regulation is one of
the most desirable goals. Despite the inability to attain freedom in many spheres, most Americans fantasize and seek to
be less constrained than they presently are. Freedom is highly
related to other values, since efforts to be active, to achieve,
and to acquire material comforts lead to the most "progress"
when they free people from the routines, controls, and constraints of everyday life.

Individualism. While Americans value freedom for
many social units—corporations, communities, religious
groups, for example—they place even more value on freedom
for the individual. In fact, all other values are influenced by
the emphasis placed upon the individual, as opposed to the
group, in American society. It is the individual who is to be
active, the individual who is to achieve, the individual who is
to acquire material well-being, the individual who is to bet-

ter his or her condition, and the individual who is to be free. Americans, then, think it appropriate for the individual to shoulder the burden of life, its achievements and its failings. Few societies value the individual as much as the United States, and few societies go to such lengths to assure at least the illusion of individual self-determination in most social matters.

Equality. Americans value equality—that is, the appropriateness of individuals having the same chance to act and achieve in a social setting. Most important, people should be treated equally and should be given "equal opportunity" to realize other values such as activism, achievement, materialism, progress, freedom, and individualism. When Americans have been convinced that equality does not exist, they respond vigorously. But equality is tempered by other values, since for most Americans it means equality of opportunity to achieve, not equality of means or income.

Morality. Americans tend to view matters in moralistic terms: there is a "right" and "wrong" in each situation. This tendency reflects the value of morality, which makes it appropriate and desirable to determine the absolute "rightness" and "wrongness" in each situation. Many overseas observers have noted the propensity of Americans to view matters in absolute terms, ignoring the subtleties of social life. The appropriateness of assuming a moralistic orientation to the social world gives added imperative to other values, because to violate activism, achievement, and so forth tends to be viewed as "absolutely wrong" and as a cause for severe judgments, if not punishments. An emphasis on morality thus escalates value standards from what is "appropriate" to what is "imperative."

Humanitarianism. Americans think it appropriate to help those who have been less successful in the "game of life." Those who are unable to be active, to achieve, and to be self-determined, or those who have been denied equal opportunity, should be assisted. But humanitarianism is highly conditional, lest the moral imperative attached to other dominant values be violated. Thus, for those who can but have chosen not to be active or to achieve, society does not "owe them a living." This highly conditional nature of humanitarianism makes Americans, to outsiders, seem at the same time the most generous and the most punishing people on earth. But when the fact that humanitarianism is circumscribed by other values is recognized, this seeming contradiction becomes less difficult to understand. Americans are, under the "right" conditions, very generous to the less fortunate, but when conditions are "wrong," they can be niggardly. Still, this value frequently comes into contradiction with others when people analyze concrete social issues.

Conformity. Not all values are consistent, and the value of conformity is an example of how people can hold what would appear to be contradictory values. Americans value conformity to dominant standards in any social situation; deviance is looked upon in negative, and moral, terms. Yet, Americans also value individualism and freedom—two values that would seem to dictate a tolerant attitude toward nonconformity. Such is not the case, although Americans have been becoming more reconciled in recent decades to nonconformity in people's lifestyles. But even in the so-called new or alternative lifestyles, it can be noted that there is a considerable degree of conformity in dress, speech, hair styles, and other features of the façades people display.

This listing of dominant core values is, of course, simplified. Yet, even so, it is evident that while there is much consistency in these values, there are also points of inconsistency. Activism, achievement, individualism, materialism, and progress form one consistent cluster that exerts, as we will come to see, an enormous influence on Americans' belief and their interpretations of social issues. The value of equality is consistent with this dominant cluster in its emphasis on individual freedom to achieve and do well, but it often is a value which is used to judge harshly inequalities that have resulted from some Americans' active efforts to achieve at the expense of others. Moreover, freedom and individualism often conflict with the value of efficiency, for people who exert their individual right to be free to be inefficient are often judged harshly. The value of morality makes inconsistency among other values more likely, since Americans are not prone to think in terms of degrees or to evaluate the world as a series of trade-offs among values. Thus, when value conflict occurs, it becomes a true moral dilemma and exacerbates efforts to deal with the source of the dilemma. The value of conformity clearly contradicts the values of individualism, freedom, and equality in many contexts and, as we will emphasize, it often places in conflict different subpopulations who conform to somewhat different standards. Humanitarianism often comes into conflict with individualism and achievement, for to "help people" frequently requires suspension of other values that are held in highly moralistic terms. Sometimes, this suspension is not possible; at other times, it is done in a highly conditional way.

One way to view these values is in terms of the dimensions outlined earlier in figure 1.1. That is, how consistent are these values, and how much consensus exists over them? Figure 1.2 represents our best effort to determine[17] where

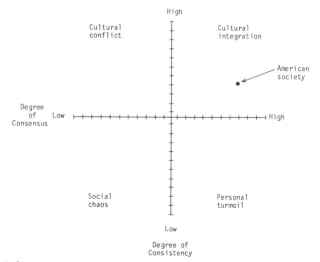

Figure 1.2 Consistency Among and Consensus Over Core American Values

these values stand along these two dimensions. Figure 1.2 must be read somewhat differently from figure 1.1. What we are trying to communicate in this figure is the degree of consistency within and among certain clusters of values and the relative degrees of consensus over the appropriateness of invoking these values as a basis for defining a situation. Individualism, activism, and achievement represent the most highly consistent cluster in America, and at the same time there is a high degree of consensus over these values. Freedom and equality represent another consistent cluster, but there is inconsistency in Americans' views about what constitutes either. Despite high consensus over the appropriateness of these values, definitions of freedom and equality are, we suspect, pulled in different directions by the activism, individualism, achievement cluster, on the one hand, and the less powerful humanitarianism, morality, conformity cluster on the other. On the progress and materialism cluster there is less consensus than there once was in America; and increasingly, there is disagreement over what "real progress" is and over the consequences of materialism. Thus, the degree of consistency within this cluster has decreased, so that progress is not always viewed as the same as material accumulation. There is also growing disagreement over efficiency. Short-term "cost effectiveness," for example, may lead to long-term problems, or vice versa. Thus, compared with previous generations, we are less consistent in our views of what is efficient, even though we all agree that efficiency is desirable. There is high consensus over the appropriateness of humanitarian responses, but little consistency over what these responses should be or how they should be implemented. Moreover, many interpretations of this value become inconsistent with rigid views on the activism, individualism, and achievement cluster, the freedom and equality cluster, and the progress and materialism cluster. With the growing awareness of the complexities of the world, Americans reveal less consensus over morality than previously, and evidence only moderate consistency in what should be viewed as absolutely right and wrong. And increasingly, conformity is seen by

Americans as less critical, particularly because there has been a dramatic decrease in consensus over what people should conform to, and abide by.

We recognize that we are imposing highly complex cognitions on a simplified two-dimensional space in figure 1.2. But our point is sufficiently served by the simplification. There is, as we have noted, relatively high consensus over American values but considerable inconsistency in people's applications of them as well as some degree of outright contradiction in their abstract tenets (conformity vs. individualism, for example). This inconsistency over the tenets of values on which there is high consensus constitutes a powerful force in American society.

Such is the case because this configuration of inconsistently held values shapes Americans' definitions of what a social problem is and what should be done about it. The fact that Americans agree over the appropriateness of the value in its most abstract form but often disagree over the value in its particulars makes for a great deal of cultural conflict about the best way to approach a solution to any problem. As we proceed to examine enduring social issues in America, we must remain attuned to the fact that these issues often pose real dilemmas for Americans.

Chapter 2

The Contradictions of Capitalism

The Dynamics of Economic Organization

All societies must create patterns of social organization that enable the gathering of resources, the conversion of these resources into usable goods and commodities, and the distribution of the products to members of the society.[1] Those processes that revolve around these activities are economic. And since they concern the life-sustaining capacities of a society, social relations and cultural patterns are to a very great extent conditioned by the way in which the processes of gathering, producing, and distributing are organized. For this reason our analysis of dilemmas in American society begins with an overview of its economy. For many of the problems that inhere in the structure and culture of American society are linked to the patterns of economic organization.

Economists have traditionally analyzed economies in terms of their "basic elements": land, labor, capital, and entrepreneurship. In our analysis of the dynamics of economic organization, we can use these terms, but will redefine and supplement them. Our view is that the concept of *land* denotes the degree of access that a society has to natural resources, whether its own or those of other societies. *Labor* concerns the properties of the human work force—its size, composition, skill levels, distribution, organization, and so on. *Capital* pertains to the "tools" used to carry out economic processes. These tools can be material implements—machines, factories, and the like—or the money used to buy these implements. *Entrepreneurship* refers to the mechanism or procedures by which other economic elements—land, labor, capital, and as we will see shortly, technology—are collated and brought to bear on the basic economic processes of gathering, producing, and distributing. *Technology* is a concept that has been added to traditional economic analysis; it denotes information about how to manipulate the social and physical environment. Technology is not the apparatus of production (that is capital) but the knowledge that is used to create such apparatus or to perform other activities. Any economy, then, involves the organization (entrepreneurship) of technology, capital, labor, and access to resources (land) around the basic processes of gathering, producing, and distributing.[2] At this generic level, all economies are alike, but far more important for our purposes, are variations in forms of economic organization.

The American economy is one form of economic organization, which we may call industrial capitalism. Like any type of economy, it reveals its own dynamics. The term "industrial" signals that the economy has technological knowledge which allows the use of inanimate sources of energy, coupled with machine capital and human labor, to gain high access to natural resources and to generate high levels of production. In turn, high levels of production of goods and commodities create elaborate distribution processes. The lable "capitalism" pertains to a particular form of industrial organization where: (1) the ownership of capital (implements and money) is to be primarily private, outside the state and government; (2) the concern for profits (that is, the desire to increase one's wealth and capital) is to be the principal motive behind the organization of land, labor, capital, and technology; (3) the pursuit of profits in gathering, producing, and distributing is to be competitive and comparatively free from political control. As we will see shortly, these three features of capitalism are often realized more in cultural ideologies than in practice, but they do describe the basic properties of capitalism, especially during its early development.

But as Karl Marx was the first to fully recognize, and as others have subsequently documented, capitalism reveals dynamics that lead to its transformation away from the three features listed above.[3] These dynamics do not necessarily lead to a "revolution of the proletariat," as Marx predicted,[4] but they do result in a revolution in the organization and operation of capitalist economies.

One of the inevitable dynamics of capitalist economies is that some individuals and corporate units "win" in the competition with others. And once they force the competition out of a particular type of economic activity, they are in a position to use their capital to prevent others from entering it. They can, for example, cut prices for a short period so that potential competitors will incur heavy losses; or, they can buy power and political influence which can give them a favorable position relative to potential competitors. Thus, there is a built-in tendency for capital to become concentrated in key economic sectors and for economic units to suppress the free competition that marks the early stages of capitalism. In response to such monopolistic and oligopolistic tendencies, political pressures mount to break up noncompetitive sectors of the economy. As a result, government regulation becomes a permanent part of economic activity.

Another basic process endemic to capitalism is the "business cycle" and other related "crises" of production. Capitalist economies tend to cycle in and out of periods of high production, employment, and consumption. When economic prosperity is followed by lowered production, high unemployment, low consumption, or related crises such as rapid inflation, political pressures mount to do something about the problem. As a result, government bodies begin to "regulate" economic units in an effort to mitigate the vicissitudes of the

business cycle or to "bring under control" crises such as inflation. In this process of intervention, "prosperity" increasingly
becomes dependent upon government intervention, so that
capitalism is transformed.

Another transforming process in capitalism inheres in
the profit motive. Capitalism is a system fueled by concern
for individual profits, rather than some cultural ideal or collective goal; and one consequence of this fact is that there is
always an economic incentive to extract labor at the lowest
cost, to manipulate and deceive consumers in order to entice
them to buy products, or to create unhealthful conditions for
workers and the broader community. Under these conditions,
as economic units seek to realize short-run profits in their
competition with others, abuses become a source of intense
resentment that lead to efforts at political mobilization to
eliminate them. The outcome is for government to be charged
with regulating industries in an effort to prevent concern with
profits from creating excessive levels of worker abuse, consumer deception, and environmental damage.

As Marx hoped,[5] perhaps in vain, another transforming process in capitalism revolves around the organization of
labor to protect its interests. In all capitalist economies, the
exploitation and abuse of workers is a potential point of conflict between those who own and those who work in economic
enterprises. Owners have an interest in keeping profits high
by maintaining low wages and rudimentary amenities in the
working conditions, whereas workers have an interest in
higher wages and better working conditions. The inherent
tension between owners/managers and workers is exacerbated with a downturn in the business cycle and other economic crises, since workers are likely to be laid off or fired
and are often left alone to cope with worsened economic conditions. Some capitalist systems, such as the one in Japan,
avoid many of these problems by the paternalistic nature of
corporate organization as well as by various liaisons with
government, whereas systems such as American industrial
capitalism have a long history of worker-manager conflict.[6]
Whether the processes are smooth or fraught with conflict,

the end result is for political pressures to mount and force government to regulate working conditions, wages, unemployment compensation, and adjudication of labor-management disputes. And in this process too, capitalism is transformed.

Yet another transforming process in capitalism is its growth. Even with periodic reversals of the business cycle, capitalism initially expands all economic activities—gathering, producing, and distributing. Capitalist economies must grow, since this is what encourages people to invest their capital; without growth and the hope for profit, there is little incentive to invest money or energy in the economy. But this very growth creates problems of coordination and control which, if not resolved, inhibit growth. For example, problems of building, maintaining, financing, and organizing communication systems, monetary systems, transportation systems (roads, rails, airlines), wholesale and retail market systems, and other infrastructures all escalate to a point where government regulation ensues. And this regulation of the economic infrastructure by government further transforms capitalism.

An additional force operating to transform capitalism stems from the activities of government to meet certain goals. All state forms of government seek to mobilize human and material resources to achieve goals that their leaders, powerful elements, and even general population demand. Moreover, goals are often thrust upon a society, as is the case when one nation wages war against another. As governments attempt to mobilize resources, they levy taxes on both individuals and corporate units and they exert control over economic activities. By selective taxation, selective budgetary priorities for spending these taxes, and selective regulation of economic activities through law and administrative agencies, government biases economic processes toward its goals. The ultimate consequence is for the general profile of gathering, producing, and distributing to be circumscribed by governmental priorities.

These transforming processes are inevitable. They are

built in to the capitalist forms of economic organization. They are defined as "good" or "bad" by people's values and beliefs. In fact, one of the most interesting facets of capitalist societies is the ideological controversy surrounding these changes. Indeed, the dynamics of capitalism itself are greatly influenced by the political battle over efforts to limit or encourage any one of these transforming dynamics. Thus, as we analyze the dilemmas inhering in the American economy, we should recognize that capitalism is a self-transforming system and that these changes create ideological controversies which feed back upon the economic system and affect its course of change.

The Dynamics of the American Economy

The Culture of American Capitalism

To understand the American economic system we must visualize its operation in the context of beliefs about "American capitalism."[7] These beliefs incorporate dominant American values, particularly activism, achievement, efficiency, materialism, progress, freedom, and individualism. And, because economic beliefs reflect core values, they sustain the perception that certain types of economic arrangements are morally more desirable than others and that serious efforts should be made to maintain them. As we can now appreciate, however, there are certain tendencies within the actual operation of the economy that often make these beliefs difficult to realize; yet, they remain a powerful ideological force. Some feel America has not adhered to its beliefs, and this is the "problem" with the economy. Others feel the beliefs are outmoded and that the problem with the economy is a failure to abandon the beliefs and the economic arrangements they support.

The beliefs regarding the economic system answer such basic questions as: (1) Who is to own and control the productive machinery of the economy—individuals, corporations, or the government? (2) How much capital—wealth that is used to buy and organize economic production—should be allowed to become concentrated in the hands of individuals, corporations, or government? In other words, how big should corporations or government become, and how wealthy should individuals who own corporations become? (3) Should corporations always be profit making? If so, how great should their profits be? Should there be some regulation of profits? (4) Should the market—the place and process of selling and buying labor, goods, and services—be free of regulation? Should corporations and individuals be completely free to pursue their profit-making interests? Or, should there be constraints?

Current beliefs about American capitalism can be labeled either conservative or liberal, depending on how each of the above questions is answered. A list of dominant beliefs and the points of disagreement between conservatives and liberals would include: (1) Capital—any asset that can be converted into money—should be concentrated in the hands of private individuals to invest as they see fit. Such a belief reflects the core values of freedom, individualism, and materialism (see chapter 1). The disagreement among conservatives and liberals in America is not over the existence of private property, or the core values of freedom, individualism, and materialism, but rather over how much capital should be held by government and whether government has any right to regulate capital accumulation among private citizens. (2) The accumulation of capital should be encouraged, since large sums of capital can be invested in economic enterprises, thereby encouraging increased production which creates jobs and income and thereby promotes the general welfare of all citizens. Such a belief reflects the general values of materialism and progress. Liberals and conservatives disagree, however, over how far capital accumulation by one corporation or individual should be allowed to go in the name of core values. (3) A corporation should use its most efficient means for accumulating and using capital for the production of goods and services—a belief that incorporates the core values of efficiency and activism. This allows for the pooling of capital, the procurement of wage labor, the development of technology, and the use of natural resources to produce and distribute goods and services to the people. Conservatives and liberals will disagree, however, over the extent to which government should control and regulate corporate activities, creating a debate over the definition of freedom. (4) Corporations must be profit-making units if investors are to be encouraged to risk their capital in various economic enterprises. Such a belief reflects the values of materialism, achievement, and activism. But conservatives and liberals will usually fail to agree over the extent to which profits should be regulated and taxed, thereby limiting the freedom to accumulate material wealth. (5) The market—the place and process where people exchange their money for goods and services—is an efficient way to allocate the resources of a society, since the people's demand for goods and services, expressed in their willingness to spend their money, will lead profit-making individuals and corporations to invest capital in those activities for which demand is high. In this way the economy can best meet the needs of the citizenry, and at the same time realize the values of freedom, individualism, activism, and materialism. Conservatives and liberals do not agree, however, on whether the supply-and-demand cycle in the market should be the only way to allocate resources. (6) A "free" market where individuals and corporations, all guided by a profit motive, can compete with each other is the best way to induce economic units to keep their costs down, and hence their prices low. This belief incorporates such core values as freedom, activism, achievement, and efficiency. Conservatives and liberals often disagree, however, on whether or not free competition will always occur, whether it will always lead to efficiency and low prices, and whether it is desirable in all sectors of the economy.

At the level of beliefs, then, capitalism can be defined as a "desirable" mode of economic organization which is presumed to provide an efficient way to organize capital, labor, technology, and natural resources so that low-cost goods and services can be produced to meet the needs and desires of people as expressed by their purchases in the free market-place. And while there is consensus over the core values, there is considerable disagreement when these values are trans-lated into beliefs about the most appropriate form of capital-ism. These divergent belief systems are summarized in table 2.1.

By reading down the right column of table 2.1, and at the same time reviewing our discussion of the structural transformations of capitalism, we see that liberal beliefs cor-respond more closely to the actual structural conditions of mature capitalism. Conservative beliefs depict early forms of capitalism. Yet, as is evident in the mid-1980s, conservative beliefs have dominated political decision-making processes. The result has been a period of ideological conflict between conservatives and liberals and strain between actual struc-tural pressures of mature capitalism and the ideological mo-bilization of conservative cultural beliefs. One of the great di-lemmas of the American economic system, then, is the ideological battle and the occasional ascendance of cultural beliefs that do not correspond to inevitable structural changes

Table 2.1 Profile of Cultural Beliefs About Capitalism

	Conservative Beliefs	*Liberal Beliefs*
(1) Ownership of capital	All capital must be private	Government must own or control some capital
(2) Concentration of capital	Increases in capital are the "just rewards" for economic success and should not be discouraged	Concentrated capital reduces economic competition and encourages monopolistic practices that must be controlled
(3) Profit-making	The desire for profits is what encourages investments and must not be regulated	Some economic activity must be directed toward collec-tive and societal goals
(4) Markets	The "law" of supply and de-mand should be allowed to operate freely	Free markets are the best allocative system for some goods and services; regula-tion and control are neces-sary for others

in capitalism. This ideological battleground has profound effects in defining the dilemmas of the American economy.

Structural Dilemmas of American Capitalism

Articulation of Government and Private Enterprise. In early capitalism, the role of government is limited. Conservative beliefs reflect, legitimate, and guide an economic system of competition in free markets among private corporate units. Over time, however, governmental involvement in the economy increases, despite the power of conservative beliefs. In most capitalist systems, this fact has been accepted and relatively clear lines of governmental control are established and legitimated by liberal capitalist beliefs, and in some societies, by quasi-socialist beliefs. In the United States, such has not been the case. Conservative beliefs have operated to distort perceptions by the public, owners of businesses, managers, and government officials about the inevitability of government intervention. In addition, the "success" of early American capitalism in the first two-thirds of this century conditioned corporate leaders and significant segments of the public to believe that, if left alone, American corporations can continue to dominate world markets.

The result of these perceptions is that, except in times of severe crisis, it has been very difficult to legitimate *systematic* and *long-term* governmental administration of economic activity. Instead, the United States reveals a system of ad hoc, jury-rigged liaisons between private corporations and government. Through a truly bewildering array of civil laws, ever-changing administrative rulings by diverse agencies, precedent-setting decisions by the courts, and subsidies through loopholes in the tax codes, government seeks to "regulate" economic activity. At any given time, there is no clear set of economic policies at the federal level; and what policies exist are subject to change depending upon political fortunes. Much of this is inevitable in a capitalist economy and a political democracy, since capitalism involves self-interested and

private decisions whereas democracy requires public assessments of political policies. Nonetheless, in comparison with
other advanced nations, the United States has not developed
clear, direct, administratively coherent patterns of communication and subsidy to industry. Subsidies tend to be indirect and hidden in the tax codes, while communication is based
on mutual distrust. As a consequence, there is enormous waste
of resources in the way that government regulates industries, and conversely, there is an equal loss of capital in efforts by industries to manipulate government. This situation
has become particularly evident in recent decades when
American corporations have found themselves competing
against foreign corporations in "partnership" with government.

To some extent, problems of coordination are inherent
in large-scale activity, especially when this activity involves
a reconciliation of societal goals and the interests of private
economic units. In addition to the built-in conflicts within
economic units between managers' desire for profits and
growth, and workers' desire for high wages, security, and good
working conditions, there is an additional conflict between
politically established societal goals, such as racial equality,
ecological preservation, national self-sufficiency, international humanitarianism, consumer safety, and the like, and
the narrow interests of owners and workers in particular economic organizations. When coupled with periodic ascendance
of the conservative beliefs portrayed in table 2.1, coordination, control, and regulation become particularly problematic. The outcome of these conflicting cultural and structural
forces is for government to seek regulation through a variety
of mechanisms, most of them indirect: (1) subsidies through
loophole provisions in the tax code (capital gains, accelerated
depreciation, tax credits, etc.); (2) cash or grant subsidies to
particular facets of selected industries, as has been the case
for airlines, railroads, and various public utilities; (3) massive purchases of goods and services in the market, including
airplanes, warships, agricultural goods, and war-related
technologies; (4) regulation of money flows through the tax

and Federal Reserve systems, as is the case, for example, when taxes are raised or lowered and when the government forces interest rates to climb by restricting money supplies; (5) export-import policies affecting the flow of goods to and from selected nations, such as the import taxes levied on imported automobiles; (6) direct control through regulatory agencies and licensing policies, as in interstate commerce and air travel; and (7) direct control of prices and wages in selected industries, and at times in all or most industries, as was the case in the early 1970s when general wage and price controls were implemented.

As is evident, the most important forms of regulation are *indirect;* only rarely does the government directly intervene. Moreover, since the ways in which the mechanisms operate can change with a new political administration or with a shift in public sentiment, they do not, in most cases, lead to the creation of stable administrative liaisons between government and industry. And given the constant political pressures of diverse segments of the economy and citizenry—large corporations, consumer groups, organized labor, environmentalists, etc.—maintaining stable political policies that encourage coherent administrative liaisons is difficult.

In one area, however, relatively clear liaisons have evolved between government and industry: national defense.[8] Over time, under the impact of both hot and cold wars, the "military industrial complex" has emerged and grown into a "defense establishment." The existence of such an establishment creates its own problems, since the technology and capital invested in its enterprises do not spill over into the domestic economy in the same way that equivalent investments do in the private sector. Moreover, the products of such an establishment do not circulate in the economy; they are stockpiled and kept secret. A study in 1982 by a private research firm[9] concludes that each $1 billion in tax money spent on military equipment causes a loss of 18,000 jobs that could have been saved if consumers had spent the money on nonmilitary goods and services. Further, this research concluded that the 1981 military procurement budget of $154 billion caused a net loss of 1,520,000 jobs to the industrial and commercial base of the United States. Of course, the military procurement budget creates jobs, directly and indirectly, but it causes a net loss of employment opportunities. A 1983 study by the New York Council on Economic Priorities concluded that military expenditures are not the most efficient way to create jobs. For every $1 billion spent by the Pentagon in the private sector, 28,000 jobs are created, directly and indirectly, but this same amount of money would generate 32,000 jobs if spent on public transit, 71,000 jobs if spent on education, and 57,000 jobs if simply used on personal consumption.[10]

In addition to these problems is added the ability of defense contractors, who have established liaisons with government, to place themselves in a favorable position to secure additional subsidies. They are often able to out-compete nondefense contractors for government subsidies, so that the economy becomes increasingly skewed toward the production of military weapons. In turn, the use of technological and capital resources for military production decreases investments in the domestic economy, and hence in the capacity of nondefense corporations to compete in the world market.

Thus, the particular pattern of government-industry relations in America will pose an enduring dilemma. American companies must increasingly compete in a world market against adversaries that, in most cases, have much more stable and coherent relations with government. In the one area where such coherence exists, namely, military weaponry, the United States is dominant in the world market. Yet, such dominance involves a rather dramatic loss of capital and technology for the nondefense economy. The curious irony of this situation is that those who hold most fervently to conservative beliefs—beliefs that inhibit a restructuring of government relations with private corporations—are also those who typically advocate a strong defense posture. Such a situation simply makes this dilemma even more intense, as we will explore further in chapter 11.

Monopoly and Oligopoly. The basic assumption of the conservative capitalist belief system is that open competition in a free market is the best form of economic organization. However, as became evident during the last century in America, if left unregulated such a system soon becomes dominated by monopolistic practices which, in turn, cut down on competitive freedom and violate the very beliefs used to legitimate early capitalism. As we noted earlier, because some corporations become profitable and as they grow in size and power, they acquire the power to cut prices, absorb temporary losses, and thereby drive less-solvent units out of the market. Or, by threatening to cut prices, they can indirectly regulate the activities of other economic units. Once economic organizations possess this kind of "overlord" power, not only can they dictate how competitors are to operate, but they can also control smaller units which depend upon powerful monopolies for their business. For example, at one time in America the John D. Rockefeller family so dominated the oil industry that it could suppress or control virtually all competitors, all small suppliers, and all buyers of oil. When this kind of market control occurs, economic units are not free, competition is suspended, and goods are no longer allocated in accordance with the laws of supply and demand.[11] Such a situation clearly violates conservative beliefs.

As we stressed earlier, this inherent dilemma has led to government regulation. Yet, increasing concentrations of capital and the growth of "successful" corporations are inevitable in capitalist systems, despite efforts to maintain competition. Several forces work against government efforts to maintain the market mechanism. First, the profit motive mandates that economic units are to increase their profits by expanding. Second, certain economic activities in modern societies (transportation, communications, utilities) can probably be performed more efficiently by large organizations controlling most of the market. Third, successful corporations which employ large numbers of workers can exert enormous political influence and thereby mitigate government efforts at regulation. And fourth, some forms of economic activity require substantial concentrations of capital, making it more profitable for corporations to be large and hence achieve the "economies of scale" that come with size, and coincidentally, market domination.

The result is for large sectors of critical resource markets to be controlled by a relatively few corporations which are subjected to only partial governmental regulation. As opposed to *monopoly,* where one corporation dominates the market, the situation of a few large corporations controlling the market is termed *oligopoly.* Competition is usually quite intense among smaller corporations in less central markets, but, with few exceptions, in markets where there is high consumer demand and where large quantities of scarce resources are utilized, the oligopolistic tendencies of capitalism are most evident. Table 2.2 presents illustrative data on the degrees of concentration of capital and market control in capital-intensive sectors of the American economy.

The basic dilemma revolving around oligopoly is how to mitigate its effects. Some would argue, of course, that control of the market is the deserved spoils of success. Others would contend that market control cannot last in a world economy where foreign companies can enter the domestic market and compete successfully with American oligopolies, as has been the case for cars, computers, steel, television and

Table 2.2 Examples of Economic Concentration in Selected Industries, 1977

Selected Sectors of Economic Activity	Percentage of Total Sales Received by Eight Largest Corporations
Grain, mill products	64%
Dairy products	63
Steel foundries	58
Primary steel production	24
Oil and gas extraction	37
Petroleum refining	61
Coal extraction	56

SOURCE: Department of Commerce, *General Report on Industrial Organization, April 1981* (Washington, D.C.: Government Printing Office, 1981).

Table 2.3 Percentage of Total Manufacturing Assets Held by 100 Largest Firms

Year	Percent Held
1950	39.7%
1955	44.3
1960	46.4
1965	46.5
1970	48.5
1975	45.0
1980	46.7
1981	46.8

SOURCE: U.S. Bureau of the Census, *Statistical Abstracts of the United States, 1982–1983* (Washington, D.C.: Government Printing Office, 1983), p. 535.

radios, and other industries that exerted oligopolistic control until the last decade or so. Yet, historically, the solution to oligopoly has been government regulation, which, in turn, creates problems inherent in "state management" of the economy.

Conglomeration. Another trend in the American economy is the process of larger companies acquiring smaller companies. Sometimes such acquisitions involve taking over competitors, or smaller corporations doing business in areas related to those of the larger corporation. Depending upon the federal government's interpretation and enforcement of antitrust laws, acquisitions can be encouraged or discouraged. In the 1980s, restrictions have been eased somewhat, and as a result, economic concentration will no doubt have increased. At other times, larger corporations diversify by buying smaller companies in different economic spheres—thereby creating a holding company or conglomerate. Table 2.3 offers some data on this process of conglomeration.

Conglomerative processes present several dilemmas for American capitalism. First, they increase the level of oligopoly and economic concentration, making it ever more difficult for smaller, and perhaps more innovative, companies to compete with the larger companies. Second, conglomeration appears to be a short-run alternative to capital reinvestment; that is, instead of reinvesting profits in existing activities, the conglomerate uses the profits to purchase another profitable company. While this strategy may increase the overall profit levels in the short term, it forestalls renovation of old production facilities and investments in new technologies that are essential in the long run, especially in a highly competitive world market. Because they have used conglomeration as their basic strategy for maximizing profits, a number of American industries have left themselves highly vulnerable in a world market composed of foreign companies that have been reinvesting profits in capital improvements and new technologies. For example, the steel and automobile industries have been in a difficult position in both domestic and world markets because of their failure to reinvest a sufficient proportion of their profits into production and research facilities. While the automobile industry appears to have mended its ways, the steel industry in America could simply be run out of business, since it cannot now afford to spend the money to retool factories and to develop new technologies.

This dilemma is inevitable in a system where processes of connecting and reconciling national priorities with the narrow interest of corporations in profits are not direct or well developed. American corporations, under pressure from stockholders for immediate profitability, have taken a suicidal path of conglomeration, which does not add to the capital stock or develop technological resources of the society. It simply consumes capital without increasing productivity, while at the same time it increases concentration and thereby reduces the level of competition in the domestic economy and makes sectors of the economy extremely vulnerable to foreign competition. The remainder of the 1980s and the 1990s will represent a critical period; unless steps can be taken to increase reinvestment as the route to profitability, basic production industries will become less and less able to operate in the world economy.

Worker-Management Tension. American industrial capitalism has historically generated tensions between line works and managers of large corporations.[12] As Marx recognized, much assembly-line and highly specialized work is alienating in that workers do not have control over the products of their labor.[13] Indeed, work is often dull, routinized, repetitious, and on occasion dangerous. Such problems are aggravated by owners'/managers' interest in keeping wages low and in minimizing other expenses that might improve working conditions. Adding to the tension is the dehumanization and uncertainty when labor "sells itself as a commodity" in a labor market for the privilege of gaining access to alienating jobs.

Marx and present-day Marxists have made much of these forces, assuming and hoping that they would lead to worker revolt and to a restructuring of the economy as a whole. Both Marx and his contemporary followers have vastly underestimated, we suspect, the capacity of capitalists to "buy off" labor. People are able to perform "dehumanizing" work when the pay, relative to other options, is perceived as adequate. They may not like the work; they often express their discontent in sloppy work performance and outright acts of sabotage; and they evidence personal pathologies such as alcoholism and drug abuse. But they perform the work, nonetheless; and they tend to perceive the costs of "revolution" as simply too high to bear. The conflicts that have marked workplace relations have typically been over issues such as pay, improvement in working conditions, fringe benefits, and the right to organize collectively. These conflicts have not involved a serious questioning of the basic patterns of ownership and organization of industrial enterprises, but they have changed the structure of American capitalism nonetheless.

Yet, even though the general nature of industrial capitalism has not been questioned, the inherent tension between workers and management poses a dilemma for all capitalist systems and a somewhat unique set of problems for the American economy. The major problem is the intense adversary relationship between management and labor. Each distrusts the other; each has little loyalty to the other; and each is guided by different ideological commitments. This situation produces a mode of production where "quality control" of products escalates, where companies will simply close a plant and move to another community (or nation) in order to save money, where "labor problems" are resolved by stricter enforcement of work rules, where workers deliberately sabotage the "system" occasionally by not performing tasks properly, and where high worker absenteeism creates problems of work continuity and quality. These tensions increase with downturns in the business cycle, but the lack of mutual commitment by workers and managers persists even in more prosperous periods. And, since the United States no longer enjoys the technological and capital advantages that it did during the middle decades of this century, world economic competition among industrial nations will aggravate tensions as managers of capital seek to cut costs and compete against foreign companies in domestic and world markets.

Much of the tension between workers and management has, during the early decades of this century, been institutionalized. Workers have organized into unions, government has protected their right to do so, and management has come to accept collective bargaining. Yet, the institutionalization of union-management relations has only made the tension routine and has done little to mitigate its broader consequences. One of the ironies of unionization is that industrial workers have now placed themselves between two bureaucracies: the corporation and the union. Work within the corporation tends to be monotonous, highly regulated, uncreative, and ungratifying, while union membership imposes restrictions on occupational mobility, job classification, and take-home pay. As industrial workers have become somewhat affluent and secure in their work, it appears that they also become more attuned to their dependent situation. Such awareness has created what has become known as the "blue-collar blues,"[14] in which the lack of individual freedom and the incessant monotony of work in large industries has stimulated a search for more meaning and satisfaction in non-work spheres.

Most of the work force in America, of course, does not belong to a union.[15] As will be emphasized in the chapters on wealth and poverty, many workers are subject to hardships generated by the business cycle, and the low wages stemming from intense competition in the unskilled labor market. Such workers experience enormous dissatisfaction and frustration with an economic system incapable of providing them with meaningful and well-paying work. The racial riots of the 1960s were, in large part, an expression of such frustration to participate in the mainstream of the economy (see chapter 8). Whites also experience these same impediments, and during times of deep recession, the marginal labor force can pose a threat to civil order.

Without union organization, marginal workers must rely on government to protect and assist them; yet, only during a deep recession or outright depression has government been willing to provide an extensive system of public service jobs. Even these jobs are defined as temporary measures to take up the slack in the employment picture of the economy. The unskilled, nonunion worker must endure constant employment uncertainty in a cyclical economy that is only partially regulated by government, which heightens frustration and at times rage against the economic institutions and the entire society. In an economy increasingly vulnerable to events in the world economic system, these problems can only increase.

Consumer Manipulation. In recent years, a considerable amount of consumer deception by American corporations has been exposed. As we noted earlier, a high degree of consumer manipulation, deception, and outright fraud is probably inevitable in an economic system structured for profit in a competitive market. Competitive markets encourage extensive advertising to induce consumers to purchase goods and services, but the drive for profits can sometimes lead corporations to deceive consumers about the nature of various products. Advertising is, of course, necessary to encourage the growth essential in maintaining capitalist economic systems. Thus, corporations seek to expand demand for goods by creating "needs" in consumers for even more goods. Instilling new needs for the latest model and a plethora of "new and improved" goods constitutes a form of corporate manipulation.

As the economy becomes dominated by large corporations and by oligopolies, advertising assumes a new function: to convince the public that giant corporations or cartels of companies are in the public's best interest. For example, oil company advertising has often assumed a "public information" format, seeking to convince consumers that oil cartel control of the world market is necessary to meet "America's energy needs" and that extensive government regulation poses a "threat to personal freedom." Thus, as competition among large corporations recedes, advertising becomes much more deliberately manipulative and seeks to persuade the public that the current state of economic affairs is desirable. Moreover, advertising costs enormous sums of money and adds little to consumer knowledge or product superiority, with the result that consumers pay more for goods whose prices are inflated by advertising costs.

In the face of conservative beliefs and the lack of coherent government-industry administrative liaisons, regulating small and large companies in a competitive market has proven difficult. Many of the regulatory problems are endemic to capitalist forms of economic organization, but some are unique to American capitalism. First, the large number of manufacturing corporations producing millions of goods makes it extremely difficult to monitor advertising integrity, product safety, and various fraudulent activities. Second, there is a tendency for regulatory agencies to become coopted by the larger organizations they are set up to regulate because day-to-day contact is not with consumers but with corporate officials. Third, the political power of corporations and unionized workers has often worked as a kind of de facto alliance to weaken regulatory laws and thus make government agencies impotent, and hence, easily coopted. As a result of these forces, a considerable amount of abuse, deception, and manipulation of consumers occurs. And without consistently effective regulation by such agencies as the Food and Drug Administration, the Civil Aeronautics Board, the Interstate

Commerce Commission, public utilities commissions, the Department of Agriculture, the Department of Interior, the Department of Justice, and the many other agencies with regulatory responsibilities, it is impossible to prevent consumer abuse.

The failure of government to effectively protect its clients, the public, has forced nongovernmental organizations (such as consumers unions and the Ralph Nader organization) to investigate and bring suits against both corporations and government for initiating and tolerating consumer abuse. This conflict between nongovernmental organizations and corporations is probably inevitable in a capitalist system like the United States where large corporations, unions, and government agencies can, at times, work against as much as for consumers' interests.

This conflict of interest in protecting the general public, and at the same time, seeking to realize conservative beliefs by deregulating industries poses an enduring dilemma in America. In conservative periods, protection of the public will typically be compromised to encourage the presumed economic growth that comes with deregulation. But as abuses mount and are given publicity by the media and private consumer groups, pressures will mount for government intervention.

Inflation. For most of the 1970s and the first years of the 1980s, America and other capitalist societies have seen steady increases in the prices of goods and services. To some extent, inflationary periods, or episodes, are inherent in forms of economic organization that rely upon forces of supply and demand in the marketplace. But recent periods of inflation in America derive from a series of forces and now pose a more enduring problem.[16] One force causing higher prices is the size of corporations that no longer need be completely responsive to competition. For example, some corporations are capable of dominating their respective markets to the extent that it is not always necessary for them to lower prices in the face of slackening demand. In light of their partial immunity to effective competition, they are likely to *raise* prices to make up for decreasing sales and hence maintain their profits. "Competitive" corporations must be careful of undercutting such corporate giants, because in an all-out price war smaller competitors could not survive. Thus, there are pressures for smaller companies to follow the leads of the larger; if larger companies raise prices, others will faithfully follow, so that prices rise across the entire market sector.

Once a sector of the economy raises prices, price increases become higher costs for companies in other sectors that use these goods or services in their manufacturing operations. Thus, should U.S. Steel raise prices, General Motors' costs increase, and GM too is likely to raise the price of its cars. Increases by resource and basic commodity industries reverberate throughout the economy, setting off waves of price increases by all the companies comprising the complex web of interconnections in a modern economy.

Another inflationary pressure comes from labor which has been able to organize collectively and to provide itself with financial compensation for ungratifying work. Capitalistic economies are generally built around expansion, creating a highly affluent standard of living for the majority of the population. Accordingly, labor becomes accustomed to an escalating standard of living (made possible by successive wage increases) and seeks to buy the myriad goods and services provided by mature capitalism. Unions constantly work for increased wages and other benefits which, from the corporation's viewpoint, represent higher costs. Unless savings can be made in other cost areas, or unless corporations are willing to decrease their profits, prices continue to increase. At times these cyclical processes escalate so rapidly as to create a *wage-price spiral* like that of the late 1960s and 1970s. Wage-price spirals would be less likely if Americans were not accustomed to ever-increasing levels of material well-being; if corporations were not oriented toward ever-increasing profits, and if markets could not be dominated by a few corporations. But as long as workers and corporations think in terms of *short-range* profits and wages, wage-price spirals easily begin in advanced capitalistic economies.

Such spirals are difficult to control by government regulation because government is not geared to establish and implement a national economic policy. First, the nature of political democracy in a society as diverse as America makes it difficult to agree on any unified policy, especially in the economic sphere, where there are so many inherent conflicts of interest. Second, even if agreement over a policy could be established by Congress and the president, implementation would be difficult because of the nature of government intervention in the economy. As we have seen, much intervention has been indirect, using the free market mechanism to stimulate or decrease demand. Government in America is not set up to *directly* control supplies, prices, and wages. For indeed, the government does not "own" the capital of the economy.

Another inflationary force is government spending itself, especially deficit spending. By spending borrowed money or by simply printing additional money, the government can create excessive demand for goods and services—thereby encouraging an increase in prices. At times, as was the case in the early 1980s, government can incur large deficits in order to placate diverse constituents, and at the same time, the Federal Reserve Board can tighten the money supply. Such policies work at cross purposes, and typically raise interest rates as government, private companies, and individuals seek to borrow in money markets where demand for money is high and the supply relatively low. The resulting increase in interest rates feeds inflation in the short run, but eventually it encourages a recession, since private citizens and corporate units find it difficult to borrow and spend money. And at some point the recession discourages inflation as unemployment increases and as demand for goods and services decreases. But as soon as controls on the money supply are lifted, inflationary pressures reassert themselves.

A final inflationary force is the international involvement of the American economy. Basic resources are now in shorter supply because of growing international demand, coupled with less accessibility of supplies for the United States. Americans must now compete with other nations for many essential resources that were formerly purchased at low cost in Third World countries. As these countries have become aware of the growing dependence of the "modern" world upon their resources, they have begun to organize and exert monetary and political influence. The OPEC oil cartel is but the first, and still the most conspicuous, example of a phenomenon that will become increasingly prevalent in the world market. Just as large corporations can begin to dictate prices in a domestic market, countries with large quantities of needed resources can begin to dictate prices in the international market. Such practices are inherently inflationary, since Third World countries are likely to raise prices in order to increase their world power and to develop their own countries.

Inflation, then, is likely to be a periodic, if not chronic, problem in America. Inflationary episodes tended to be of short duration and were self-correcting as long as the Third World countries "sold" their resources cheaply, the American corporations were small and competitive, corporations were national in character, labor was less accustomed to ever-increasing wages, Americans were used to some shortages, and government was not a large purchaser of goods and services. But it is now clear that there are persistent inflationary pressures built into modern capitalist systems like that of the United States.

Economic Cycles. Capitalist forms of economic organization are subject to what we termed earlier the *business cycle,* where periods of economic prosperity (high profits, full employment, and higher wages) are followed by recessions and depressions (declining profits, high unemployment, and lower wages). The American economy has experienced many such vacillating cycles. But despite their inevitability and methodical frequency, economists still debate their causes.[17]

Since the 1930s government policies have been directed at mitigating the consequences of the business cycle. Various programs sought to assist unemployed workers, and government policies have been designed to keep demand for goods high enough to prevent a severe cutback in production. Recently, in the 1970s, recession has been accompanied by inflation. In previous recessions, unemployment and decreased production caused prices to go down; individuals and corporations did not have money to spend, and the demand for goods and services decreased. But because of the built-in pressures for inflation discussed above, recent recessions have not always lowered prices. The result is *stagflation*—an economy where production is down, unemployment remains high, and prices are rising.

This situation is perhaps inevitable in economies where (1) unions are able to keep wages high even in the face of unemployment, (2) oligopolies, multinationals, and international cartels can control domestic and world markets, and thus need not lower prices (and in fact may raise them) with less demand for their goods, and (3) government is not structured for direct control of wages, prices, and employment.

Future Prospects for the American Economy

From one perspective, the prospects for the American economy do not appear bright. The technological lead that American companies have enjoyed for much of this century is no longer very great; and in fact, some American industries lag considerably behind those in other countries. The infrastructure of the American economy—from steel plants to roads and bridges—is aging and will need to be repaired and replaced. The wages of the skilled and semiskilled labor force are high relative to those in many other countries with whom American companies must compete. Resources are limited, especially since foreign cartels and nations now regulate access to many of them. And, relative to nations against which the United States must compete in the world's markets, a far greater proportion of the gross national product in the United States is devoted to military production.

Many of the dilemmas discussed in this chapter are inherent in the nature of capitalism and are not unique to the

United States. We should not assume that only the American economy is beset with problems. Also, it should be stressed that since the United States can no longer dominate the world economically as it did for the middle decades of the century, we should not compare the economy of today with the one which dominated the world in the post–World War II era when most industrial nations were rebuilding in the aftermath of the war. Our apparent "leadership" ensued as much from the good fortune of not being attacked as to any great industrial superiority; hence, it is unrealistic to assume that the American economy could have maintained its lead over other industrial nations after they rebuilt their economies.

In the long run, then, the major challenge to the American economy is its capacity to adjust to the realities of a new world where resources are not easily secured and where competition for markets is intense. To a great extent, the capacity to make this adjustment will depend on how well the United States can effect at least partial resolution of the dilemmas discussed in this chapter.

While the mid-1980s have seen the ascendance of conservative economic beliefs, it is unlikely that the situation can endure. In fact, the more government is seen as a hindrance and even an "enemy" by economic units, the less able the economy will be to adjust to the new realities of the world economic system. Conservative beliefs have ascended as a reaction, we suspect, to the perceived ineptitude, inefficiencies, and inequities of present government liaisons with industry. It will be critical to develop a new set of administrative linkages with economic units, and at the same time, to abandon rigid adherence to beliefs that do not, and cannot again, correspond to economic realities. The rebuilding of America's industrial infrastructure and the recapitalization of declining industries will involve massive government subsidies. Probably the most important steps that can be taken revolve around the abandonment of indirect subsidies through the tax code and their replacement by direct subsidies and a complete overhaul of an overly complex and unfair system of taxation in America (see chapter 7 for some suggestions).

At the same time, it must be recognized that in some

industries, oligopolies will persist. The critical issue will be how to regulate their activities in order to encourage profitability, efficiency, and equitable treatment of workers. Other industries, particularly in high technology areas, will need to remain highly competitive, since they represent the best potential for effective penetration of world markets. Moreover, small businesses, especially those in small-scale manufacturing, need to be protected from encroachment by large conglomerates and subsidized, since they offer a vital source of creativity not found in the research and development laboratories of big companies.

Probably the most difficult change to implement is in the worker-management tension that exists in almost all companies, large and small. The United States can never emulate the Japanese system, as some have naively suggested. The history of tension, perceived betrayal, and ideological divergence of workers and management is too long. Much more viable than the ideological loyalty to the company, bordering on religious commitment, so evident in Japan is direct worker involvement in ownership and management of companies. Only when companies are about to go bankrupt is this option considered. But instead of being the option of last resort, it should be seen as essential. Workers must be given a financial stake as well as a sense of psychological involvement in the activities of companies. Thus far, most corporations have been reluctant to do this. Instead, they aggravate problems by shutting down plants and/or moving production facilities overseas where a cheaper and currently more docile work force can be found.

Another difficult change that will need to be implemented is a decrease in the excessive concern of many American corporations for the short-term "bottom line." In most American corporations, the incentive system for stockholders, boards of directors, and managers is for short-term profitability. Long-term investments in new technologies and capitalization programs are not made, nor are enduring commitments to workers seen as a wise corporate strategy. Instead, profits are paid back to stockholders or they are used to buy out other companies in order to extract their profits.

In neither of these processes is capital reinvested in a consistent way that allows an industry—whether cars, steel, or plastics—to maintain a competitive edge on foreign competition.

Problems of inflation and the business cycle will never be satisfactorily resolved in capitalism. They can be mitigated if the general guidelines discussed above are followed. But realistically, these guidelines seem difficult to achieve. How can the role of government be redefined? How can the tax system and administrative linkages of industry and government be radically revised? How can long-standing management philosophies and worker-management hostilities be wiped out through radical corporate reorganization? And how are lay persons, economists, and politicians to abandon a conservative belief system that once "made America great" but which will now take it to its economic grave?

Perhaps there is time to implement these changes slowly. One of the great strengths of the American economy is that it is the world's largest market. Through careful use of this fact to control the destructive impact of foreign competition, government can encourage and provide the necessary time for industries to readjust and reorganize. Another great advantage of the American economy is its knowledge system, particularly its structure of higher education. As a resource for new social and material technologies, as well as skilled workers, it can provide corporations with the needed competitive edge while other, more difficult changes are initiated. If these advantages are not utilized to implement more long-term changes in government-industry liaisons, to change radically worker-management relations, to alter dramatically management philosophies and incentive systems, and to generate a productive mix of regulated oligopolies, high technology industries, and subsidized small manufacturers, then the prospects for the American economy are not bright. And since the economy is so central to events on the rest of the society, the dilemmas and problems in other structural components of American society will only intensify.

Chapter 3

The Dialectic
Between Democracy
and Governance

The Dynamics of Governance

$\mathbf{A}$ll populations of humans face problems of coordinating their activities, allocating tasks and duties, distributing resources, and maintaining order.[1] These problems are "political" in that, except in the simplest hunting and gathering societies, they involve the mobilization and use of "power." The concept of power has been the topic of great conceptual controversy in the social sciences, but fortunately for our purposes in this chapter, we need not get heavily embroiled in ongoing debates.[2] For our needs, we can simply view power as the capacity of one social unit to control the actions of other social units.[3]

When we examine an entire society, our concern is with the creation and use of power to coordinate activities, allocate tasks, distribute resources, and maintain order. That is, what social units possess power, and how is it used to resolve these basic human problems? Historically and to the present day, power has been mobilized in many different ways at the societal level. Indeed, we have a rich vocabulary of overlapping terms to describe this variation—chiefdoms, empires, monarchies, dictatorships, democracies, feudal systems, and the like. Underlying these diverse terms, however, are just a few simple dimensions of power: first, the level of power possessed by decision-makers in a society (that is, how much control can be exerted on the internal affairs of a society); second, the degree of centralization or concentration of power (that is, how many or few decision-makers relative to a population are there in a society); and third, the degree of democracy in the use of power (that is, how much do those who are subject to power have to say about who shall use that power and how it shall be used).

Some of the most interesting dynamics of a society revolve around the forces that increase, or decrease, the level of power, its degree of centralization, and its democratic or undemocratic implementation. Inevitably, many of a society's most pressing problems will revolve around these three dimensions. It is little wonder, then, that power is often viewed as an evil that corrupts its holders and subjugates its victims. Yet, the increasing concentration of power is, to some degree, necessary under certain general conditions. One of these is the increasing size of a population, for after a certain size is reached, interpersonal contact and informal sanctions become inadequate means for coordinating and controlling activity.[4]

Another general condition causing an increase in the level of power and its degree of centralization is the perception of a threat—whether real or imagined—by a population or its leaders.[5] Warfare is the prototypical case, but other threats to a society typically result in higher power levels and greater centralization for coordinating activities, allocating tasks, distributing resources, and maintaining order in the face of an "enemy." (Conversely, the level of democracy typically decreases at such times.)

Yet another critical condition of power is an economic surplus.[6] Power cannot be effectively mobilized in a society unless there is sufficient productivity to free people from purely economic activities. Decision-makers cannot be effective when tied to the day-to-day routines of surviving; police and armies cannot be sustained without the ability to produce a large economic surplus. Moreover, with an economic surplus, a society possesses more options that require decision-making procedures. And, as we will observe in chapter 7, surplus production is almost always usurped and used to buy power.

Thus, we can conclude that as societies grow in size, raise their levels of productivity, and successively deal with threats in their environment, the level of power and its degree of centralization will increase. These processes are self-reinforcing. Large societies that are politically integrated can grow even larger, forcing increased growth of political authority to control the actions of the larger population. Societies that have been politically centralized under conditions of threat can seek out new enemies in order to justify and sustain political unity.[7] And once increases in productivity are coordinated politically, an important condition for further increases has been met. These processes can also be mutually reinforcing. For example, a politically unified population that sees another as a threat will sometimes conquer and incorporate enemy populations in order to sustain itself—thereby increasing the size of the population and the need for further political centralization. Or, escalating productivity can create options for defining other societies as enemies; or it can create demands for their resources or their use as markets. In either case, an increase the the level of political power is the likely result.

As power is mobilized, consolidated, and centralized, it presents a paradox. Power is necessary "to get things done" in large and productive societies; but at the same time it is a source of resentment, tension, and opposition. Those with power usually wish to keep it; those without power often covet it, or resent those who have it. Thus, the conditions that create power set into motion one of the most volatile and fascinating dynamics of a society: the inherent tension between those with and without power.[8] Those with power seek to legitimate their right to make decisions and control the activities of others; those without power are ready to question its use. The stability of a political order thus rests on its capacity to be defined by those without power as legitimate—that is, the belief that those with power have the right to rule. While populations can be coerced through force for considerable periods of time, the use of force generates opposition, consumes enormous quantities of resources, requires constant monitoring, and makes a society vulnerable to outside forces. In the long run, then, societies held together by coercion collapse or are destroyed by outside forces.

Historically, legitimacy has been achieved through a variety of mechanisms:[9] appeals to religious sanctions, invocation of the weight of tradition and all that went before, appeals to patriotism or nationalism, mobilization of charismatic and revolutionary leadership, and creation of legally defined procedures for citizen representation in decision-making processes. Modern democracies represent one use of this last legitimating mechanism. As people come to believe that their views have at least some representation in political decisions, they are more likely to accept the use of power as legitimate. Such is not always the case, for political democracies have historically crumbled. But among the larger, highly productive societies of the world, appeals to the ideology of democracy and efforts to install some kind of legally defined representation have become dominant modes of legitimating power. Democracy, we can hypothesize, is most likely when other procedures for legitimation—religion, tradition, charisma—become unviable and when coercive force is not considered an acceptable option. The viability of these other modes of legitimation is, we believe, related to the size and productivity of a society. That is, larger societies with highly productive economies can rely less and less on religion, tradition, or charisma to legitimate the ever greater concentrations of power necessary to sustain a large society with a surplus. Highly productive societies constantly alter people's daily routines, create secular orientations, increase levels of education (knowledge), and in other ways make religion, tradi-

tion, and charisma less appealing and viable means of legitimation.

In modern industrial societies, then we are likely to
observe a political system that reveals high levels of power,
that evidences centralization of decision-making, and that
reveals democratic processes in selecting decision-makers.
Societies vary, of course, in the *degree* and *pattern* of political
organization. These variations represent different approaches to resolving the dilemmas of governance in large and
productive societies. We need to examine some of these general dilemmas in order to appreciate fully the extent to which
political problems in America are endemic to the governance
of large-scale industrial societies.

One of these dilemmas concerns the degree and pattern of political administration in a society. At one extreme
is a highly centralized bureaucratic state that seeks to regulate virtually all internal activity, while at the other extreme
is a loose confederation of self-governing regions and prov-
inces. Highly centralized political systems tend to reveal bureaucratic rigidity and unresponsiveness to changing conditions, low levels of democratic representation, and inefficiency
in administration. Yet, they are able to make rapid decisions,
to mobilize resources quickly for achieving a given societal
goal, and to bend internal activities to collective purposes.
Decentralized systems reveal problems of achieving coordination of activities and of mobilizing resources to meet societal goals. But, in contrast to centralized systems, they tend
to be more flexible and democratic.

The USSR and United States represent the best examples of two societies that have sought to resolve problems
of large-scale administration in different ways. The USSR is
a highly centralized state, whereas the United States is,
comparatively, at least, decentralized. Thus, as with all *relatively* decentralized systems,[10] we would expect the major
problems of governance in America to revolve around (1)
achieving a sufficient degree of coordination, control, and
regulation in efforts to meet societal objectives, and (2) man-
aging the ways in which diverse interests are to achieve rep-

resentation in decision-making processes. Conversely, to the extent that a trend toward centralization of political power is evident in America, we would expect problems of bureaucratic rigidity, unresponsiveness, and unrepresentativeness to surface.

Another set of related dilemmas revolves around the pattern of democratic representation in a society. There is always the dilemma in democracies of effecting a balance between, on the one hand, a representative body that is too responsive to volatile shifts in public moods and, on the other hand, one that is unresponsive to and unrepresentative of the public. A wide variety of legislative approaches have been attempted to resolve this problem—from representatives who merely "rubber stamp" policies made by party leaders or monarchs to unstable multiparty systems that frequently reconstitute the balance of political power. The USSR and Italy probably represent the present-day extremes of this continuum, with Western societies in general tending toward high degrees of representativeness and with Eastern European societies moving toward less responsive legislative bodies that merely approve policies decided by elites. We should expect, therefore, systems which have truly representative legislatures to present a number of common problems, including: periodic shifts in political policies, frequent inability to enact comprehensive legislation or make society-wide decisions, and constant ideological debate. Conversely, less representative legislatures can make decisions more rapidly, will engage in considerably less debate, and will tend to stay with policies until party leaders change them. The legislative system in the United States is somewhat unique, highly visible and open to the public and to vested interests.[11] Thus, it is inevitable that it would evidence problems in maintaining stable policies, developing long-term political programs, subordinating blatantly ideological issues to concrete problems, and insulating itself not just from powerful vested interests but also from sudden shifts in public sentiments. But such dilemmas are not aberrations; they are endemic to multiparty legislative systems. We would do well to stress this last point as we approach an analysis of the American system of governance.

The Dynamics of American Government

Cultural Dilemmas in the American Political System

Americans hold a number of somewhat contradictory beliefs about government.[12] These beliefs reflect the realities of governmental processes and at the same time contribute to the maintenance of the realities by circumscribing what people see as possible or desirable. Moreover, they reflect the contradictory application of core values to concrete social processes. One very powerful complex of beliefs concerns people's desire to maintain "local control" and to limit the capacity of "big brother" to intervene in their lives. This complex involves the application of the core values, freedom and individualism. Contradicting this system of beliefs is another set which holds that the federal government "should do something" about various problems. This set of beliefs invokes the value of activism, which, in this context, contradicts the way the values of freedom and individualism are applied to political affairs. Thus, beliefs hold that social affairs should be managed at the local level, but that the federal government must use its power to intervene in persistent and pressing problems.

Mediating this contradiction to some extent is another complex of beliefs, ratified in the U.S. Constitution, that advocates a "checks and balances" system of government where the branches of local, state, and federal government—the legislative, administrative, and judicial branches—circumscribe each other and set limits on each other's power. Strong local government, Americans implicitly argue, operates to check the powers of the federal government, whereas the intervention of the federal government mobilizes local governments to address significant problems. In this way, the values of freedom, individualism, and activism are made to seem politically compatible.

Yet, there remains considerable contradiction among these values. Depending upon the issue, they can be selectively mobilized to legitimate or condemn virtually any governmental action. As we noted earlier, this contradiction both reflects and helps to perpetuate the actual structure of government. For as we will see, the administration of power in America is an unsystematic, eclectic, and somewhat chaotic mix of federal, state, county, and city programs which do indeed check and balance each other, while at the same time, they can also duplicate, overlap, and inhibit each other's implementation. American governance typically reveals considerable controversy over the "proper role" of federal, state, and local government, assuring that much energy is consumed in working out jurisdiction disputes among the levels and branches of government.

In addition to this contradictory cluster of beliefs about the administration of government is a strong set of beliefs about how the electoral process should occur. Over the years, Americans have increasingly become suspicious of ideologically unified parties and of closed party politics. Indeed, in accordance with the values of individualism, achievement, and activism, a candidate should therefore be evaluated on the basis of his or her personal qualities, a belief which weakens party structure in America. The overall consequence of beliefs in this "candidate democracy" is that the unsystematic character of political administration is compounded, somewhat, by a diversity of elected decision-makers who, without strong party identification, have difficulty formulating, and acting upon, comprehensive political programs.

The existence of these beliefs reflects Americans' historical distrust of government as well as strongly held values. But at the same time, the invocation of these beliefs to limit political programs represents a self-fulfilling prophecy that sustains people's distrust in government—their sense that it "can't get things done." For when elected decision-makers are each responding to local and diverse interests, and when the administration of government continually rekindles jurisdictional and ideological disputes, it is inevitable that formulating clear national policies will be difficult—a fact that, however inevitable, furthers people's doubts about government and reinforces their conviction that government intervention must be monitored—and that, perhaps, yet another candidate with other personal qualities can "get the nation out of this mess."

Structural Dilemmas in the Electoral Process

Unlike other political democracies, the United States does not have a strong party system. Two general parties dominate the electoral process, but they are not highly structured administratively, unified ideologically, or secure financially. Candidates will affiliate with a party, but, they must raise much of their own campaign money and must state *their* views, as opposed to the party's, on issues. In addition, parties often rely upon the charisma of prominent candidates to raise money and to formulate programs. In most other societies, the party is much more prominent in forming the issues, raising money, and selecting candidates.

The primary system of selecting candidates who will run in the general election further weakens parties. If a candidate is to be its party's representative, funds must be secured and positions taken in the primary election before the candidate becomes closely identified with the party. By the time a candidate becomes the party's nominee, he or she has usually developed a nonparty base of support and has selected issues on which to take a stand. As a result, the party's fate often depends more upon the candidate than the candidate upon the party.

Federal financing of campaigns has also contributed to the weakening of unity in parties. To secure federal matching funds, candidates must limit the size of individual donations and engage in a full reporting of contributors. As a consequence, the party loses some of its financing functions, since federal guidelines as much as party fiscal formulas determine the amount of money a candidate will receive in an election. And if a candidate wishes to pass up federal financing, then he or she probably has a base of financial support outside the party, which weakens the party's control over the candidate.

This system is consistent with Americans' belief that

one should "vote for the candidate more than the party." But it has a number of consequences against which the citizenry often objects. First, since candidates operate as much outside as inside the party, loyalty, as we mentioned earlier, is to those narrow interests that financed the campaign and to the often parochial views of a limited constituency. Any comprehensive piece of legislation will inevitably encounter resistance from an ad hoc coalition of interests which may have nothing more in common than their opposition to a particular program. Second, bringing in the vote on an issue can often prove difficult when legislators might have to go against those interests who financed, and those constituents who supported, their election. While such a situation may represent a democratic ideal to many, it makes the Congress less effective in dealing with national problems. And third, as a result of this fact, the executive branch and even judiciary have increasingly become far more significant in formulating national priorities and programs than has the Congress, which now can, at best, only react to initiatives from nonelected officials and agencies.

The irony of this situation is that the more elected officials remain responsive to local constituents, the less able they are to be unified by party discipline, and hence the more legislative initiative is taken away from Congress. Americans' belief in the candidate democracy and their distrust of strong ideologically unified parties has resulted in congressional indecisiveness, thereby forcing legislative initiatives to come from the executive branch of government—the very embodiment of "big brother."

The Structural Dilemmas of Congressional Decision-Making

The problems of initiating and enacting comprehensive legislation also result from structural features of Congress. Party leaders can and do allocate their members to various committees in the House and Senate, and thus have some power to exact conformity. But this power has been weakened considerably over the years as various "reforms" have weakened the positions of leaders who, if they are too autocratic, can find themselves replaced through a party caucus vote. Moreover, since the parties themselves are not ideologically unified, there are always shades of interpretation for any issue within the party, with the result that conservative Democrats and middle-of-the road Republicans are more likely to agree with each other than with the liberal wings of their own parties.

The structure of the legislative process reinforces these problems, especially when legislation is controversial, since comprehensive and change-oriented legislation is almost always subject to the mobilizing of lobbies by diverse interest groups. Without strong party discipline, legislators are extremely vulnerable to lobbying efforts not only from private sectors but also from all the executive branches of government. These efforts are well financed and orchestrated, and as a consequence, they can swing votes one way or the other, especially when the personal convictions of a legislator are not strong or when constituent sentiment is weak or evenly divided. For legislation that is change-oriented or national in scope, lobbying pressures from the private sector will have the net effect of opposing the legislation; typically a larger number of vested interests wish to preserve the status quo than to change it. Both in the relevant congressional committees and on the floor of the House or Senate, the pressures typically work to make passage of change-oriented legislation difficult unless it is strongly supported by the executive branch, whose lobbying can counteract that of private interests.

Figure 3.1 presents one way to visualize the pressures against comprehensive and change-oriented legislation, listing the roadblocks at each stage of the legislative process. From the figure it is clear why legislative initiatives in Congress are not radical and why presidential support for legislation must be extremely strong if it is to become law.

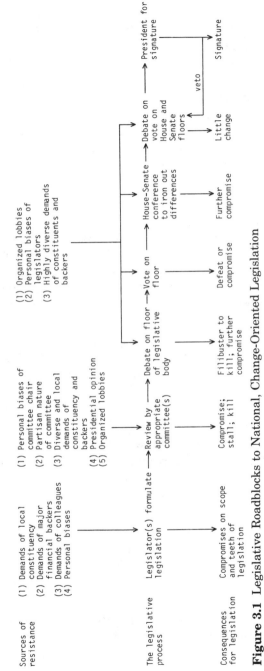

Figure 3.1 Legislative Roadblocks to National, Change-Oriented Legislation

Sources of resistance
(1) Demands of local constituency
(2) Demands of major financial backers
(3) Demands of colleagues
(4) Personal biases

(1) Personal biases of committee chair
(2) Partisan nature of committee
(3) Diverse and local demands of constituency and backers
(4) Presidential opinion
(5) Organized lobbies

(1) Organized lobbies
(2) Personal biases of legislators
(3) Highly diverse demands of constituents and backers

The legislative process
Legislator(s) formulate legislation → Review by appropriate committee(s) → Debate on floor of legislative body → Vote on floor → House-Senate conference to iron out differences → Debate on vote on House and Senate floors → President for signature

veto

Consequences for legislation
Compromises on scope and teeth of legislation → Compromise; stall; kill → Filibuster to kill; further compromise → Defeat or compromise → Further compromise → Little change → Signature

Dilemmas of Federalism and the Administration of Government

Compared with most industrial nations, America is a decentralized, federalist system, with fifty individual states, their constituent counties, and thousands of local communities supposedly determining much of their own destiny. The decentralized system is the original concept of the federal government as one that will perform best when its duties are restricted to "housekeeping" chores: defense and security, coinage of money, and regulation of trade. Complementing this concept are beliefs in the desirability of local autonomy. Moreover, conservative economic beliefs (see table 2.1) stressing that free enterprise is necessary for progress further buttress this concept of good government. In contradiction to beliefs in federalism, local autonomy, and laissez-faire, however, is a second feature of American government: the trend toward centralization. Increasingly, decision-making power is passing from states and local communities to the federal government, and within the federal government, into the hands of the president and away from Congress and the judiciary.

In all federalist systems, problems of arranging national priorities are a reflection of the contradictions between local control and a large, centralized government. A decentralized federalist system is attuned to local rather than national interests, with the result that, as we noted above, efforts by Congress to create national programs are likely to encounter resistance by coalitions of local interests. Furthermore, when national programs are enacted, the federalist structure of government has the potential to neutralize them. When there is an attempt to work through local governments and utilize the private sector of the economy (in accordance with conservative economic beliefs), many federal programs can be rendered less effective by waste, inefficiency, graft, and corruption at the local level. Thus, national planning is inherently difficult in a political system that values competition as well as "checks and balances" among different levels of government.

Despite intense resistance, centralization of government into the hands of federal agencies has been one response to this problem. But while resolving some problems, national centralization creates others. First, large bureaucracies can often be inefficient themselves. Once created, they are difficult to dismantle, even if their effectiveness is questionable. Second, centralized bureaucracies can become less sensitive to local needs while remaining attuned to their internal bureaucratic traditions and the dictates of the central authority structure. Third, in large, centralized bureaucracies the potential for the abuse of power is greater than in smaller systems, since it is more difficult to oversee and regulate their activities.

A fourth problem with centralization concerns the issue of national priorities. Once large bureaucratic establishments are created, changing priorities becomes more difficult, since bureaucratic agencies have considerably greater political power to lobby for their own interests than the public. In the recent American experience, for example, the military establishment—the Pentagon and related agencies—poses constant problems over military versus domestic priorities. While the establishment of a centralized federal government during the 1930s revolved around domestic programs (social security, housing, and welfare), the post–Korean War period has seen domestic programs consume a smaller proportion of the budget, although they still represent a majority of expenditures. Meanwhile, the military budget in the 1970s and 1980s has risen to support levels equivalent to what before the 1960s would have constituted mobilization for war.[13]

Structural Dilemmas in Maintaining the "Balances of Power"

The U.S. Constitution originally defined the powers of the presidency rather ambiguously. But over time, in response to a long series of national crises ranging from war to economic depression, this ambiguity has become translated into far-reaching powers: to appoint and remove administrators from office, to direct administrative agencies, to initiate most legislation for Congress, to direct and control the military, to make war, to regulate the budget by selectively administering funds granted by Congress, and to appoint and direct cabinet officers and the administrative bureaucracy under them.

This centralization of power has occurred in the face of strong beliefs about local control and about balances of power. To overcome these traditions powerful forces have been operating to create a centralized political system. One of these has been the sheer growth in the size of the nation from a small, agrarian population to an industrial, urban populace of over 200 million. Large urban and industrial societies probably cannot be governed locally, since a proliferation of nationwide problems makes decentralization most difficult. A second force leading to government intervention has been the movement toward destruction of the capitalist economy through monopolization by a few corporations. The boom-and-bust cycles of the economy, culminating in the Great Depression, have also necessitated further control (see chapter 2). Still more pressure for centralization has come from the redefinition of citizenship and civil rights for formerly disfranchised groups who have demanded federal intervention in the social and economic spheres.

Another source of pressure for centralization has come from war. From 1776 to 1900 American army units participated in an estimated 9,000 battles and skirmishes, and naval units engaged in 1,100 missions involving violent conflict. These figures average about 90 violent conflicts per year for the first 125 years of American government.[14] When twentieth-century conflicts are added to this inventory, the military involvement of American government becomes clear: aside from World Wars I and II, the United States, in recent decades, has engaged in military actions in Korea (1950–53), Indochina (1951–53), Guatemala (1954), the Congo (1960), Cuba (1961), Laos (1961), Vietnam (1962), the Dominican Republic (1965), Cambodia (1970), Laos (1971), and Grenada (1983).

Whether the involvement is full-scale or limited, people and resources are mobilized on a national scale. War activities create both social problems (protests, hardships, debate over veterans' benefits, etc.) and economic problems (such as inflation), increasing the need for even more centralized power. And once a large military establishment is created, economic, social, monetary, and political policies become interwoven with this establishment (see chapter 11). The interconnections with the military increase the power of the president as commander-in-chief, and the power of the Pentagon. They also make the redirection of national priorities toward domestic issues by the executive branch of government a divisive issue for Americans, as has clearly been the case in the 1980s.

In the original system of checks and balances, Congress was to mitigate the powers of the executive branch. Under the provisions of the Constitution, Congress was empowered to initiate most legislation, to establish national priorities, to set up and regulate executive agencies, and to determine the structure of federal courts. Since Congress was set up as a representative body, the will of the populace was to guide the form and direction of the federal government. However, the growing centralization of government has led Congress to abdicate much of its power. Now the president and executive agencies establish national priorities and initiate the most important legislation. This shift in the balance of powers has resulted from Congress's inability to enact consistently change-oriented and/or comprehensive legislation. One of the great ironies, then, of a highly representative legislative branch—which, despite the opinion of its critics, does respond to both organized interests and the ideological biases of constituents—is that it has lost much of its capacity to act. It is a *re*active force; Congress can fail to pass programs initiated by the President, refuse to confirm key appointments, block efforts at government reorganization, and withdraw funding for programs. Yet, in being a reactive force, Congress contributes to the lack of consistency in federal actions, since when it exerts its power to block legislation it is likely to decrease the overall level of coherence in government programs. The result is more concerted efforts by the executive branch to consolidate power in order to avoid congressional "interference" in its legislative programs.

One of the interesting consequences of the growing imbalance in the powers of the Congress and the executive has been the increase in influence of the federal judiciary. Indeed, an important source of programmatic change in America over the last thirty years has been the federal court system, culminating in the Supreme Court. The list of changes initiated by the Supreme Court, from school desegregation and protection of civil liberties in criminal cases to draft reform and reapportionment, is extensive and comes close to equaling that of Congress and the presidency combined. In passing on the consitutionality of various laws and practices, the Supreme Court has been able to legislate new, reform-oriented, comprehensive laws. This legislative function of the Court is not an abuse of its power but rather an obligation imposed by the Constitution. For the disfranchised, poorly financed, and loosely organized segments of the population, the sympathy of the Supreme Court has represented one of the few legitimate channels for redressing grievances. With comparatively few resources and only a small organization, groups can initiate test cases to challenge unfair laws and practices. In many ways, the court system has represented a counterforce for the public and small interests against the well-financed and well-organized interest groups exerting a disporportionate influence on Congress. Further, the Court has forced consideration of controversial issues (civil rights, abortion, busing, etc.) that Congress might prove incapable of resolving in a forthright manner.

Naturally, there are limits on the Supreme Court's capacity to initiate change in society. First, the Court rules on the constitutionality of practices, but it cannot administer the details of the required action. The courts are not regulatory agencies. In fact, they must often await a lawsuit to determine if rulings are being carried out properly. The result of this fact has been, at times, inefficient, reluctant, and even subversive administration of court rulings. Probably the best example is in the area of school integration; some thirty years after *Brown v. Board of Education,* integration is still resisted, often with considerable violence by the public. And as long as public resistance is high, representative bodies at all levels of government will be reluctant to enact clear administrative guidelines and to enforce those established by lower federal courts.

Second, the Court rules on *specific* issues brought before it; it cannot always establish comprehensive policies that take related issues into consideration. Such comprehensive policies are best established through action by Congress, but as we have discovered, the structure of government presents a number of roadblocks to change-oriented legislation that might reorder national priorities.

Third, the composition of the Supreme Court determines, to a great extent, just how change-oriented decisions will be. The Supreme Court is ultimately a political body that can evidence a liberal, moderate, or conservative profile. Over the last thirty years the Court has evidenced a liberal profile, but in the late 1970s and into the 1980s its composition appears to have shifted toward a more moderate profile. While specific decisions can still be labeled "liberal" or "conservative," the cumulative impact of many decisions appears to have shifted judicial policies away from major change.

These limitations suggest that the court system is inherently less capable of generating national planning and reordering national priorities than either the executive or legislative branches. It is only in the face of the growing power of the executive branch, coupled with the structural impediments to congressional concensus, that a reliance on the courts has been so necessary for those who want a definitive set of policies on an issue. But the appropriate limitations on the power of the courts simply dramatize the current dilemma of maintaining balances of power and at the same time implementing coherent programs.

The Dilemma of Concentrated Power

One of the great dilemmas in human affairs is that the concentration of power usually increases both the capacity to get things done and the potential for the abuse of this power. In societies that value political democracy, this potential for abuse is seen as particularly problematic, since such societies emphasize legal definitions of, and limitations on, power that can be used by government. Another irony of Congress's inability to get things done as a result of the diverse influences on its members has been an increase in the illegal activities by government agencies frustrated by perceptions of congressional inaction. During the early 1970s, for example, a number of such illegal activities were exposed: The FBI was found to have attempted character assassinations of Dr. Martin Luther King, Jr., while keeping files on politicians in order to blackmail them for their support. The CIA, against its charter, was discovered to have engaged in domestic spying, while maintaining extensive files on citizens. The Pentagon was revealed to have a file on those who, exercising their constitutional rights, had protested the Vietnam War. The IRS was found to have audited people's income tax returns at the request of politicians, while giving favorable treatment to key political figures. A president was exposed as having condoned illegal staff activities against "enemies" of his administration, while lying to the American people about his involvement.

These activities clearly violated people's beliefs about what government should be, confirming for many the dangers of "big government" and "big brother." Initial shock, surprise, and dismay have now in the 1980s become transformed into apathy about these illegal activities. But the abuse of power that these activities represent will remain an enduring problem of culture and structure in America.

Most abuses of power revolve around activities to gather and store information on citizens in order to neutralize their resistance to the use of power—activities that go against basic American values of freedom, but that are made inevitable by the desire to preserve centralized power. Power is best exercised when resistance can be overcome, and agencies of the government have an interest in knowing the potential sources of resistance to their policies. The Pentagon, FBI, CIA, and other agencies given the necessary power will, unless constantly checked and monitored, seek the information that will allow them to expand their power.

With technologies such as electronic surveillance devices and computer data banks, it becomes possible to acquire, process, store, and retrieve information with much greater efficiency than ever before. Thus, the temptations for illegal data collection are much greater. Moreover, these new technologies allow for greater freedom from detection on the part of outside investigators than was at one time possible.

Why are people in agencies willing to engage in covert activities in a society valuing individual freedom? The answers to such a question are manifold: (1) Those engaged in these activities often do not view them as illegal or immoral, but as necessary and proper. (2) The organizations where such activities are most likely to occur are often charged with the tasks of defense of the nation; hence it is often easy to justify questionable activities in the name of the higher goal. (3) Congress and the American people have traditionally held in high esteem those organizations that have engaged in illegal activities, and thus, monitoring and supervision have been minimal. (4) These agencies have been given considerable power, and power begets efforts to increase power. That is, power often becomes its own goal.

This dilemma revolves around the question of how much power should be bestowed on any agency, and on what amount of information is necessary for that agency to perform its function. In a modern society with a myriad of programs and agencies charged with their administration, a considerable amount of information is necessary if the agency is to do its job. But how much information? And of what kind? And who is to decide what is and what is not necessary?

There are no easy answers to these questions. People appear to desire the protection of federal agencies despite their beliefs about big government and about local autonomy. They want the services that centralized, concentrated power allows, but they want to preserve individualism and freedom. Thus, most seek monitoring procedures that would, in all likelihood, create another centralized agency with considerable power. Moreover, in the face of a Congress fraught with internal problems, and subject to lobbying pressures from the very agencies it seeks to regulate, it may prove difficult to establish effective or permanent congressional oversight of federal agencies. Therein lies one of the more enduring dilemmas of America's governmental structure.

Chapter 4

Control
in a Free Society

The Dynamics of Social Control

In all societies, there is a tension between forces generating disorder and those operating to maintain order. As societies increase in size and complexity, this tension greatly escalates, with the result that modern, industrial societies always reveal widespread deviance and conflict, on the one hand, and an elaborate system of social control, on the other. The process of social control thus becomes one of the most visible and controversial features of contemporary society.

In contrast to the situation in complex, industrial systems, social control processes are not centers of public debate in simple, traditional societies. Socialization of individuals into a common culture, the use of informal, face-to-face sanctions, the performance of religious rituals, and the embeddedness of activity in cohesive kin groups and peer groups are sufficient to maintain order. At times, of course, feuds erupt among kin groups, individuals come into conflict, and deviant acts require formal sanctions by tribal leaders. But in comparison with modern societies, the process of social control in tribal societies is recessive.

It is with urbanization, growing inequality, expanding specialization of roles, increased economic productivity, and other interrelated forces that conflict, deviance, and potentially disruptive tensions escalate. Large preindustrial systems always revealed widespread deviance and an extensive system of police, courts, and corrections to deal with disorder. Industrialization has simply accelerated this situation, primarily because it weakens primary processes of social control—socialization into a common culture, group involvement, face-to-face informal sanctioning, and emotionally charged rituals. As the number of people in a society increases, as their escalated rates of mobility break ties to neighborhoods, kin, groups, and community, as their assumption of specialized occupational roles reduces their common world view, and as their shares of resources divide them into distinctive social classes, it is inevitable that conflict among individuals, groups, and subpopulations should increase. Early sociologists tended to view this inevitability with dismay; and they worried about social pathologies and the breakdown of society.

Such worry was excessive, perhaps because the changes brought by industrialization were compared to a rather romanticized view of traditional society where primary control processes were seen to prevail. In the present day, we need to examine social control, deviance, and conflict more realistically. Primary social control processes are still the most crucial, and if they ceased to operate, modern social systems would soon collapse. Yet, these primary processes are inadequate to the control problems of a modern industrial system; as a result, supplementary control processes have evolved in human societies.

One of these is the elaboration of the political state, or government. As problems of coordination become acute, power becomes concentrated to facilitate the increased volume of transactions among segments of the society and to maintain order in the face of conflict. The expansion of the state creates a new source of tension, as people and groups resent the constraint that comes with expanded power. Nonetheless, political power is extended into an elaborate legal apparatus.

Thus, any modern society will reveal (1) an elaborate system of legislative and administrative bodies—legislatures, councils, supervisors, administrative heads, and regulatory agencies—that creates laws; (2) a system of enforcement—federal, state, and local police, security forces, military, and militia, enforcement arms of regulatory agencies—to maintain some degree of conformity to the ever-expanding body of law; (3) a system of adjudicating bodies—federal, state, municipal courts, administrative tribunals, and military courts—to cope with the detected offenders of laws as well as to resolve purely civil disputes among private parties outside the enforcement system; and (4) as offenders are found guilty of violations and as the general rates of deviance inevitably increase, a system of incarceration structures—prisons, juvenile halls, mental hospitals, local jails, security farms—to remove deviants from the mainstream of the society.

In some societies law-making, law-enforcing, law-adjudicating, and incarceration structures constitute a true "system" in the sense of relatively unambiguous spheres of authority and clear lines of articulation among organizational units, whereas in other societies, such as the United States, there is considerable ambiguity, overlap, duplication, and conflict among social control agencies. But in all societies, whatever their degree of systemization, social control becomes a prominent institutional feature, and at the same time poses a series of contradictions and dilemmas for the members of the society.

The Dynamics of Social Control in America

Secondary Social Control

In most political democracies where an emphasis on individual freedom and equality is a paramount value, the concentration of power in an array of social control structures poses a dilemma. By itself, concentrated power is always resented because it limits options and imposes constraints, but when juxtaposed with the values of freedom and individualism, social control structures will often be viewed in ambivalent, if enigmatic, terms. Such is the case in the United States, where Americans hold contradictory beliefs about the social control system and where their responses to this system are tinged with a recognition of its necessity, and at the same time, a distrust in its fairness and efficiency. As we come to appreciate, this ambivalence of the citizenry toward the social control system in America marks one of its most dynamic features.

The structure of the control system can be summarized as follows:

1. *Law-enacting processes* occur at the federal, state, county, and city level. Bodies of lawmakers are elected. In addition to the elected legislative bodies are a wide variety of agencies at all levels which enact laws through the creation and enforcement of administrative procedures. The Internal Revenue Service, the Civil Aeronautics Board, the Federal Trade Commission, the armed services, the city planning commissions, the state alcoholic beverage control boards, and other administrative units are examples of law-enacting bodies.

2. *Law-enforcing processes* are also carried out by a diverse array of federal, state, county, city, and other governmental units. The armed services, the national guard, the FBI, the enforcement arms of regulatory agencies, the federal marshalls attached to federal courts, state troopers or highway patrols, county sheriffs, city police, and even legally sanctioned private enforcement organizations such as collection agencies all show the diversity of the enforcement process in America.

3. *Law-adjudicating processes* revolve around a hierarchical system of federal, state, and municipal courts, culminating in the U.S. Supreme Court. Supplementing this hierarchy is a system of military courts and a collection of quasi-courts consisting of administrative hearing boards or review

boards, such as parole boards, review panels of most regulatory agencies, the hearing procedures of the IRS, and the like.

4. *Incarcerating processes* consist of government financed and controlled federal prisons; various types of state prisons, juvenile halls, and farms; county and city jails; and state and county hospitals or care centers for varying types of deviants. Alongside of these publicly financed structures is a host of private homes, hospitals, care centers, sanatoriums, treatment centers, and the like which incarcerate people for various forms of deviant behavior.

The diversity of structures signals that formal, secondary social control processes are not a coherent "system" but a loose array or confederation of agencies, organizations, and bureaus performing a wide variety of law-enacting, enforcing, and adjudicating functions and engaging in varying amounts and degrees of incarceration. Such is inevitably the case in a society that is built on federalist principles (see chapter 3), which values decentralized authority, and which emphasizes personal freedom and protection from arbitrary and unequal applications of power. Yet, as we noted in chapter 1, Americans also value rationality, efficiency, and cost-effectiveness which, in essence, contradict their desire for a loosely structured control system without Big Brother overtones.

Nowhere is this set of contradictions more evident than in the criminal justice system, which is probably the most controversial portion of the secondary social control process in America. The remainder of this chapter will therefore examine this system in greater detail.

The Criminal Justice System in America

The Political Economy of Defining Crime. There is little agreement over what basic concepts like "crime" and "criminal" mean.[1] The safest course is to adopt the common Western legal definition, in which "crime" is behavior that violates formally enacted criminal law and a "criminal" is a person found guilty by a legally constituted court of violating a criminal law. This definition represents in symbolic form the gradual takeover by governments of the exclusive right to define crime and of the police to administer reactions to criminal behavior. Yet, even in the face of the elaborate crime-fighting machinery, there is always more crime than the legal system can effectively handle. Officials are forced to narrow their working definition of crime so that it encompasses only common behaviors like murder, forcible rape, robbery, aggravated assault, burglary, larceny, auto theft, arson, and a few other offenses. Even after doing this, most legal systems are still overrun by the volume of crimes that they are required to process.

Compounding this inability to deal with common crimes is the apparent incapacity of the justice system to deal with "elite crimes" committed by political officials and others who are rich, powerful, or notable members of the elite classes. Such criminals are hard to catch and most difficult to convict.[2] As we noted in the last chapter, the wealthy exert more power than the less affluent in defining the goals of government. Hence, it could be expected that crimes committed by the less affluent would be defined as the major part of the "crime problem" in America. Thus, the definition of crime offered earlier must be qualified by the political realities of a society. In accordance with distribution of power, some law-breaking behaviors are going to be defined as more criminal than others. Moreover, since the wealthy possess the resources to fight enforcement of laws in the courts, they are less likely than those without resources to be defined as criminals. Such is not always the case, for indeed, the wealthy do not exert absolute control over the justice system; but we should note that they are able to exert disproportionate influence in determining the operative definitions of "crimes."

Cultural Beliefs About Crime. Deviant acts in general, and criminal behavior in particular, are always culturally embellished by emotion-arousing beliefs. To an extent, these beliefs are imposed by political processes that favor the wealthy and work against the poor, but they are also the result of nonpolitical processes. Daily experiences, religious convictions, social ideology, educational attainment, social class position, and core values all condition people's beliefs. As a result, no single set of beliefs dominates Americans' thinking about crime. Instead, most societal members subscribe to several beliefs at once, even though they are often contradictory. For example, Americans hold at least some of the following beliefs simultaneously: "Crime is caused by a devil, demons, or a rival god." "Criminals are at birth a distinct physical or mental type and cannot help but engage in crime." "Humans decide, through rational thought processes, whether or not to engage in crime." "Crime is a byproduct of social disorganization" (that is, otherwise normal persons engage in crime when exposed to rapid social change, poverty, mass migration, and broken homes, for example). "Crime is caused by personality disorder." "Crime is caused by culture conflict." These beliefs rise and fall in popularity, but none wither away; in fact, all these ideas about crime have considerable support.

There are also competing societal beliefs about the best way to control crime and to deal with criminals. Again, there is disagreement about the best method of crime control, and most members of American society hold somewhat contradictory beliefs: "Criminals should be punished, for society must seek retribution." "Criminals should be isolated and held separate from the rest of society." "Criminals should be rehabilitated through therapy, education, and job training." These contradictions are translated into contradictory and vacillating policies in the courts and prisons. Sometimes reactions to criminals are punitive and harsh; at other times, reactions are rehabilitative and benign. And frequently, they are both punitive and rehabilitative. It should not be surprising, in light of the cultural contradictions in people's beliefs, that the structure of criminal social control is also filled with contradictory procedures.

The contradictions among beliefs about criminals, as

well as contradictions between these beliefs and the actual
structure of the justice system, are aggravated by the American ideals of justice. Built into the Constitution, and reinforced by general values of equality and freedom, these ideals state that all citizens are "equal under the law," that all
criminals are "innocent until proven guilty," and that all accused criminals have a right to a "speedy trial by their peers."
Such ideals often come into conflict with beliefs in the moral
and mental inferiority of criminals and with beliefs about the
need to punish and isolate criminals. For in the haste to rid
society of the criminally inclined, it is often difficult to sustain beliefs in their "innocence until proven guilty" and other
tenets of justice. More fundamentally, as we will come to see,
these ideals are difficult to maintain in the face of the enormous volume of criminal cases in relation to the physical and
administrative capacity of the justice system to process these
cases—creating yet one more contradiction between cultural
ideals and structural realities.

   *The Structural Contradictions in Criminal Social Con-
trol in America.* Law-enacting, law-enforcing, law-adjudicating, and criminal-incarcerating components of the American
justice system are, on the one hand, separate subsystems
comprised of organizations with their own bureaucratic imperatives; and yet on the other hand, they are supposed to
coordinate their activities. The bureaucratic imperatives of one
subsystem often operate at cross-purposes to those of another.
   Indeed, each subsystem of the overall criminal social
control system has its own historical evolution; each recruits
different kinds of personnel with widely varying social backgrounds, educational credentials, and social philosophies; and
each is subject to different kinds and degrees of political and
financial pressure. For example, legislatures may suddenly
"get tough" on alcohol-related crime and pass new laws requiring mandatory prison sentences for convicted offenders.
However, police departments are overloaded in just trying to

respond to citizen calls for public service and for protection from common criminals, with the consequence that street-level police officers might not have much time to enforce the new laws. The courts are overloaded with pending civil and criminal cases, so that they may not be able to process new types of criminal cases. Or, the prosecuting attorney may be reluctant to charge offenders with crimes that carry mandatory, strict penalties, because this would retard the plea-bargaining process that keeps the court system operating. In the same political jurisdictions correctional agencies might be committed to rehabilitation through counseling, education, and job training; they may not welcome additional new offenders because their caseloads are already too extensive and because their rehabilitative beliefs require commitment of time and energy to each inmate.

Problems of bureaucratic articulation among the components of the justice system are aggravated by the contradictory beliefs that Americans hold about criminals. In fact, varying incumbents in each bureaucracy are likely to reveal a different profile of beliefs, creating cultural conflicts within a bureaucracy about how it should proceed with its tasks and how it should deal with other bureaucracies. When these conflicts are added to the enormous work overloads and underfunding of each component in the system, then it is not difficult to predict considerable chaos, variability, and inconsistency in how justice is administered in America.

These, then, are some of the general dilemmas that inhere in the criminal justice system. They are not easily resolved, and they are a constant source of controversy. As we now proceed to examine the operation of this system in more detail, we will come to appreciate the extent to which the general cultural and structural contradictions discussed here are built into the structure and operation of criminal justice in America. We will also come to understand more fully why crime and justice in America will continue to represent an enduring dilemma.

Crime and Justice in America

Definitional Dilemmas

In 1930, Congress authorized the FBI to begin collecting data from American municipal police departments on the number of crimes known to the police and the number of criminal arrests made by the police. In order to do this, the FBI asked the Executive Committee of the International Association of Chiefs of Police to specify the most serious crimes confronting American citizens. The chiefs identified seven Index Offenses (now called Part I offenses)—homicide, rape, robbery, aggravated assault, auto theft, larceny, and burglary. Also identified was a larger set of "lesser" crimes, such as forgery and drunk driving, now called Part II offenses. Part I and Part II offenses have come to dominate official thinking about, and public perceptions of, crime in America.[3]

The *Uniform Crime Reports* of the FBI are the only long-term, official source of information available about crime in the United States. Each year the number of crimes known to the police and the number of arrests made are reported by the FBI for Part I offenses. The only information on Part II offenses is the number of arrests made. As a consequence of this differential reporting, Part I offenses have become the major basis for the public's perception of crime in America. Yet, Part I offenses account for only around 20 percent of the arrests made by American police officers. Thus, U.S. citizens have been implicitly conditioned to focus on only a minority of crime, if we take recorded arrests as a valid indicator of crime. This strong emphasis on Part I offenses has also led most Americans, as well as social scientists, to believe that serious crime is most often committed by poor persons, since it is the poor who are usually arrested for Part I offenses.[4] Omitted from an equivalent scrutiny by governmental agencies are, for example, corporate crimes (price-fixing, monopolistic practices, bribing public officials), organized crimes (loan sharking, gambling), and many white-collar crimes (most of which are under Part II offenses).

This situation aggravates general problems of inequality in America (see chapter 7); and it violates the ideal of justice that people are to be treated equally under the law. As the public's perception of crime is subtly biased toward the *lower class* crime problem, inequity increases.

These definitional problems are compounded by efforts to delineate what should and should not be defined as "criminal." Most Americans believe that persons who physically harm others and who steal valued material objects should be defined as criminals. Many Americans also maintain that criminal law should uphold the value of morality; and hence, those who violate certain moral codes, regardless of whether they have harmed another person or taken property, should be subject to the sanctions of the criminal law. From this perspective, for example, prostitution, gambling, drug use, and unusual sex practices should be crimes, even though some combination of these are committed by persons who are generally law-abiding, and even though such crimes usually do little physical harm to others or to their property.

In contradiction to these beliefs are those of a smaller number of Americans who assert that only deviant acts that tangibly harm others or property should be defined as criminal. Such beliefs represent application of the broad American cultural values of individualism and freedom to many deviant acts, for they emphasize the right of individual citizens to be different.

As we will see, much of the structure and general functioning of criminal law in America reflects the contradiction between a moralistic criminal code and libertarian beliefs. This contradiction in the legal system mirrors the broader cultural conflict in America between the values of conformity, on the one hand, and freedom and individualism, on the other. Thus, many of the problems in defining "real crimes" and in dealing with crime by various agencies stem from contradictions in the culture of American society. And when Americans' contradictory beliefs in what causes crime and in what should be done to criminals are added to the moral issue of what crime is, we can see how difficult it is to develop a consistent approach. Indeed, these cultural dilemmas as they affect definitional problems are intimately connected to the substantive dilemmas confronting the American criminal justice system. These definitional dilemmas have created a system that defines as criminal more acts than can be monitored; they have led to a class bias in enforcement; and they have clogged the courts with cases to the extent that all the ideals of justice must be violated.

Dilemmas of Overcriminalization

The legislative bodies that enact the criminal codes are, by their nature, political and subject to pressure from diverse sources. Hence law-enactment reflects, in large part, the pressures on legislatures of the public and various vested interests. Over time, these pressures cause the expansion of the criminal codes, since the general public, narrow vested interests, various moral entrepreneurs, and religious and civic groups all press for new laws. These pressures are coupled with the personal biases of legislators as well as their respective party platforms, further assuring that the body of law will expand. Rarely are old laws taken off the books, and so, as new laws are enacted, a problem of overcriminalization begins to emerge. That is, there are simply too many laws, many of which cannot be enforced.

This process is inevitable in a political democracy. But as the number of criminal laws expands, the legislative component moves out of syncronization with the enforcement and adjudicatory components of the justice system. For as the volume of laws begins to exceed the capacity of enforcement and adjudication, the police and courts must alter their internal procedures. And, as we will come to appreciate, they must do so in a way that violates the ideals of justice, while aggravating problems of inequality.

Overcriminalization is most problematic for "crimes without victims." Such crimes do not directly harm others, damage property, or challenge the government, but they do offend some portion of the public's sense of proper conduct. Thus, drug use, certain sexual behaviors, gambling, and prostitution are all criminal acts and represent a large portion of the criminal legal code, while at the same time, they consume a significant amount of enforcement and court resources.

In a large, industrial-urban society emphasizing values of individuality and freedom, we should expect enormous diversity in tastes and lifestyles, and as a result, we can anticipate constant and vigorous conflict over lifestyles among different segments of the population. The outcome of such conflict is a mixture of one segment imposing its morality on another through effective lobbying for "moral codes" and reluctance by the police and courts to enforce these codes as a result of pressure from another segment of the society. For even in the face of scores of legal codes reflecting the morality of only some, many people still gamble, use drugs, and enjoy a wide variety of sexual activities. Most persons run little risk of legal sanctions because many morals laws—especially with respect to sexual conduct—are not strenuously enforced. As Thurman Arnold caustically observed, they "are unenforced because we want to continue our conduct, and unrepealed because we want to preserve our morals." But many of these laws *are* enforced, even though little harm to property, others, or the state results. The persistence of a large body of "crimes without victims" generates several dilemmas for the criminal justice system.

First, laws denoting morals crimes—such as those concerning certain forms of sexual activity, drug use, public drunkenness, gambling, and vagrancy—are so broad that they make potential criminals of most Americans. In effect, morals laws hold criminal sanctions over many American heads for behaviors that often do no tangible harm, except to the moral precepts of a dominant segment of the population. In doing so, such laws potentially limit people's rights to self-determination and to self-expression, while violating deeply held American values of individualism.

Second, since many Americans appear to drink large quantities of alcohol, to use unprescribed drugs, to engage in unorthodox sex, and to gamble, laws prohibiting these activities go against widespread behavior patterns. Having vast bodies of laws on the books that many citizens insist on violating creates law enforcement problems. It is possible, for example, that as "normal" citizens violate morals laws, they lose respect for the rest of the criminal codes and for those who enforce them.

Third, legal prohibitions against prostitution, drugs, and gambling create and maintain a vast illegal marketplace for organized crime. Since millions of Americans demand these services, they tend to be provided by illegal syndicates that derive enormous untaxed profits and have little regard for preserving and strengthening other important aspects of American society. Profits from the "morals industry" are used to subsidize and expand other harmful crimes such as loan sharking, extortion, and bribery. These profits are also used for investment in legitimate corporations and other business enterprises. Mergers between criminal syndicates and normal businesses make the distinction between law and lawlessness even more difficult to maintain. From this perspective, the existence of morals crimes supports organized crime. It is no coincidence, for example, that organized crime in America emerged as a significant social problem during the Prohibition era. Criminals became highly organized in order to deliver the illicit goods demanded by a large and willing public and in order to avoid prosecution. Today, a similar situation exists with respect to drug use and gambling, for as long as legal prohibitions against these widespread acts remain, organized crime will continue to enjoy a ready market for its services.

Fourth, the existence of victimless crimes consumes large quantities of resources that could otherwise be devoted to dealing with crimes with victims. In any large urban area, for example, public drunkenness and disorderly conduct offenses constitute close to one-half of all arrests. This keeps the local police busy with morals offenders and overloads the jails and courts. Or, to take another example, close to one-third of all police detective hours are spent on drug-use violations in large urban areas, while constituting an equal portion of criminal court cases (see table 4.2 below).

Fifth, the persistence of a large body of morals laws creates a situation in which not all American laws can be enforced; there are simply too many morals offenders in American society and they currently consume most criminal-legal resources. When not all laws can be enforced, then police, court, and correctional *discretion* is inevitable. The existence of unenforceable laws can issue the police a license to enforce selectively all laws, a situation that goes against all basic American tenets concerning due process. Thus, the greatest danger of granting excessive discretion to the police, or to any other legal agency, in one area is that such selective enforcement can easily be extended into other areas. Furthermore, to encourage excessive discretion in police enforcement sets the precedent of granting the police autonomy from their legislative mandate.

And finally, the existence of a large body of unenforced laws can, on occasion, allow the police to use such laws to prosecute persons on grounds unrelated to the act prohibited by the law. For example, vagrancy laws have been traditionally used by American police officers to arrest "suspects" from lower socioeconomic groups who cannot be arrested or detained on other criminal charges. Thus, morals laws not only give the police, and many other legal agencies, the power to selectively enforce the law; they also enable the police to change the intent of law and to use it for purposes other than those dictated by the law.

Thus, overcriminalization poses a number of difficult dilemmas. To the extent that we want a large body of laws and to the extent that we want to prohibit widespread acts that do little if any harm to others or to property, then the police must selectively enforce the law; at the same time, the courts and prisons will be jammed. In taking this course, we violate many cultural values, due process tenets of the legal system, and most of the ideals of American justice. These problems are simply compounded by the taxpayers' reluctance to pay for the processing of the large numbers of criminals created by an overcriminalized set of legal codes. Yet, the public believes the legal system is "soft on criminals"— an inevitable belief when the legal system must devote one-third to one-half of its resources to crimes without victims.

Dilemmas of Biased Criminalization

As we just emphasized, overcriminalization gives the police discretion as to *which laws* to enforce, so that they assume law-making (as opposed to law-enforcing) functions. As they become a law-making agency, they are also subject to political and public pressure as to which laws they will enforce. The definition of "the crime problem" has come to revolve around Part I offenses and morals crimes, as is reflected in tables 4.1 and 4.2 where arrest frequencies are

Table 4.1 Persons Arrested in the United States, by Charge and Gender, 1980 (in thousands)

Crime	Total Arrests	Male	Female
Part I Offenses			
Murder	17.8	15.5	2.3
Forcible rape	27.8	27.5	0.3
Robbery	134.2	124.5	9.7
Aggravated assault	241.9	211.8	30.1
Burglary	448.6	421.0	27.6
Larceny theft	1,065.0	754.6	310.4
Motor vehicular theft	122.3	111.8	10.5
Arson	16.9	14.9	2.0
Part II Offenses			
Other assaults	425.9	366.7	59.2
Forgery and counterfeiting	66.9	45.6	20.7
Fraud	224.5	131.3	93.2
Embezzlement	6.9	4.9	2.0
Possession of stolen property	106.6	95.4	11.2
Weapons	146.9	136.2	10.7
Prostitution	83.0	24.9	58.1
Sex offenses	59.5	55.0	4.5
Drug abuse	489.2	422.9	66.3
Gambling	45.5	40.9	4.6
Offenses against family and children	42.9	38.0	4.9
Driving while intoxicated	1,133.0	1,024.1	108.9
Liquor law violations	382.8	324.8	58.0
Drunkenness	989.8	914.0	75.8
Disorderly conduct	689.1	581.5	107.6
Vagrancy	28.1	24.1	4.0
All other offenses	1,539.2	1,308.5	230.7

SOURCE: U.S. Bureau of the Census, *Statistical Abstract of the United States, 1981* (Washington, D.C.: Government Printing Office, 1981), p. 180.

Table 4.2 Crimes for Which Persons Are Most Commonly Arrested in the United States, 1980 (in thousands)

Crime	Total Arrests
All other offenses	1,539.2
Driving while intoxicated	1,133.0
Larceny theft	1,065.0
Drunkenness	989.8
Disorderly conduct	689.1
Drug abuse	489.2
Burglary	448.6
Other assaults	425.9
Liquor law violations	382.8
Aggravated assault	241.9

SOURCE: U.S. Bureau of Census, *Statistical Abstract of the United States, 1981* (Washington, D.C.: Government Printing Office, 1981), p. 180.

reported. The police themselves are likely to enforce laws pertaining to these crimes because lower-class criminals and moral violators have fewer resources to fight arrests than do members of organized syndicates, white-collar criminals, large corporations, and corrupt public officials. Thus, as the police selectively enforce, they also rewrite the law. The law then assumes a bias against certain social classes and certain life-styles.

The bias of the law is perhaps most dramatically revealed in the area of "elite crime." This area has not been formally defined by government, but we can provide a general characterization by viewing it as serious law violations committed by important private citizens, government officials, private organizations, and government agencies. Very often elite law violations are not considered criminal by government; thus, data in this area are fragmentary and describe only certain types of elite crime. On the basis of no-contest pleas and fines paid without criminal conviction, we must make inferences on the nature of such crime, since in the vast majority of cases, elite crimes are not reflected in Uniform Crime Report data. In table 4.3 some interesting information about public officeholders who have been caught violating federal criminal statutes is presented. This table presents data

Table 4.3 Federal Prosecutions of Public Corruption, 1970, 1975, and 1980

Prosecution Status	1970	1975	1980
Total: Indicted	63	255	723
Convicted	44	179	551
Awaiting trial	—	27	213
Federal officials: Indicted	9	53	123
Convicted	9	43	131
Awaiting trial	—	5	16
State officials: Indicted	10	36	72
Convicted	7	18	51
Awaiting trial	—	5	28
Local officials: Indicted	26	139	247
Convicted	16	94	168
Awaiting trial	—	15	82

SOURCE: U.S. Bureau of the Census, *Statistical Abstract of the United States, 1981* (Washington, D.C.: Government Printing Office, 1981), p. 184.

about the numbers of local, state, and federal officeholders who have recently been indicted, convicted, or are awaiting trial for federal criminal law violations. No information is available about the numbers of these persons who were arrested.

We see from the table that the numbers of public officials processed by the legal system for federal criminal violations have increased steadily. But we also see that the American legal system processes very few public officials for criminal violations, since in 1980 only 723 public officials were indicted.

Another way to look at elite crime is to focus on the law violations of large corporations. Considerable evidence suggests that most stealing and injury caused by corporations goes undetected and unlabeled as crime, that corporations cannot be arrested, and that their administrative employees and owners spend very little time in jail. "Nolo contendre" pleas and payment of "civil penalties" are to corporations what plea bargaining is to common criminals. In table 4.4 some of the criminal activities during 1976–83 of larger U.S. corporations are listed, with special attention on the civil penalties and settlements in excess of $50,000 and the criminal convictions, including no-contest pleas. As the

Table 4.4 Civil Penalties or Settlements in Excess of $50,000, and Criminal Convictions, Including No-Contest Pleas, Involving Large U.S. Corporations, 1976–1983

Corporations	Date	Allegation	Conviction or Plea	Amount Paid Back	Fine or Penalty
Exxon	1978	Overcharges	None	$508,000	—
	1983	Overcharges	—	$895 million	—
Mobil	1980	Violation of Natural Gas Act	No contest	$19 million	$500,000
	1979	Overcharges	—	$2.2 million	—
Container Corporation (Mobil)	1976	Price fixing	No contest	—	$50,000
Montgomery Ward (Mobil)	1980	Dumping[a] Japanese TVs in U.S.	—	$1.9 million	—
Southern Bell	1978	Using corporate funds for political donations	Guilty	—	$310,712
Texaco	1978	Overcharges	None	$7.8 million	—
Standard Oil of California	1981	Overcharges	None	$82.5 million	—
Standard Oil of Indiana	1980	Overcharges	None	$100 million	—
	1978–79	Overcharges	—	$55 million	—
Gulf Oil	1977	Violation of Bank Secrecy Act	—	—	$229,000
	1977	Providing free trips to IRS agents	Guilty	—	$36,000
Atlantic Richfield	1979	Overcharges	None	$82,727	—
Sears, Roebuck	1980	Dumping[a] Japanese TVs in U.S.	—	$19.8 million	—
Sheraton Hawaii (ITT)	1979	Illegal payments overseas	(Suit settled)	—	—
	1979	Price fixing	Convicted	—	$50,000

Company	Year	Offense	Plea/Verdict		
Phillips Petroleum	1978–79	Overcharges	—	$26 million	—
	1977	Illegal political donations	Guilty	—	—
	1977	Failing to report $2 million income	No contest	—	$30,000
Tenneco	1979	Violations of Natural Gas Act	—	—	$1 million
Tenneco Oil	1981	Overcharges	—	$16.2 million	—
	1978	Bribing a sheriff in Louisiana	Convicted	—	$300,000
Packing Corp. of America (Tenneco)	1976	Price fixing	No contest	—	$50,000
Sun Company	1980	Overcharges	None	$30 million	—
Occidental Petroleum	1981	Illegal political payments	(Suit settled)	—	—
	1981	Pollution by subsidiaries of Love Canal, N.Y. and Lathrop, Calif.			Agreed to clean up pollution
Oxychem (Occidental Petroleum)	1978	Pollution and false reports	No contest	—	$38,000

[a]That is, selling goods for less than their cost of production.

SOURCE: *U.S. News and World Report* (September 6, 1982), 93:26–27: 1983 data from (Denver) *Rocky Mountain News*, March 26, 1983, pp. 1 and 34.

data indicate, corporations simply pay fines to avoid criminal penalties for their officers. Such fines, we should note, are passed on to consumers in the form of higher prices. Yet, as we can see from table 4.2, elite crimes of this nature are considered far less dangerous to the society than, for example, drug use and intoxication by less elite citizens.

Dilemmas in Law Enforcement: The Police

In principle, laws define crimes. This means that the police are to enforce all criminal laws and thereby control crime. During enforcement, the police are supposedly guided by the rule of law (procedural law) which, in accordance with the general societal values of freedom and equality, guarantees the civil liberties of suspects and makes the police accountable for their actions. Ideally, just as substantive codes and statutes define criminal behavior for the public, procedural laws define what is criminal for the police. While these principles are easily stated in the abstract, and are reinforced by the public's values and beliefs, they are often violated in practice. The potential dangers of this situation in a free society—police abuse of citizens' rights, police discrimination, excessive police brutality, the police as lawmakers through selective enforcement, and the police as a political force with so much power they can overrule other types of law—need not be dwelled upon, but they contradict widely held and value-laden beliefs in freedom, equality, fairness, and limitations on power.

A wide discrepancy between the operation of the police in theory and in practice is perhaps inevitable in light of two general conditions. First, as we noted above, the broad scope of the criminal law makes impossible the enforcement of all the laws, which leaves to the police decisions about which ones to enforce. Second, even though most Americans highly value law and order, the financial resources made available to municipal police departments are typically inadequate. Without adequate resources, and at the same time burdened with a vast body of unenforceable morals laws, the police must inevitably begin to establish their own priorities; as they do so, they can begin to divorce themselves from legislative mandates, from public scrutiny, and from the constraints of procedural law. Such is one of the ironies of legislation that gives the police more than it can handle, for as the police are overwhelmed by legislative mandates, they increasingly isolate themselves from that mandate.

While these two conditions help account for police deviations from their legal mandates and procedural law, several other conditions contribute to the situation: (1) police and community relations; (2) the internal structure of the police; (3) police ideology; (4) police professionalism; and (5) police political power. Each of these is examined below.

Police and Community Relations. In spite of the vast array of services the police provide for American citizens, according to public opinion polls and other sources of information, the general public holds them in comparatively low esteem.[5] Yet, great expectations and demands are placed upon the police within any community. One of these expectations forces the police to engage in a wide range of social service and peacekeeping activities, many of which have little to do with law enforcement. For example, one study found that nearly one-half the requests for assistance received in a police station are for help in health care (such as ambulance service), in handling problems with children and incapacitated persons, and in supervising recreational activities. While such tasks need to be performed by public service agencies in most urban areas, they are a burden on the police. Peacekeeping and social service tasks can divert resources and attention away from enforcement of laws prohibiting crime. As one social scientist said, the police officer is thus "philosopher, guide, and friend" in addition to being a "crime fighter."[6]

One danger in requiring the police to provide so many social services is that their duties are often extended beyond the bounds of substantive and procedural criminal law. As the police assume the ambiguous role of public service agents (e.g., helping with stalled cars, pets in trees, etc.) and peacekeepers (family disputes), they are granted enormous discretion in defining what is necessary in order to preserve the peace (not necessarily to uphold the law). One potential consequence of this situation is that some suspects, usually from the lower socioeconomic classes, can be arrested in order to preserve the peace; others, usually from the middle and upper classes, can be let free in similar situations; and still others can be illegally detained. Thus, the public demands of the police non-crime-fighting services which, ironically, reduce their crime-fighting ability and increase the dangers of law violations by the police—consequences the public does not condone and yet sets in motion.

The police in any community are subject to pressures from the public and from local political leaders, both of whom demand that the "streets be kept clear of crime." In any community the police are highly responsive to this form of pressure, with the result that they can at times violate procedural law by arresting various deviant and outcast persons, such as homosexuals and skid-row drunks, under "cover charges" to demonstrate their efficiency statistically, even though to do so diverts resources away from action on crimes involving injury to persons and loss of property. This need for the police to constantly demonstrate crime-fighting efficiency is one of the most persistent conditions promoting procedural shortcuts in the name of maintaining an arrest record that will satisfy the public and various community pressure groups. And it remains one of the enduring dilemmas of police-community relations in America.

Internal Structure of the Police. Partly in response to pressures to demonstrate crime-fighting efficiency, and partly as a result of the volume and variety of activities expected from them, police forces inevitably become extensively bureaucratized. Police bureaucracies are command hierarchies basically like the military, arranged into major units. Bureaucratization of the police has at least two consequences for the rule of law. First, bureaucracies tend to develop their own internal rules and procedures in order to generate greater efficiency. However, since these rules are established to increase efficiency, they can sometimes cause violations of the due-process principles of the law, which are not designed for efficiency. In fact, as Skolnick has noted, the efficient administration of criminal law will always be hampered by the adoption of procedures designed to protect individual liberties.[7] The second consequence is that bureaucratization sometimes allows the police to obscure their own illegal acts. For outsiders, bureaucracies are always difficult to move; and quasi-military bureaucracies present special problems. As a result, private citizens, legislators, judges, and other concerned persons, such as members of civilian police review boards, have great difficulty in penetrating or investigating the policies and practices of large police departments. In addition to formal rules limiting outsiders' access to information, a large number of informal rules have emerged. Emphasis on police secrecy and keeping matters "within the department" can be found in any police department. This autonomy from public scrutiny can allow the police to remain aloof, if they choose, from much of both the substance and the procedure of criminal law, posing a dilemma for a democratic society that is to be governed by procedural law.

Police Ideology. In any large, bureaucratic police department, there exists an internal ideology which, stated in extreme form, commands the police to *(a)* maintain secrecy about practices from the hostile public; *(b)* get respect from the public, even if it must be coerced; and *(c)* by any means, legitimate or illegitimate, complete an important arrest. Putting the tenets this bluntly certainly creates an overstatement. Yet, behind much police activity—especially where it involves the lower socioeconomic classes—these beliefs are prominent. It is easy to characterize this ideology as an outgrowth of the authoritarian personality of each individual officer, but studies reveal that raw recruits to police forces are about the same in beliefs and attitudes as their counterparts in the general population.[8] Furthermore, at many police academies a civil libertarian viewpoint, stressing procedural law and the rights of the accused, is a prominent part of the curriculum. Thus there appears to be something about the bureaucratic structure of most municipal police forces in America, and about the nature of police work per se, that soon changes young recruits into veterans who can, at times, harbor somewhat antidemocratic views. This antidemocratic tendency underscores a basic contradiction of police work: the nature of police work and its bureaucratic organization create a set of practices among the police that sometimes violate American ideals of justice and the intent of procedural law.

Three facets of police work appear to be responsible for the existence of an antidemocratic ideology. First, the dangers of police work make the police suspicious of the general public, especially in urban, lower-class neighborhoods. The suspicion isolates police officers from many of those whom they serve, while driving fellow officers together as a body of close-knit comrades engaged in mutual protection. Second, at times the police will have to assert their authority physically in order to perform law enforcement duties against a hostile segment of the public that holds them in low esteem. Maintaining this high level of power frequently becomes the credo of police on the beat, for, as recruits are told again and again by seasoned veterans, "you gotta be tough." This combination of suspicion and the desire to be tough can become volatile when it shapes police behavior toward segments of the population, such as low-income racial and ethnic minorities. The police are already suspicious of these persons, since they tend to reside in high-crime areas; and when the police attempt to assert their authority they are resisted, often violently, by minority group members who see a get-tough attitude as one more abuse not to be endured. Third is the internal bureaucratic structure of municipal police forces. The bureaucracy must continually demonstrate its efficiency in the eyes of the public and politicians. A prime indicator of efficiency is the number of criminal cases "cleared" by an arrest. Since the department as a whole and often individual officers are gauged by their arrest efficiency, the police are often anxious to make arrests, even at the expense of some aspect of procedural law.

A police practice arising from the need for high arrest statistics is the emergence of arrest quotas. One way to fill a quota is to arrest suspects without much evidence, or to arrest drunks, vagrants, and prostitutes. Most police authorities vehemently deny the existence of quotas, but there is too much evidence suggesting their use in some police departments to accept such denials without some skepticism. The concern for arrests is perhaps inevitable in light of the bureaucratic imperative to demonstrate efficiency. The service function of the police, or the role police officers play in preserving civil liberties, is difficult to document statistically and convincingly. By default, the arrest record often becomes the yardstick of police efficiency.

Thus, the nature of police work, its bureaucratization, and its performance in local communities foster an ideology among the police that violates the very tenets of procedural law—as embellished by more general beliefs and values—that the police are supposed to uphold. The situation represents a severe contradiction in a democratic society and poses an enduring dilemma for Americans.

Police Professionalism. The current drive in the United States toward police professionalism represents an attempt by police administrators to meet the excessive demands for service made by the American public as well as to overcome the widespread corruption and inefficiency that once characterized American police departments during their brief history. For example, big city political machines and other corrupt organizations have, over recent decades, lessened their influence on the municipal police; civil service exams have become the basis for promotion; and the educational credentials of officers now weigh more heavily. Moreover, in a society where high technology is a sign of sophistication, the use of new machines—from computers to infrared night telescopes to newer and better police cars—inevitably becomes a symbol of police efficiency, professionalism, and progressiveness. While many of these changes have increased efficiency and helped cut down on many types of police corruption, they also risk causing the police to overstress a few crimes of the poor, easy arrests, and technological efficiency. In most police departments there is strong temptation to define professionalism as the use of technical gadgetry—wiretaps, miniaturized communications devices, bugging devices, dum-dum bullets, helicopters, computerized files, and so on—in fighting crime. Politicians at all levels of government have supported the technological bent of police professionalism by allocating, with little hesitation, funds to buy equipment to be used for riot control and for surveillance of citizen activities.

While new technologies and higher levels of training can help make the police more competent, a potential danger resides in overstressing this aspect of police professionalism. Too much stress on simple crime, easy arrests, and technical gadgetry in the name of law and order can create a social climate in which technology, rather than basic human rights and procedural law, dictates the way law enforcement will occur. Skolnick notes that, if freedom and individualism are to be maintained, the use of newer, more technical equipment will have to be balanced by a new and harder to achieve professionalism which is firmly committed to the ideals of a democratic order.[9] Yet, under grants from the Law Enforcement Assistance Administration, and more recently from Congress and the Department of Justice, most federal funds made available to municipal police departments are for technical equipment and basic training in fighting common crime.

A further danger of a technologically defined professionalism is that reliance upon gadgetry further isolates the police from the community. As the police become remote from day-to-day contacts with the public, they often lose the informal, interpersonal exchanges that could help them prevent or solve crimes, as occurred when the police walked a beat. Thus technological escalation, ironically, interferes with an even more important crime-fighting technique.

Police Political Power. To a very great extent, the police are caught in the middle of public demands for law and order, political pressures, the perception of rising crime, and recent Supreme Court rulings stressing the civil liberties of defendants. Under these cross-pressures, the police have at times retreated behind walls of bureaucratic technocracy. They have become disposed to think of themselves as persecuted from all sides. Undeniably the police are subject to a wide variety of pressures; but often the police themselves have exerted pressure on politicians and the public about common crimes of the poor and created the sense of a crisis over rising crime in America. Even though municipal and other police organizations can become defensive, many are not passive, and some have become powerful political lobbies. While lobbying activities are perhaps necessary for any organization charged with performing many tasks on very limited resources, the current direction of much lobbying appears to be pressure for even more discretionary powers. If these powers are granted, they could violate the tenets of procedural law which emphasize the rights of the accused over the needs of the state for power and order. Thus, another irony of a modern, highly professionalized, bureaucratic police force in a free society is that the police become an effective political force advocating their narrow interests rather than the broader interests of the public and the accused.

In sum, we should not view these trends in police work as the fault of "evil," "corrupt," or "authoritarian" persons. They are the result of an interplay among various forces: the enactment of too many laws by legislatures; the basic contradiction between protecting the accused and the safety of officers doing a dangerous job; the excessive demands on the police for non-crime-fighting services; the low esteem in which the police are held by the public; the constant public and political pressure on the police; the inevitability of bureaucratization of police forces as they increase in size; the current cultural definition of professionalism as technological sophistication; and the availability of channels of political influence to all segments of society. It is out of the interplay of these forces that the dilemmas of law-enforcement in America have arisen.

Dilemmas of Adjudication: The Courts

As we noted earlier, American courts are a complicated mixture of local, state, and federal courts as well as various tribunals and commissions. There are three principal consequences of such a complex and loosely structured judicial "system." First, there are often several tribunals or courts to which a particular case may be taken. Second, multiple court systems encourage differing interpretations of law from one jurisdiction to the next. And third, cases involving the wealthy and powerful rarely find their way into criminal courts, but instead are processed through a separate, elite system of justice composed of civil courts, commissions, and review panels.

Since there are thousands of courts in the United States, it is impossible to estimate accurately the number of criminal cases that they handle on a year-to-year basis. We do know, however, that the number is very large, much larger today than the creators of the American judiciary could possibly have anticipated. Moreover, the courts must deal with a very large volume of both civil and criminal cases, so that both the volume and diversity of cases coming to American courts exceed their capacity to process them. Such is particularly evident with criminal cases, where the government rather than the litigants must pay court costs and where the number of law violators dramatically exceeds the resources of the courts.

This situation is an enduring dilemma because it forces plea-bargaining, in which most defendants plead guilty in exchange for reduced criminal charges. In 1980, for example, among the 36,000 criminal cases brought before the federal courts in America, 23,000 involved pleas of guilty typically in exchange for reduced charges.[10] The plea-bargaining system is, on the one hand, necessary in light of limited resources, but on the other, it violates all tenets of American ideals of justice. The presumption of innocence until proven guilty is hard to maintain when the goal of prosecutor and defense attorney is to negotiate a guilty plea. The right of equality under the law is also suspended, since the poor have little choice but to "cop a plea" when they cannot pay for a defense; and the right to a trial by one's peers is obviated because guilty pleas are handled by the prosecutor, defense attorney, and judge.

Yet, when asked, the American public perceives the real problem of the courts as their leniency. In fact, conviction rates are very high in a plea-bargaining system—around 70 to 90 percent in urban areas—and punishments are rather severe, especially since the defendants in a case have little chance to demonstrate their innocence—unless, of course, they have the financial resources to fight a lengthy court battle. The dynamics of these problems can best be illustrated by examining in more detail the various phases of adjudication: (1) arrest and detention, (2) arraignment and plea, and (3) sentencing.

Arrest and Detention. According to American procedural law, within a short time after arrest a suspect must be brought before a lower court, such as that presided over by a magistrate or justice of the peace, for a preliminary examination of the case. If the offense is minor, the magistrate often has the authority to determine the guilt or innocence of the suspect and to prescribe punishment or other corrective measures. However, if the case involves a serious crime (a felony), the function of the magistrate is quite different: to determine if sufficient evidence exists to hold the suspect over for trial, and if there is, to set the amount of bail so that defendants can exercise their right to freedom before trial.

Even at this early stage violations of the ideals of American justice frequently occur. First, criminal suspects are often detained for long periods of time before a preliminary examination is held. In fact, one study of Chicago felony suspects revealed that half were held for at least 17 hours before being formally charged.[11] In America, by the time a preliminary hearing before a lower court judge rolls around, many suspects have been held for days in jail—a situation which violates the presumption of "innocence until proven guilty."

Second, many pretrial maneuvers by prosecuting attorneys and presiding judges can be highly unfair. The Eighth Amendment to the U.S. Constitution provides that bail shall not be excessive, but what constitutes reasonable bail is determined by judges whose standards and decisions vary widely, even in the same geographical area. Sometimes lower court judges are poorly trained and at times set bail in accordance with their own personal, political, and moral biases. Furthermore, the practice of bail discriminates against the poor, since they do not have the collateral to put up their own bail or the money to pay a bail bond. If individuals cannot meet the bail set by lower court judges, they must remain in jail until the trial, which can mean serving several months in close proximity to convicted criminals, some of whom are awaiting transfer to prison. It becomes difficult to presume people innocent when they must stay in jail with those who have been proven guilty. In fact, one recent study of the processing of felony suspects in Los Angeles County revealed that defendants who await trial in jail have less chance of being dismissed or acquitted, and they are under tremendous pressure to plead guilty in order to avoid maximum punishment.[12] In most cases in America, rather than endure months in overcrowded, substandard jails, suspects plead guilty to a lesser charge and thereby get their cases more quickly adjudicated by a judge, without the benefit and protection of a trial by jury. Thus, bail can be used as a means of detaining suspects in violation of the Eighth Amendment and as a form of coercion.

Third, a further injustice stems from the lack of formal legal training and criminal law experience among many lower court judges. They are usually elected or appointed; they are usually middle-aged white males from the business community who have fixed social ties and set political attitudes. As a result, the lower courts in many American cities are less than impartial, especially where the poor and unconventional individuals are concerned.

In sum, then, the process of arrest and detention is filled with bias. Yet, the dilemma revolves around reconciling the need to use limited resources to process large numbers of cases with the need to uphold the ideals of American justice. At present and into the future, this dilemma will endure and represent a source of inequity in America.

Arraignment and Plea. When the crime is serious, the defendant and counsel, the prosecutor, and judge face each other in a court of record in a pretrial hearing where written transcripts of the encounter are made. The formal charges are read by the prosecutor, and the defendant is asked to enter a plea of guilty or not guilty. However, it is behind the scenes outside the courtroom, away from the presiding judge, that the real drama usually takes place in American criminal courts. The pretrial appearance in court is typically a formality that finalizes a bargain between the attorneys, the presiding judge, and the defendant concerning what the charges, plea, and punishment will be. As we noted earlier, 70 to 90 percent of all criminal cases are resolved before arraignment, where the prosecutor has negotiated with the defendant's lawyer in order to secure a guilty plea in exchange for a reduced charge and/or sentence.

There are four major parties in criminal plea negotiations: the prosecutor, the defendant's lawyer, the judge, and the defendant. The most powerful and important of these parties is the prosecuting attorney, who is empowered by law to drop a case, negotiate a plea, or push for maximum punishment. The prosecuting attorney, therefore, has considerable discretion in dealing with criminal cases. However, prosecutors operate under two heavy constraints that limit their effectiveness as law enforcement agents. First, they are officials, elected or appointed, who often use their prosecutor's role as a stepping-stone to higher office. Prosecutors are thus under public, political, and media pressure to appear effective, even under a staggering caseload. They must win the major cases and dispose of the multitude of minor ones. This means that the charges brought against criminal defendants, and the willingness of prosecuting attorneys to negotiate pleas, often reflect political considerations—a fact that would seem to run against the tenet of equal and impartial justice. A second constraint on prosecutors comes from the large administrative bureaucracy in which they work and the massive numbers of cases they now process. Bureaucracies need to appear efficient; but each court bureaucracy faces an overwhelming caseload. If even one-half of criminal cases were adjudicated by actual trial, efficiency would be impaired. Under these constraints, the only way to maintain the appearance of efficiency is to process rapidly, without trial or other legal frills, as many criminal cases as possible. In most instances prosecutors must negotiate a plea of guilty in exchange for a lesser penalty to keep cases from jamming already crowded courts.

To negotiate pleas successfully, prosecutors use a number of strategies, many of which hold great potential for violating basic tenets of American justice. For example, in serious felony cases prosecutors usually recommend high bail pending trial, and hence force the incarceration of the poor. In this way, prosecutors can put pressure on defendants to plead guilty. Prosecutors can also exert an influence in the selection of judges; and by moving to select one who is tough on a particular type of crime, defendants can be coerced into negotiating. Prosecutors also decide how the indictment will read at the pretrial hearing. They can use the practice of "multiple indictments," or filing several different charges for one criminal act, to their advantage in forcing a guilty plea. For example, a typical indictment for possession of an eighth of an ounce of heroin could read as follows: Count 1, felonious possession of a narcotic; Count 2, felonious possession with intent to sell; and Count 3, unlawfully possessing a narcotic. Or a typical list of charges for armed robbery might read: Count 1, robbery, first degree; Count 2, assault, second degree; Count 3, assault, third degree; Count 4, grand larceny; Count 5, carrying a dangerous weapon; and Count 6, petty larceny.[13] Thus, by threatening to "throw the book" at criminal defendants, prosecutors pressure suspects to seek a compromise—usually a quick guilty plea to one of the lesser charges. Finally, prosecutors can delay bringing cases involving obstinate defendants to court; when this practice is coupled with a high bail forcing defendants to remain in jail, the prosecutor can exert extra pressure on defendants to plead guilty.

In the ideology of American justice, defense lawyers are to have an adversary relationship with prosecutors. In practice, however, defense lawyers readily enter into negotiations with prosecutors, even though they are often at a disadvantage. If defense attorneys bargained only for their clients, it might be possible to maintain better the illusion of an adversary system of justice; but defense lawyers are often "double agents" who represent, in addition to their clients, themselves and the need of the court system to adjudicate speedily without trial. Defense lawyers may have ties to specific prosecutors and to the court bureaucracy which can be much more binding than those to a succession of poor clients charged with common crimes. For example, a defense lawyer who had been an assistant district attorney might know the prosecuting attorney personally, and might have background and friendship ties to his/her "opponent." Even when this is not the case at first, defense lawyers and prosecuting attorneys who see each other frequently are likely to establish ties that can supersede the transitory needs of one client. Most important, prosecutors must rely on defense lawyers to negotiate in order to keep too many cases from going to trial; and conversely, most defense lawyers must rely on the cooperation of prosecuting attorneys to secure their fees.

The vigor that defense attorneys reveal in criminal cases is best assessed outside the courtroom, where defense lawyers can push extra hard for a favorable negotiated plea, and reduced punishment, or where they can accede to a quick deal proposed by the prosecuting attorney. In important cases the defense lawyer is likely to draw upon the past favors owed by the prosecutor. However, since these common negotiations are hidden from public and in most cases judicial view, they are not subject to the tenets of procedural law. Indeed, they are most likely to be subject to the prosecutor's need to process cases quickly and the defense attorney's desire to justify and secure a fee. To justify high fees, defense attorneys are often allowed a public performance in the courtroom which involves a profusion of rhetoric and perhaps some display of emotion. In this performance, defense lawyers are sometimes aided by judges and prosecuting attorneys who tolerate such excesses. The overall result is for defense lawyers to acquire a vested interest, much like prosecutors, in a system of negotiated rather than adversary justice, since a real adversary trial would have enormous costs in time, energy, and money, for both defense and prosecuting attorneys. Thus, busy criminal lawyers come to rely on pleas negotiated outside but staged within the courtroom. To the extent that criminal lawyers rely on this informal system, loyalties to clients are badly compromised.

This system works well for the affluent, who can afford attorneys with good courtroom ties who will bargain effectively. But for the poor, who must rely on a court-appointed lawyer or a public defender, "copping a plea" works to the benefit more of the prosecutor and court than of the defendant. Court-appointed lawyers are seldom at the top of their profession. Many have "pull" with prosecutors, and they are most typically interested in securing quickly their small fees without preparing for a full-blown trial.

Some public defenders, who are supported by government funds or charitable organizations, are highly competent. But much like the courts and their prosecuting counterparts, they are overburdened with cases, making it necessary to negotiate pleas to keep up with their caseload. When public defenders can defend clients only through negotiation, they lose the very weapons that could make them effective in such negotiations: their competency as trial lawyers and a credible threat to go to trial and tie up court time and personnel. In most cases, therefore, public defenders have less leverage than do lawyers for affluent Americans, resulting in a situation where the poor are more likely to be found guilty without trial. Because the vast majority of poor defendants are presumed guilty (for they must eventually plead guilty in a negotiated system), it is clear that they do not have equality before the law.

The final party to a negotiated plea is the judge. It is in the courtroom that pretrial hearings and arraignments occur, and it is the judge who will ask defendants how they plead. If a defendant pleads "not guilty," the judge is forced to set a trial date. But if the accused pleads "guilty," the case can be disposed of quickly. Thus, judges clearly have a vested interest in adjudicating criminal cases without trial, for, like prosecutors and defense attorneys, they are part of a system which demands the efficient processing of enormous caseloads. The popular public image of the dispassionate judge, especially at the lower-court level where most cases are heard, is not entirely accurate. In reality a working judge "must be politician, administrator, bureaucrat and lawyer in order to cope with a crushing calendar of cases."[14] As such, judges actively, although discreetly, enter into plea negotiations by implicitly agreeing to abide by the decisions of prosecutors concerning charges and sentence. In fact, under some circumstances, actual meetings may be held behind closed doors in the judge's chambers as deals are concluded. Judges must participate in negotiated pleas, for they must make room for civil matters and they must not accumulate too great a backlog of criminal cases. Once an agreement has been struck between a prosecutor and a defense lawyer, the judge allows a defendant to plead guilty at the pretrial hearing, and this consummates the trial stage of a criminal case.

The vast majority of criminal cases brought before American judges are resolved in this manner. Thus, most judges will have difficulty in remaining impartial, since inevitably they will have an interest in facilitating negotiations. The fact that judges enter into wholesale negotiations makes it hard to visualize them as neutral protectors of justice; and the fact that they are likely to encourage plea negotiations reveals a presumption of guilt on the part of the American judiciary, an inability to grant defendants a trial by their peers. Given the large numbers of common criminals processed by American police and court systems, it is likely that many clearly guilty persons can use the bargaining system to avoid the full impact of the law. It is also likely that many innocent poor persons admit guilt to avoid extensive pretrial punishment and the threat of long-term incarceration. But it is difficult to separate the guilty who fare well from the innocent who must plead guilty. Such is one of the great dilemmas of plea-bargain "justice."

Sentencing. After a trial in which a defendant is found guilty, or as is more often the case, after a pretrial plea of guilty, a judge must pronounce sentence or decree some form of corrective action. In a general sense, judges must do so within the limits of the law, but they have wide discretionary powers in sentencing. Many legal innovations, such as the indeterminate sentence, probation, and other putative reforms have greatly increased judges' discretion, as has the general movement in America toward individualizing the treatment of criminals. Discretion gives room for bias on the part of judges. Contrary to their public image as impartial officials who coldly apply the law, judges have many of the same prejudices as other Americans. Nowhere is this more evident than in sentencing. Since so much crime is processed by the legal system and since prisons are overcrowded, probation is the most probable sentence for those convicted. If a person has been on probation before, or if the offense is extremely serious, some other form of sentence will be considered. All too often the availability of prison space determines whether a serious criminal will be incarcerated, but personal biases of the judge and other court officials can also have an influence.

Judges can usually legitimate sentences by reference to presentence reports, usually compiled by probation department personnel. In fact, a presentence report can be the sole basis upon which judges make sentencing decisions. A presentence probation report is compiled by a social worker who collects both factual data, such as previous arrest records, and impressionistic information on a defendant from some combination of local social agencies, relatives, friends, schools, police, employers, or any other available source. Often, presentence reports are based on uncorroborated or even on hearsay information that would not be admissible in a trial guided by procedural law. And yet, judges regularly use this "evidence" to justify sentencing decisions; and to the extent that judges use presentence reports as the principal basis of their decisions, they are granting enormous power and authority to a grossly overworked employee, the probation officer, who is unlikely to last more than three years on the job and who often has only the slightest familiarity with defendants and their cases.

The U.S. Supreme Court has generally upheld the use of presentence reports, on the assumption that probation departments function autonomously from criminal courts and can therefore mediate between courts and defendants. But in reality, probation departments are often adjuncts to criminal courts and are subject to many of the same pressures. The budget, the recruitment of personnel, the operating policies, and the administrative directives all tend to flow from the criminal court. As a part of the court bureaucracy, probation departments are involved in the caseload demands; and although most probation officers stress concern for the unique problems and needs of defendants, their administrative mandates usually force expedient processing and stereotypical categories. To incarcerate defendants on the basis of such stereotypes, or to use them to justify biases of judges, violates the basic ideal of justice and represents another enduring dilemma for the justice system.

The problems of the courts are, to a very great extent, an extension of those of law-making and law enforcement. The courts are underfunded and overcrowded; yet, they are charged with upholding lofty ideals *and* with meeting public demands for efficiency and effectiveness in dealing with the criminal element. It should not be surprising, therefore, that plea-bargaining, discrimination against the less affluent, and partial suspension of the ideals of justice have emerged as "solutions" to the contradictory cross-pressures. But in a society that values freedom and equality, these solutions are only another facet of the dilemma.

Dilemmas of Incarceration

Nowhere is America's cultural conflict over what should be done about crime more evident than in the treatment of convicted criminals. Correctional theories are at the same time oriented toward punishment and toward rehabilitation. The opinion polls tell us that most Americans want criminals punished "to teach them a lesson" and to serve as a deterrent to others. Such beliefs have been translated into a penal system composed of underfinanced jails and prisons which simply hold prisoners for the duration of their sentence. At the same time, however, many Americans want criminals rehabilitated before they reenter society, and as a consequence, probation for convicted criminals and parole for inmates in correctional institutions have increased in recent decades. Those with a punishment orientation see these measures as "coddling the criminal element," while those oriented more toward rehabilitation point out that incarceration does little to deter crime or reform prisoners and costs the taxpayers a great deal of money. These conflicts in beliefs are implemented in contradictory treatment of convicted criminals.

Problems in the Jail System. City and county governments each have a system of jails which hold prisoners before trial, and in some cases, those convicted of crimes involving relatively short sentences. Jails are by nature punitive, since they make virtually no effort at rehabilitation. Most American jails are overcrowded, understaffed, and physically deteriorating. Moreover, they are often dangerous and unhealthful.

As we noted earlier, the jail and bond system work, in concert, to discriminate against the poor, since those who cannot post bond are forced to stay in jail while they await trial. And because of the punitive nature of American jails, it is difficult to maintain a presumption of innocence when unconvicted defendants must do time before trial. The fact that the affluent can buy their way out of jail by posting bond also obviates the doctrine of equality before the law.

Problems in the Probation System. Probation costs much less, perhaps 20 percent as much as incarceration in jails or prisons. As a consequence, it is becoming an attractive correctional alternative. Probation is the process whereby convicted criminals serve their sentences in American communities, ostensibly under the direction of a probation officer; but in reality, few probationers are closely supervised and most have little contact with their supervising officers. This alternative is less punitive than jail because it does not sever ties to family, job, and community.[15] Yet, since probation is the most frequent sentencing choice of judges, most probation officers are saddled with extremely large caseloads, making it difficult to monitor, let alone help or rehabilitate probationers.

Moreover, what is to be done with probationers is left vague. Are probation officers "cops" who must enforce the law and the exact conditions of probation, or are they psychologists/social workers who extend a helping hand to persons in their care? As one criminologist remarked, "casework implies no specific technique of corrections; hence its prescription for crime is as unclear as if medical students were told no more than surgery was the appropriate response to appendicitis." Also, as we stressed earlier, probation is usually ordered by a judge who has read a hastily prepared report that contains unsubstantiated evidence and much inaccurate information. Many criminals who should be incarcerated are thus put on probation, while conversely, some who should be set free are also put on probation. Because of the caseload burden in both the courts and the probation bureaucracy, the use of probation has become somewhat indiscriminate, negating its rehabilitative potential. And probationers are subject to the same potential biases, arbitrary actions, and variable policies of individual officers that operate in police and court systems. Abuses of authority are likely, since probation officers operate largely unnoticed under a vague mandate which allows for considerable discretion. Finally, although most probation officers are committed to rehabilitation, with such heavy caseloads it is difficult for them to establish a frequent or intimate relationship with more than a few of their clients. Many probationers are supervised by mail or over the telephone; most see their officers only occasionally at standard office interviews; and a few are simply lost in the bureaucratic shuffle. These problems dramatically reduce the effectiveness of probation as a rehabilitative tool.

Problems in the Prison System. Prisons are places where persons are sent to be incarcerated for more than one year. There are many types of prisons, but most are hidden from society in small rural towns and other unvisited places. Each state has its own system of prisons, and they come in several varieties, such as maximum, medium, or minimum security prisons for men, separate prisons for women, male and female juvenile halls and farms for those under age, and special "hospitals" for heroin addicts and psychologically dangerous persons. There is a separate system of federal prisons, where a few particularly dangerous prisoners are held. Among prisons there is wide variability in critical features such as the physical facilities, the guard-to-prisoner ratio, the ratio of correctional officers to prisoners, the availability and qualifications of training staff, the emphasis on rehabilitation as against punishment, and the types of prisoners incarcerated together. Even in view of this variability, however, prisons usually share a number of general features:

1. Inmates are housed under severe conditions of inactivity and overcrowding. They are confined to small cells, with virtually every aspect of their personal lives and daily routines subject to control by the custodial staff.

2. Prisons make at least token efforts to "treat" and "rehabilitate" criminals. Job training, counseling, and educational programs are the most typical, but in most American prisons, treatment and rehabilitative services are sufficient for only a small minority of inmates. Indeed, most prison inmates work at menial jobs and sit around in their cells.

3. There is always a conflict between the custodial and the treatment staff. Guards can undermine the work of treatment staff by tightening security or by engaging in other repressive actions.

4. Prisons are authoritarian hierarchies, where those high in the command structure are forced to make operating decisions without adequate information from the lower levels, namely guards and other staff members. Moreover, directives from the prison command are often selectively implemented by the custodial staff. As a result, prison operations are guided by an ambiguous mixture of explicit goals, formal rules, and administrative directives made in relative ignorance and only selectively enforced.

5. Prisons always evidence a viable and vibrant inmate subculture of different groups with clear leadership and patronage hierarchies. This structure has its internal conflicts—as the incidence of violence in prisons attests—but it has considerable power to influence the actions of not only most inmates but also most guards and staff members. The interaction between the inmate subculture and the formal bureaucracy is another source of ambiguity and potential conflict.

6. Prisons are political organizations subject to legislative fads and erratic budgeting policies at both the state and the federal level. As a result, prison administrators, goals, priorities, and policies can change quickly and dramatically, causing greater disruption to a prison system where there are already tense relations between guards, staff, and elements of the inmate subculture.

7. Prisons tend to produce high rates of recidivism—that is, the proportion of felons who commit crimes after their release is very high. Indeed, as many as 50 percent of all inmates—and more from maximum security prisons—commit fresh crimes. While prisons clearly punish, they do not effectively rehabilitate many. The reasons for such wholesale failure are not hard to discover:

    a. American prisons have become little more than holding pens for masses of violent persons and social misfits. Each year there is relatively less treatment, training, and education available for the typical inmate.

    b. Prison life is highly regimented and unlike life in American communities. It is hard to learn how to live a normal life in such a repressive environment. In fact, there is mounting social psychological evidence that behaviors learned in such settings do not generalize well to more open settings.

c. Prisons expose criminals to each other, reinforcing criminal orientations and encouraging the teaching and acquisition of new criminal skills. This situation also creates intense anger in many inmates toward normal society and the legal order, which are seen as the causes of the demeaning inmate violence they must endure.

d. Prisons stigmatize their inhabitants, making it difficult to get a job or otherwise become an accepted member of communities outside the prison. Without a job or community acceptance, former prisoners are far more likely to turn again to crime.

The recognition of these problems, and the rising cost of prisons, has led to increasing efforts by courts and correctional systems to avoid the incarceration of convicts whenever possible. Today this means that close to two-thirds of convicted American criminals are on probation or on parole. Yet, as we noted earlier, the extensive use of probation and parole has generated among the public the sense that the criminal element is being coddled and is not sufficiently punished. Such beliefs are, unfortunately, a reaction to the failures of an overloaded probation system and a prison system which, in its present form, cannot deter crime. Ironically, to the extent that these beliefs force the courts to put criminals in prison, they will increase the likelihood of recidivism, and hence of criminal behavior in American society.

Problems in the Parole System. When prisoners have served part of their court-assigned sentences, they become eligible for parole and serve the remaining part in the community under the supervision of a parole officer. Moreover, in some 22 states, it is possible to release prisoners during the day to attend schools or to hold jobs in the community. Such programs reach only a small number of inmates, but recidivism appears to be lower where they have been tried.[16] Recidivism figures for regular parolees are subject to considerable ambiguity of interpretation, but they tend to be extremely high. In fact, parolee recidivism appears to be about the same, on the average, as that of prisoners released without parole at the end of their sentences.

Upon release from prison, parolees are assigned a parole officer in their community. The parole officer is in charge of overseeing the conditions of parole and helping the parolee adjust to the community. Yet, with caseloads varying between 50 and 200 parolees, supervision is difficult, and parolees often fall back into the lifestyles which encouraged their criminality in the first place. Whether parole will be revoked and a convict sent back to prison depends upon a number of factors, including: (1) the beliefs and biases of parole officers, (2) the nature and size of the officer's caseload, and (3) the number of technical and behavioral conditions imposed on a parolee. A parolee can be returned to prison because one parole officer is more authoritarian than others, because the officer has a lighter caseload, or because so many behavioral limitations are imposed as conditions of parole that violations mount to the point where they cannot be ignored. Appealing a parole revocation is very difficult, and few inmates do it successfully. Because of the increasing number of people on parole in America, because the parole officer is a vague mix of law enforcement officer, counselor, and friend to clients, and because of the arbitrary nature of most state parole systems, parole very likely contributes to the high recidivism rates. Yet, parole and probation are relatively inexpensive alternatives. This contributes greatly to their persistence, despite the public's misgivings. The same public is unwilling to pay the costs of incarceration or rehabilitation—another signal of the many contradictions in the public's reaction to crime.

Social Control and Justice: A Final Comment

Any large, complex, rapidly changing social system will reveal high rates of deviance, for primary processes of social control—socialization into a common culture, stable group affiliations, long-term face-to-face interaction, and solidarity rituals—become inadequate. Yet, deviance is always defined as a problem, since it challenges the social order, even in societies like the United States, where deviance is inevitable and where strong values emphasize freedom. As secondary social control compensates for the decline in effectiveness of primary control, new dilemmas surface for these new control processes.

These problems are most evident in the criminal justice system; and in this chapter we have tried to document the inconsistencies, ironies, and contradictions within and between Americans' cultural beliefs and the structure of lawmaking, law-enforcement, adjudication, and incarceration. These inconsistencies and contradictions have created a long list of dilemmas which resist resolution and will continue to create an arena of conflict in American society.

Chapter 5

Dilemmas
of Kinship

With industrialization, family life is transformed. Sometimes this transformation is extensive, as is the case when the elaborate descent systems linking hundreds, if not thousands, of kinfolk together are destroyed.[1] More often, these elaborate systems of kinship have already been weakened by the time industrialization occurs, and thus the changes in kinship patterns are not so dramatic.[2] But the change is, nonetheless, fundamental and revolves around the increasing isolation of the nuclear family unit of husband, wife, and children from extensive economic and political ties to other kindred. For in more traditional kinship systems, this nuclear unit is embedded in a web of other kinfolk, but with changes in the organization of the economy toward an industrial-urban profile, the ties to other kin are attenuated and the nuclear family is left to fend for itself. While personal ties to close relatives, such as parents, grandparents, aunts, uncles, and cousins can remain, these are not typically economic, nor do they involve political authority and other strong ties typical of more traditional kinship systems. It is in this transformation to a more isolated nuclear unit that many of the dilemmas confronting American society can be found. And thus, we need to know more about the underlying structural changes in kinship.

Structural Changes in the Family

At one time, husbands and wives settled with or near one of their families, and in many cases, both families, creating a kind of quasi-corporate unit with extensive economic, personal, and political ties. But the migration of Europeans who had broken many family ties, as well as the rapid urbanization of indigenous Americans and the subsequent "conquest of the frontier," generated a normative climate where freedom of residence became the dominant pattern. Families in America are now free to move when and where they wish. Today, the average American family moves every five years in response to economic opportunities.

With the increased mobility of the urbanized family, the size and composition of American families has changed. In 1850, for example, the average family had almost six children; today it has less than three. It is clear, then, that family size has shrunk, and so has its composition: grandparents, aunts, uncles, cousins, and other kin have been formally excluded. These changes reflect the industrial-bureaucratic urbanization of the population. Large families organized to perform farm labor are not needed in an urban setting. In fact, they are a liability, since it is harder to move a large family (with diverse kindred) in response to changing economic opportunities.

In early rural America, the division of labor was fairly clear: women performed household work—cooking, clothesmaking, cleaning, child care; men performed tasks related to labor on the farm. With industrialization, however, women became employed outside the home in factories, especially in tasks that were considered "women's work," such as looming in textile mills. With increased industrialization, and the resulting bureaucratization of administrative tasks, women began to perform many clerical roles in the business economy. Today women have expanded their economic activities outside the home into many spheres, even some defined earlier as "men's work," and around 50 percent of adult females now participate full time in the labor force.

The traditional division of labor between household and economic tasks for men and women has thus changed dramatically during the last century. This fact would indicate that the division of labor within the household unit is under pressure to change. Questions about who should do the housework, care for and feed the children, shop, and perform other household tasks are increasingly asked. And as we will see shortly, ambiguity over the appropriate answer to these questions represents a source of family conflict in America.

In a small, mobile family where the wife is often in the labor market and where debate over household chores has increased, authority patterns become another arena for potential conflict. Such was not the case in preindustrial America, where the husband dominated almost all decision-making. One indicator of male dominance in the household was the lack of legal rights possessed by women. Women could not vote until 1920; they could not sit on juries in most states until after World War II; women could not own their own property in a marriage; and a married woman could not enter into legal contracts without her husband's signature. Today women possess these rights, and as they have become economic partners with males, the dominance of males in the family is often an issue, with more equal sharing of decision-making clearly the trend. Yet, as we will see, the tradition of male dominance still prevails and can create many tensions in the family.

In America, where ties to other kindred are weak, the family unit is not established, maintained, or changed by traditional rules of descent, but by marriage and divorce patterns. The boundaries of the family unit are created by marriage and dissolved with divorce. In contrast, in preindustrial

America some form of family unit existed before and after marriage and divorce, since it embodied several generations of relatives who could carry on the family of a son or daughter who died, divorced, or remained single.

Since marriage is no longer a part of a larger kinship system, its control by other relatives has decreased. For as the family has become isolated from other kin and economically self-sufficient, mate selection has become more open and free. Mates are selected for their appearance, personality, sexual attractiveness, and other qualities related to mutual compatibility. Whether or not the family approves has become a less salient—not irrelevant, however—criterion of mate selection. Mate selection is thus a personal rather than kin decision and is based on a "love" relationship involving considerations of personal feelings and compatibility. But free choice in terms of the vague, and sometimes unrealistic, criterion of love creates many problems of adjustment for the family as husbands and wives begin to cope with the practical problems of maintaining their own household. One result of the modern love-oriented marriage is an increase in divorce. And because divorce occurs outside a broader kinship system, it presents many problems of adjustment for the couple and their children.

As the structure of the family has changed, the relative importance of various functions of the family has shifted. At one time in America almost all socialization occurred in the family. By the early 1800s, however, many children were enrolled in either church or public schools, and today, over 98 percent of younger children go to school. The school has taken over some of the socialization functions once performed by the family. Many skills, especially those relating to future job opportunities, are now acquired almost exclusively outside of the home. While important aspects of children's personalities, such as their self-concepts, basic values, aspirations, and motives, still appear to be acquired primarily in the family, children learn much outside the kin unit. As a result, many uncertainties about how to reconcile children's diverse socialization experiences with the views of parents prevail in the modern family.

The family is no longer a productive group; it is now a consuming unit. As people left their family farms they worked outside the home in autonomous industries where they earned wages that could be spent by family members. While this change in the family may appear obvious, it is nonetheless profound, since virtually all family activity revolves around consuming. Moreover, much of the consumption is "individualized," as each family member spends much of his or her income (whether earned or received as an allowance) independently of other family members. For example, children spend their allowance and time with other children; fathers with other males; mothers generally by themselves for both personal and family needs. Such individualized consumption represents a dramatic change from the economic functions of the rural and even early industrial family where all pitched in to produce a living and where consumption was primarily a collective enterprise.

Today, as in past times, the family still provides for the regularization of birth and the maintenance of its members. Yet, the isolation of the modern nuclear family from other kin creates problems of how to support the aged. While maintenance of the young is still a vital function, the old are often cast out into a society that makes few provisions for their health and well-being.

The impersonality of an urbanized, industrialized, and bureaucratized society has often been noted. Much emotion must be suppressed when working in a "rational" world, making the family one of the few structures in modern society where emotion can be released and where personal feelings can be communicated. At times the family suffers emotional overload from the demands placed on it by its members, because now a much smaller unit must absorb the emotions of, and provide support for, people who by necessity must participate in many neutral, impersonal, and frustrating situations outside the family. Thus, the American family has assumed increasing social support functions. And as a result, the small, isolated unit is often put under considerable emotional strain.

The extensiveness and rapidity of change in both the

structure and the functions of the American kinship system have created much uncertainty among family members about how they should act. The ambiguity is reflected in the cultural beliefs pertaining to family activities; the application of core values to family structures has created a system of beliefs that is at times outmoded. Moreover, as new beliefs more consonant with the structural realities of family life have been codified, they have come into conflict with the old. The situation compounds the dilemmas inhering in the American kinship system.

Changing Cultural Beliefs About the American Family

Beliefs about what the family is and should be are presently in such flux that it is difficult to discuss a unified "culture" of the family. Even for a particular family, we can often observe conflicting beliefs that are at odds with other people's basic values—attesting again to the human ability to segregate and hence tolerate inconsistent cognitions.

Much of the debate about the contemporary family depends upon individual beliefs. For example, among those adhering to traditional beliefs, free and equal sharing of economic and household tasks between men and women can spell "destruction" for the modern family and therefore reveal what is wrong with it. For those holding modern beliefs, concerns with male economic dominance and female confinement to home represent "the enslavement of women"—another conception of what is wrong with the family. Thus, what is problematic is ultimately a matter of personal belief, and nowhere is there more conflict over definitions than with respect to the family. These beliefs are intensely held because they represent different interpretations of core cultural values. In general, though, traditional beliefs in husbands as "breadwinners" and wives as "homemakers" violate key American values, because their application has denied females equality with males, and more important, the freedom to be active and to achieve outside the home. And, as we will see in chapter 9, when women do leave the home, they are victims of occupational discrimination. Thus, this cultural contradiction represents an increasing source of conflict and poses a severe dilemma for American society.

At a more specific level, there are three crucial areas where existing systems of beliefs, revealing varying degrees of compatibility with core values, present problems for the American family: (1) beliefs about marriage—that is, the creation of a family; (2) beliefs about family relations or the "proper" roles of husbands, wives, and children; and (3) beliefs about divorce, or the dissolution of the family.

Beliefs About Marriage. In America, the initiation of the family unit is guided by "romantic love." While love may seem an obvious universal, mate selection in other times and places has often been influenced by wealth, family background, kinship rules, health, strength, and only after these factors have been considered, love. In early America, this was often the case, although in America romantic love has always been a prominent consideration. The tenets of belief in romantic love provide the criteria for selecting mates as well as for forming conceptions about marriage. These tenets are summarized below:[3]

1. Whether to marry is a decision those seeking mates must make, and other kin are not to make the partner selection.

2. Marriage partners are to be assessed in terms of personal qualities and traits—appearance, personality, responsiveness—and not in terms of utilitarian considerations—money, power, social connections.

3. When partners are selected on the basis of their personal qualities, complete attraction and compatibility are more likely to result. Life together is seen as unbroken compatibility, with conflicts and troubles capable of being ironed out.

4. Love is to be an emotional "oneness" in which the compatible couple insulates itself from corrupting influences.

5. Sexual bliss is assured under the above conditions. Complete sexual attraction can only augment love, happiness, and compatibility.

Stated in this form, these tenets may appear naïve, but in fact most Americans seeking partners adhere to them. While the beliefs may be held in more sophisticated form, the underlying assumptions remain intact. Such assumptions are compatible with both core values and evolving structural arrangements in the modern family. Values of individualism, activism, and achievement are consistent with individuals' actively seeking to achieve marital harmony. Moreover, the values of freedom and equality would dictate that those seeking partners should be free of constraints in selecting mates, and that selection on the basis of personal rather than utilitarian qualities will assure greater equality and openness in the formation of family units. As we have discussed, the family has increasingly become a small, comparatively isolated unit. Romantic love beliefs are consonant with such a small unit, since it is the marriage partners who must, in the end, form and maintain a relationship with each other (as opposed to other kindred). Such a concentrated relationship would require considerable freedom for individuals to choose their partners in terms of qualities that they feel they can live with.

An emphasis on romantic love, however, can pose problems: It can establish unrealistic expectations about the harmony of the conjugal family unit. Romantic love can mask many of the problems of a day-to-day, working marriage; it can create false expectations about sexual relations; it provides few guidelines for resolving problems; and it overestimates the degree of insulation from external influences—work, finances, relatives, and the like. These problems, built into the tenets of romantic love, are further compounded by the ambiguities in beliefs pertaining to how relations are to proceed once the family unit is formed.

Beliefs About Family Relations. In examining beliefs about "proper" family relationships, it is necessary to separate the beliefs concerning males and females and, after examining them independently, indicate the conflicts and ambiguities that they reveal.

Until recently, beliefs about the husband's role have been relatively unambiguous.[4] Husbands are to (1) work steadily and provide an adequate income for the family; (2) express kindness and tenderness for the family; (3) "help out" around the house, although just what constitutes "helping" is ill defined and often causes conflict; and, (4) make major economic decisions and those pertaining to major purchases, but it is desirable that he consult with the family. These beliefs reflect values of activism and achievement in "providing" for the family; and to a limited extent, they exhibit some emphasis on equality in decisions and household chores. In many ways, however, the emphasis on husband dominance of "major" decisions and the vague definition of "helping out" underscore the fact that these beliefs also violate basic values of equality among people. Such becomes particularly clear when these beliefs are juxtaposed with those governing wives.

Three sets of beliefs concerning wives are presently evident in America:[5] (1) those beliefs emphasizing the wife-mother-homemaker role in which values of activism and achievement are to be realized in the narrow spheres of bearing and raising children and in the maintenance of the household for a husband and children; (2) beliefs emphasizing the companion role of wives who are to relinquish some child-rearing and household chores to others, such as schools, domestics, and day care centers, while being active in recreational activities; the wife can demand emotional responses and admiration from her husband, but there are limits to her equality since she must act in ways that facilitate her husband's economic and social dealings; and (3) those beliefs, which have only recently gained wide acceptance, emphasizing the appropriateness of the wife as partner, actively seeking to achieve in the job sphere while "equally" sharing child-rearing and household responsibilities with her husband.

As can be seen, beliefs about women in the family are in conflict and flux. At one time in America, wife-mother beliefs dominated, even though they violated values of freedom and equality. Companionship beliefs became prevalent among the affluent middle classes, and while they allowed some "freedom" and some capacity to achieve outside the household, they did so within rather narrow boundaries. Partner beliefs are, of course, reflections of the growing economic involvement of wives and the political activities of various women's groups. They are the most consistent with basic American values, but most in conflict with more traditional beliefs concerning the wife's role and those dealing with the traditional husband's household role. This conflict, along with the realities of the working wife, basic values of equality, freedom, individualism, activism, and achievement, and long-standing beliefs about the proper family roles for men and women, poses one of the most difficult dilemmas facing the American family.

Beliefs About Divorce. At one time in America, marriage was seen as permanent. Even in unhappy marriages it was considered desirable for a couple to stay together, if only for "the sake of the children." Such beliefs were consistent with romantic love beliefs that preclude the possibility of marital discord. These beliefs also reflected the conditions of marriages in early America, where other kin were involved in mate selection; husbands, wives, and kin were economically interdependent; small communities exerted social pressure on a couple to remain married; religious sanctions against dissolution were severe; and the legal system made divorce difficult. The creation of the urban, economically self-sufficient conjugal family, coupled with the reality of increasing divorce, has changed beliefs rapidly and dramatically. Although divorce is still considered regrettable, it is also accepted as "best" for the parents and children involved in an unhappy home. Yet, the older traditional beliefs have not disappeared; rather, they stand in conflict with more liberal beliefs about divorce. These new beliefs are, however, more consistent with dominant American values of individualism than are traditional beliefs about divorce. They are less likely to pose cultural conflicts for marriage partners than highly restrictive traditional beliefs that emphasized conformity to the tenets of romantic love and wife-husband roles, even if such conformity meant sacrificing one's freedom.

In sum, then, the structure and culture of the American family contain the potential for many dilemmas. Family structure is small, isolated, and involved in increased social support functions. At the same time, dominant beliefs create unrealistic expectations about what marriage and family life will bring, and they give rise to ambiguous and conflicting beliefs, many of which contradict basic values and realities. Given new, liberalized beliefs about marital dissolution, the potential for family disruption in America has increased. Thus, it is in this contradictory cultural and structural context that the dilemmas of families in America must be analyzed.

Dilemmas of American Kinship

While the list of "what ails" the American family is long, especially since contradictory beliefs influence people's definitions of the issues, we can group these problems under three general categories: (1) the problems of divorce and dissolution, (2) problems of internal family relations, and (3) problems of the aged in a nuclear kinship system.

The Dilemma of Divorce and Dissolution in America

One indicator of the cultural and structural strains on the American family is the rising divorce rate. Popular commentaries notwithstanding, divorce is probably not out of hand, nor is it even clear just how high divorce rates have become. Even today, the U.S. government does not collect complete data on divorce rates for all states in a given year. Every ten years questions about marital status are asked during the national census, but these concern only people's marital status at the time, not their status over the last ten years. Other sources of data include periodic samplings of the population by the census bureau, as well as compilation of data from other agencies (such as divorces and marriages from state and local government agencies).

Even if complete data were collected each year, there would be problems in presentation and interpretation. For example, one way to present divorce data is by the number of divorces per 10,000 people in the population. From such data it is possible to discern that before the turn of the century there were about 3 to 4 divorces per 10,000 people, and over 50 per 10,000 today. But since neither children nor all adults are married, variations in the marriage rate and age composition of the population make such statistics rather meaningless. The most popular way to report divorce data is the number of divorces per 100 marriages in a given year. Thus, in 1982 there were over 49 divorces per 100 marriages, which, in the public's eyes, means a marriage has about a 50 percent chance of failing. Such is not necessarily the case, since the number of divorces in a given year is not the result of marriages in that year, but of marriages in all preceding years. Depending upon the age groupings of the population, earlier marriage patterns, the propensity to seek divorce, and the number of marriages in a given year, the number of divorces from the past (as a proportion of present marriages) can vary enormously and distort divorce rates.

To avoid some of the statistical pitfalls of reporting divorce data, the most accurate, but still incomplete, way to report divorce rates is to report the number of divorces in a year as a proportion of the entire married population, fifteen years or older. Most typically (because of the way the government collects the data), only females are in these comparisons, so that the data will reveal the number of women who get a divorce in a given year as a proportion of the number of married women, fifteen years or older. These data do not, of course, say anything about the chances of a successful marriage; no data currently collected by the government can do this. But this procedure enables us to examine divorce trends as far back as 1920. They are reported in table 5.1.

Table 5.1 Divorces per 1,000 Married Women, Age 15 and Over, for Selected Years

Year	Divorces
1920	8.0
1930	7.5
1940	8.7
1946	17.8
1950	10.3
1960	9.2
1970	14.9
1974	19.3
1975	20.3
1976	21.1
1977	21.1
1978	21.9
1979	22.8

SOURCE: U.S. Bureau of the Census, *Statistical Abstracts of the United States, 1982–1983* (Washington, D.C.: Government Printing Office, 1983), p. 82.

As can be seen in the table, divorce appears to have fluctuated. It remained low until the post–World War II period, when so many hasty marriages ended in divorce. Divorce rates declined until the 1970s, then rose sharply. The data reveal that the divorce rate has increased, but it is not that much higher than in the decade after World War II. And to argue that these divorce rates signal a "pathology" in the family is premature, for we must assess additional information.

One important piece of needed information is: how long have those who seek a divorce been married? If long-standing marriages where children are involved end in divorce, this fact would have different implications than if divorces occurred only among the newly married. The data reveal that most marriages, if they are going to be dissolved at all, end before the seventh year. But most divorces occur in the second year, which, because of the time lag involved in getting a divorce, indicates that most marriages really end in the first year. Apparently the realities of marriage simply do not correspond to the expectations of romantic love, and when conflicts over other family beliefs surface, the tension leads the newly married to seek a divorce.

What about children and divorce? While the research on the impact of divorce on children is far from complete, the available evidence indicates that children are not so negatively influenced by divorce as public opinion argues.[6] Moreover, many youthful marriages that end within the first year are childless, and many late-in-life marriages are also childless. From 1920 to 1950 about 65 percent of all divorces involved no children, but over the last twenty-five years, this figure has shrunk to over 45 percent.[7] To some extent, the increase in divorces involving children reflects the post–World War II "baby boom" that had subsided by 1965 and now appears to have vanished as birth rates have dropped dramatically. With a decline in the birth rate, the percentage of childless divorces in the future should increase. Thus, while children have increasingly been involved in divorce, it is not so harmful for them psychologically as was once believed, and there is good reason to believe that fewer children will be a party to divorce in the future.

What happens to divorced parents? If people did not remarry, then this fact might signal a decline in the institution of marriage and family. But if they did remarry, this would indicate strength and vitality in the family. The evidence clearly argues for the attractiveness of marriage and family, since in accordance with romantic love beliefs, divorced partners seek new marriage partners. As the demographer Kingsley Davis summarized:[8] "At such rates . . . [of remarriage] . . . the divorced population would soon be consumed if it were not constantly fed by newly divorced recruits." While people are more likely to seek a divorce, they are also more prone to desire remarriage and the reestablishment of the family unit.

Understanding which social categories seek divorce can help us find an explanation for increasing divorce and remarriage in America. One of the most important factors in predicting dicorce is the age of the partners at the time of their marriage. The evidence is clear that the younger the age at which partners are married, especially if they are under twenty, the higher the incidence of divorce.[9] The economic

situation of a family also influences divorce patterns: the lower
the income, the higher the divorce rate, regardless of age.[10]
Similar findings can be found for the prestige of the male's
occupation (which, of course, is correlated with income): the
higher the prestige and status associated with the husband's
occupation, the lower the divorce rate. A final category concerns the issue of previous marriage: if marriage partners have
been previously married and divorced, then the new marriage is more likely to end in divorce, although the data on
this matter are incomplete and sketchy, and should thus be
interpreted carefully.[11]

These data can perhaps offer some clues as to why the
divorce rate appears to have increased. For the young married couple who are most likely to hold romantic love beliefs,
the realities of family life, especially as they are exacerbated
by conflicting beliefs about male and female roles, can generate such frustration and tension that the partners immediately seek family dissolution. For the less affluent, financial problems can present additional tensions with which
marriage partners have difficulty coping. Such tensions can
be aggravated with the working wife whose income may lessen
the financial burdens of the family, but whose *combined* work
and household burdens create other sources of tension. Since
the working wife is most likely in lower-income families where
husbands most typically hold traditional beliefs about male-
female roles, the working-class wife is subjected to enormous
pressure to perform both a full-fledged labor market role and
the wife-homemaker role. Under these conditions, maintaining a tension-free household proves difficult.

The sketchy data on divorce and remarriage would indicate that people do not necessarily learn from their mis-
takes. Apparently, divorced people seek remarriage in accordance with romantic love beliefs, but they also fail to alter
other beliefs, or at least fail to recognize them as a potential
source of marital discord. Thus, many of the authority conflicts are repeated in second marriages, and when they are
aggravated by economic circumstances, another divorce becomes increasingly likely.

In response to the inevitability of divorce in a society where unrealistic romantic love beliefs, coupled with ambiguous and conflicting beliefs over male-female family roles, prevail, divorce has increasingly been simplified. Until very recently divorce law and court procedures were complicated and usually involved adversary procedures where damages by one party had to be demonstrated in a court of law. But over the last decades states have been liberalizing their laws so that divorce is increasingly a "no fault" matter in which partners simply agree to dissolve the marriage. Slackening of rigid divorce laws has, no doubt, encouraged people to seek the divorce option in an unhappy marriage. And as beliefs have begun to shift toward a more tolerant view of divorce, the inevitable tensions of the small, conjugal unit can now, with little stigma and fewer legal obstacles, be resolved through divorce. Moreover, as people have sought more personal freedom in accordance with basic American values, divorce is increasingly defined as a more viable solution than staying in an unhappy marriage. Such changes in beliefs have also encouraged liberalization of public attitudes about, and legal sanctions concerning, the process of divorce.

In sum, then, it is clear that high divorce rates are inevitable in American society. Family beliefs are in great flux, creating severe problems of adjustment for Americans and increasing the likelihood that they will seek marital dissolution. Just whether increasing divorce per se is a problem becomes a matter of definition—a definition that will reflect people's personal beliefs. High divorce rates are inevitable, but as the remarriage rates of those who have been divorced reveal, they do not indicate a weakening of people's interest in family life. Rather, they underscore Americans' desires to have the harmonious family life that their beliefs lead them to perceive as attainable. From one perspective, divorce does not represent the weakening of the family but its reaffirmation as couples seek new family ties.

Dilemmas of Family Relations in America

Even though divorced partners seek remarriage, the increase in divorce reveals that considerable tension is exerted on relations between husbands and wives, as well as on children, in the American family. In order to understand the root causes of divorce patterns and the dynamics of American kinship, it is critical to examine key sets of relationships, namely those between spouses and those between children and parents (relations with other kin are less critical because of the isolated nature of the American family). While the family is comparatively isolated from other kin, it is subject to situational pressures from the outside that influence relations among family members.

Husband-Wife Role Relations. Relations between husbands and wives in the American family are greatly influenced by the cultural beliefs that they hold and the situational pressures that they must endure. In turn, the age or maturity (as well as affluence) of the partners affects, to some degree, their ability to reconcile these pressures. With maturity, people are more likely to perceive, talk out, and discuss their problems, and with affluence, they can buy counseling assistance and other services—such as household help—that can cut down on pressures. For husbands, cultural expectations are, as we noted earlier, relatively unambiguous. There is some conflict between basic values such as equality, on the one hand, and beliefs about male dominance and avoidance of domestic chores on the other. This conflict, however, only becomes severe when the wife's actions deviate significantly from the wife-mother-homemaker profile. In contrast to males, it is clear that females are subject to multiple and conflicting cultural pressures. Three contrasting beliefs exist, and it is increasingly rare for wives to adhere to only one. Most are likely to "believe" in elements of all three—thus setting up pressures on the wife, and indirectly, creating ambiguities, frustrations, and tensions in the relationship between husband and wife. And to the extent that these conflicting beliefs are also perceived as violating the basic values of activism, achievement, individualism, freedom, and equality, additional pressures are brought to bear on the wife and relations with her husband.

There are two types of situational pressures compounding these cultural forces: those revolving around household obligations and those existing outside the household. For husbands, household pressures usually involve maintaining the car, yard, and outside of the house (painting, repairing plumbing, etc.). If the couple does not own or rent a house but owns a condominium or rents an apartment, then these obligations are reduced. But since there are always household chores inside the house, the wife's obligations are not proportionally reduced. With affluence, of course, the pressures of home ownership are lessened as "help" is hired, and they are often turned over to the wife, who becomes the overseer of hired household labor. In all types of households, husbands are also obligated to spend time with their children in spontaneous encounters at night and on weekends and in organized recreational activities. Most of the day-to-day care, feeding, transporting, helping, and disciplining, however, is turned over to the wife. Outside the household the husband's major role is that of "breadwinner" on the job. He may also have recreational roles (golf, bowling, tennis, watching T.V. football) which are relaxing in themselves, but which can represent sources of pressure on relations with a resentful wife who is left to "hold the fort." Husbands may also have community service roles, such as civic clubs and organizations, that can exert the same kinds of pressures on the marital relationship. On the wife's side, the household chores of cleaning, laundry, meals, and dishes represent a drain on her time and emotions, especially if she must also perform work roles outside the house. Monitoring of children represents an additional burden, as does the time spent talking with the children. When community service and recreational roles also exist, they can create additional time pressures on the wife. The extent of such pressures depends upon whether or not she must hold a job and whether she has the affluence to relieve herself of many time-consuming tiring household chores. It is clear, then, that the female partner is potentially subjected to considerably more pressure than the male. These situational pressures can be compounded if she holds contradictory beliefs.

Parent-Children Role Relations. In an extended kinship system, where other relatives live with or close to a family, much of the children's family interaction is with adults other than their parents—grandparents, aunts, and uncles being the most immediate kin. But as the family has lost many of its functions and shrunk in size and composition, parents represent the sole emotional support objects for young children. Even as children grow and increasingly participate in the broader society, parents and the family unit still remain the vital center of social support. This structural situation, coupled with beliefs that parents should be loving and devoted to their children, places a heavy burden on husbands and wives. As the principal love objects of children, they must maintain individually warm relations with their children, even when under stress. Numerous studies have revealed, and parents implicitly recognize, that the nature of the relationship between parents has profound implications for their children's emotional well-being. As we have seen, however, maintaining a tension-free relationship between parents is often difficult. Moreover, the demands placed upon parents by constantly maturing children who also spend increasing amounts of time outside the home makes harmonious relations with children difficult while frequently placing strains on the marital bond. Thus, the problems of relationships between parents and children inhere in a set of inevitable structural relations: (1) There are few adults other than parents in the American family with whom children can relate emotionally. (2) Parents are under enormous pressure to be good and loving to their children, and yet, the husband-wife relationship has potential sources of strain that can make this difficult. (3) The young move quickly, within fifteen years, from highly dependent children to biologically mature but emotionally and financially dependent adolescents, who participate in peer groupings and organizations that are often ill-understood by their parents.

Each of these structural forces requires some elaboration. First, the reliance of children for emotional support is great, since most interactions outside the home, including many peer relationships, are more neutral. Clubs, schools, competitive play with friends, and various organizations—scouts, baseball, football, dance, recreation centers, and the like—put much emphasis on performance, creating the tensions that must be relieved in the more relaxed and supportive home environment. As numerous studies have indicated, basic personality traits such as self-esteem, achievement motives, aspirations, and emotional security are acquired in interactions with parents in an emotionally secure home environment. This state of dependency, and its importance for basic characteristics of children, is recognized by parents who, as we noted above, experience a great deal of strain over how to be good parents.

This brings us to the second point listed: parents have many sources of strain that can make it difficult to provide a loving environment. Moreover, norms of child-rearing in America are unclear; parents are somehow supposed to know instinctively how to raise children. But in reality, parents usually must grope and experiment in how to relate to their children, a situation that can create the inconsistent and ambivalent responses from parents that can undermine the security of the home environment. Or, parents can disagree over how to treat children, compounding the problem. And when such ambiguities and outright disagreements are accompanied by marital tensions, then strained relations between children and their parents will create even further tensions which, in turn, compound existing tensions in an escalating cycle. The end results are for the marriage bond to be subjected to additional strain and for children to endure the harmful consequences of a stressful home environment.

The third structural problem listed revolves around the simple fact that children grow up. As they grow, parents must adjust their responses to a changing being, but this can often prove difficult when tensions already exist between husband and wife, between parents and children, or both. As adolescence approaches, this adjustment process can prove difficult even when harmonious relations have previously existed because now the children are biological adults with many out-of-the-home activities, and yet, they remain emotionally and financially dependent on their parents. Parents often have difficulty understanding the adolescent youth culture—dress, music, language, and the like—and the independence-dependence conflicts of their children for freedom from parental domination and for love and emotional support. Adolescents, on the other hand, have difficulty recognizing the problems that their parents have in visualizing the transition of their children into young adults. This dependence-independence process, and all its accompanying confusion, is protracted in American society because of the extensive "credentialing" activities performed by schools. While prolonged involvement in educational structures is often unnecessary in terms of actual job requirements, parents, children, and employers believe that education is necessary. Thus, children are often required to remain financially tied to parents well beyond their adolescent needs to be emotionally supported by parents. Thus, the "need" for education can often create additional problems of adjustment for parents and children as they leave an already long adolescence and enter adulthood—an adulthood which can still involve independence-dependence conflicts with parents.

In viewing the relations between parents and children, it is clear that the potential for strain is great. The small nuclear unit is expected to absorb an enormous tension-management load in a society where most nonfamilial contexts are either neutral or competitive. This load is even more difficult because parents are given few cultural guidelines as to how they are to be good parents. For both parents and their maturing children, these built-in sources of strain can become highly problematic, especially as children mature, making a constant readjustment of children-parent relations necessary. At times these pressures harm both parents and children, emphasizing again the extent to which parent-child problems inhere in the structure of American kinship.

Dilemmas of the Aged in America

In societies revealing an extended lineage system, with elders living in the household unit (or with the young family living in the elders' house), "old age" is not a problem. In fact, it is often a venerated position with many important functions, such as keeper of lore and religion, owner of family property, political leader of family units connected by lineage, and caretaker-teacher of grandchildren. The early American family often included the elderly, who could assist with household chores and child-rearing while providing a knowledge resource for both the husband and wife in their economic and household roles. With the creation of the small, mobile, conjugal family, however, kinfolk were excluded, including parents and grandparents, and this change in the structure of the family has contributed to the problem of being old in America.

Many elderly must endure loneliness, a sense of worthlessness, low prestige, poor health, and povery without the support of either kin or government. While the forces of change have radically altered the kinship system, these same forces have yet to create a place for the elderly in a society of isolated nuclear family units. And the problem has assumed major proportions. There are now over 25 million over 65 years of age, who constitute close to 11 percent of the population. By the year 2000, they will represent over 12 percent of the population. To put these figures in historical perspective, the population of the United States has experienced a 100 percent increase since 1900, but the number of people over 65 years has increased by 500 percent. The reasons for this shift are varied, but are related to the fact that the life expectancy of the average American has increased, while the massive immigration of the young from Europe has ceased.

Large proportions of elderly in a society do not constitute a problem per se. They become a problem when they are subject to negative stereotypes, are excluded from participation in society's institutions, are forced to endure loneliness, and are subjected to the vicissitudes of poverty at greater rates than the younger population. The very industrialization and bureaucratization of the economy which created the conjugal unit that excludes the elderly has also forced the elderly out of the economy at age 65. The nature of jobs in the economy changes so fast that experience in work is less critical than recent training, with the result that the older employees of a company can become a liability. Despite recent civil rights legislation, many companies will not hire those over fifty; they often encourage their employees to take early retirement; and most try to force 65-year-old workers to retire.

When the elderly are excluded from the economy, they can become the victims of negative beliefs that portray them as nonproductive, mentally slow, physically feeble, and a burden on their families and society. Such beliefs are perhaps inevitable applications of basic values to a population forced by economic policies to be "nonactive," "non-achievement-oriented," and because of its stage in life, "incapable of progressing." Thus, the old are excluded from meaningful work roles which, in turn, makes them vulnerable to the harsh application of dominant American values. Such treatment is particularly severe in a society where the elderly are denied access to kinship ties that could make their exclusion from the economy more bearable. It is, therefore, in this context that their problems must be understood.

Conclusion

The dilemmas of family in America are the result of dramatic alterations of kinship systems under the related pressures of industrialization and urbanization. The basic contradiction in this alteration is that as kinship evolves toward a nuclear profile, it must still perform many of the most vital functions in any society. As a result, the pressures on the small nuclear family are often enormous, and they are compounded by changing beliefs and by ambiguous norms about the respective roles of father, mother, and children.

In such a mixture, divorce, family tension, and isolation of the elderly are inevitable. This inevitability is what poses a dilemma, for on the one hand, tension, conflict, divorce, spousal abuse, and the isolation of the aged are all defined as "problems" about which "something should be done"; while on the other hand, the structure of the family is not geared to resolving these problems. Indeed, it inevitably must generate them. Thus family issues will remain a prominent arena of controversy.

Chapter 6

Problems
of Education

The Dynamics of Education

In traditional societies education is fused with kinship, religion, and community. In such societies it is difficult to isolate educational structures and processes from the routine groupings of social life. In contrast, education is a highly visible, controversial issue in modern societies. Indeed, in most of the contemporary world, education occupies a central place in the dynamics of a society. The reasons for this centrality reside in the fact that as societies become more complex, traditional structures—extended kinship, community, caste, manor, and other social forms of preindustrial systems—become inadequate in performing crucial social tasks.[1]

In complex societies, where individuals acquire many skills and dispositions outside the kinship system, education becomes an important part of the secondary social control system. Through their long-term participation in the educational system, people become committed (i.e., motivated, oriented, and willing) to enacting formal and informal roles, while they learn the specific skills necessary to fulfill the normative demands of these roles. In traditional societies, acquiring commitment and skills is, to a great extent, an informal by-product of interacting in the family and community. However, as the economic environment of the family becomes more complex, education within the family becomes inadequate to impart all the skills and commitment necessary for participation in the growing number of nonfamilial roles.[2] New values, orientations, interpersonal styles, skills, and levels of knowledge are required of societal members; and as a consequence, educational organizations carry out the increasingly complex task of social control through socialization.

As we noted in chapter 1, culture is a complex of interrelated symbols, such as language, beliefs, values, ideologies, knowledge, lore, tradition, customs, mythologies, dogmas, and technology. One way to visualize culture is as a storehouse filled with a symbolic inventory. Some of this inventory is constantly involved with the roles individuals play, but much of it remains more remote. In industrial systems, some values, beliefs, ideologies, scientific knowledge, and technology are intimately involved in day-to-day economic and political processes, whereas other cultural symbols, such as those about history, lore, and religious dogma have become less relevant in the political and business world. All societies find ways to preserve and store cultural symbols which are seen as immediately useful, but they also preserve and store some cultural systems which have passed from fashion. In hunting and gathering systems of the past, or today in relatively isolated parts of the world, cultural storage usually occurs in the family or in religious rituals. In these societies culture is unwritten and stored in the minds of men and women. It is preserved through family socialization and, at times, through instruction by religious practitioners. In more developed societies, cultural preservation and storage are increasingly removed from the purview of the family and religious practitioners. Instead specialized educational structures are charged with preserving and storing components of culture. Currently, in the more industrial and postindustrial societies, these roles have proliferated and become incorporated in a wide variety of organizations such as libraries, museums, computer banks, schools and colleges. In these organizations culture is written down, coded, catalogued, cross-tabulated, and otherwise deposited. It is thereby preserved and stored.

Social systems always evidence means for retrieving cultural symbols and for disseminating these to at least some members of the society.[3] Throughout most of the history of human societies and in many places in the contemporary world, cultural retrieval and dissemination have occurred primarily within familial structures. Yet, the long-run trend is for cultural storehouses to become sufficiently complex and filled so as to necessitate separate educational organizations to assume many of the retrieval and dissemination functions formerly performed by the family. Today in the most modern societies, families disseminate only general values, beliefs, histories, and dogmas, while school systems impart an increasing portion of a society's symbolic culture.

At some point in a society's development, education begins to have consequences for expanding the inventory of culture.[4] Expansion and innovation through education are most apparent in societies with large universities and scholarly centers that are staffed by applied theorists and researchers, technicians, students, and other professionals. Such persons are explicitly charged with the task of expanding culture through scientific innovation and other creative processes. While educational centers tend to generate new technologies for large-scale economic, military, and other governmental interests, they also generate innovation in other areas, such as music, literature, and social philosophy outside direct governmental and economic control.

There are two general mechanisms for inserting individuals into the larger social structure: ascription and performance. Ascription is the process of placing people into economic, political, legal, and class positions on the basis of characteristics inherited at birth. In traditional societies, for example, family background is usually the most important of the ascribed characteristics; and in such societies, where children end up in the economic, political, religious, legal, and other social class spheres is in large part a direct reflection of where their parents have been located. Depending upon other ascribed characteristics, such as gender and birth order, more specific allocation occurs: women occupy different positions from men; oldest sons and daughters hold different positions from youngest, and so on. Thus, in traditional societies social placement and allocation are processes intimately connected with kinship. However, as technological and economic requirements on people become more varied and complex, new mechanisms for allocating people to positions emerge; and these revolve around performance criteria. The period from birth to adulthood involves attending schools where performance is judged and evaluated and where credentials for occupational placement are acquired. Schools thus become arenas for proving one's ability to assume certain positions; and as a result, mechanisms (such as testing, counseling, and tracking) for identifying and developing the capacity of students become elaborated.[5] Thus, in modern societies the social placement consequences of education become extensive.

As social processes are transformed under the impact of industrialization, education comes to have profound consequences for problems associated with such societal transformation. Initially educational development is sporadic, unplanned, and resisted. Yet, once education becomes a dominant institution, it is often used as a deliberate vehicle for social change and reform. Because of its importance for storing, disseminating, and expanding culture, as well as for social control and placement, education can be an effective means for implementing programs of social transformation and reform. The nature of the changes that can be brought about in this manner, and the extent to which education can be seen as the means for their implementation, varies. In many Third World nations, for example, education is seen by governments as a major key to economic transformation and to other forms of development; in Russia after the Revolution, education was considered crucial by political leaders for economic development and for creating a new type of Soviet citizen; and in the United States, education has been touted by governments and other groups as one of the principal means for creating social equality. Thus, once the potential of education for altering the dynamics of a society is recognized, it is often used as a deliberate vehicle of social change.

The dynamics of education, then, increasingly revolve around the processes of social control, cultural preservation and storage, cultural dissemination, cultural expansion, social placement, and social transformation. Because these processes are so critical to the viability of a society, education increasingly becomes viewed as a central institution. And as is inevitably the case with structures so critical to the operation of a society, education becomes the center of controversy. Such is the case in the United States, where education is one of the most visible and vital institutions.

The Dynamics of Education in America

The Structure of American Education

American education is a vast hierarchy of primary and secondary schools, community colleges, technical schools, state universities and colleges, and private schools of every kind. From region to region the profile of this hierarchy differs, depending upon a myriad of circumstances. For example, the degree of population density, affluence, cultural diversity, and ethnic heterogeneity will all affect the pattern of education in a region. These and many other circumstances make education in the United States highly diverse. The diversity is amplified by the lack of a national educational program and the consequent control of education by state governments and local communities. The result of this situation is that school facilities and curricula, teachers' salaries and credentialing, and students' cultural backgrounds vary not only from state to state but from community to community. In fact, it is somewhat surprising that education in America displays a national character, a consistency from region to region. This consistency probably results from three forces: (1) Growing professionalism of many school employees and their national organizations force upon states and schools certain common standards. (2) Various national associations communicate policies, methods, and teaching techniques to most educational professionals. (3) High rates of mobility among urban Americans generate, to some degree, common outlook about the elements of a good education; as a result, parents bring pressure on local school organizations to provide certain common educational facilities and programs.

As an outcome of these forces, and as federal funding (and hence, control) of school programs has increased in the last decades, it becomes possible to draw a very general portrait of education in the United States. Primary schools display six grade levels following a year in kindergarten in which children become accustomed to the school environment without intense demands for academic performance. Primary schools tend to be small in size and located within delimited residential areas. In other words, they are "neighborhood schools." Upon completion of primary school, most students go on to junior high school, which lasts two to three years. Junior high schools can help mitigate the severity of transition felt by many children as they transfer from the small, neighborhood elementary school to the much larger, consolidated high school. Junior high schools draw students from several elementary schools and yet maintain some of the neighborhood atmosphere of the elementary school. High schools usually draw students from several junior high schools and encompass the physical boundaries of an entire community or large sections of a metropolitan area. High schools are highly bureaucratized and represent the end of formal education for many Americans.

At each of these levels there are both public and private systems. Under the impact of state, and to lesser extent federal guidelines, curricula and standards of these schools are sufficiently similar so that many students readily move between parts of the public and private systems. The public school system is run by state and community governments; private schools are run by a variety of organizations including churches, foundations, and businesses. Among states, the broad outlines of the lower educational system—primary, junior high, and high schools—are somewhat similar, with movement from school to school within or between states less problematic than might be expected in light of the relatively decentralized political and economic character of American education.

Completion of high school is very important for most Americans, because it is at this juncture that a major status transition occurs. Students either go out into the work force, or they go on to higher education, or they join the ranks of the unemployed. For many students this transition is delayed for a while by attendance at a junior or community college. Community colleges are usually tied administratively to a local school district; they provide a general liberal arts curriculum as well as extensive vocational programs; and they can be used as a place of transition into either the work force or four-year colleges and universities.

Overlapping with junior and community colleges are various universities, colleges, and vocational technical schools. Vocational schools tend to exist on the periphery of higher education, but in terms of curriculum and other features, they have much in common with many community colleges as well as with some university programs. Beyond community colleges and trade schools are colleges and universities which vary enormously in terms of size, curriculum, libraries, computing and tele-media facilities, extensiveness of specialites, and research vs. applied activities. In both the public and private sector are small liberal arts colleges, technical and scientific universities, full-scale universities, and large multiuniversities.

It is through this hierarchy of primary schools, junior high schools, junior and community colleges, vocational schools, and colleges and universities that American students pass. In the educational hierarchy are built many dilemmas for the students passing through the system, for its permanent employees, and for the broader society. These dilemmas present American society with a series of enduring controversies, fueled by cultural beliefs. It is from the perspective of people's beliefs about education, as these follow from the application of general societal values, that the definitions of "problems" in the educational systems are formed.

The Culture of Education in America

The intensity of feeling over the educational process stems from the strong beliefs that Americans hold about what schools should be and what they should do. As with crime, these beliefs are, to an extent, imposed by economic and political processes that favor the affluent and work against the poor, but they are also the product of other important processes. Daily experiences, religious convictions, social ideology, and educational attainment all operate to condition people's beliefs about education. No simple set of beliefs dominates American thinking about education; instead, most members of American society subscribes to several beliefs at once, even though they are often contradictory.

Beliefs in Equality of Opportunity. Basic values of freedom, equality, achievement, and activism have become translated into a cluster of beliefs that schools should provide all citizens with "an equal opportunity" to acquire the learning and skills necessary for success. Public schools are to negate inequalities in wealth by giving all a chance to achieve, and thereby to acquire educational credentials commensurate with their abilities. Those who hold this set of beliefs see schools as providing freedom of opportunity for all; but as the value of individualism stresses, individuals must seize their opportunities.

Much of the current public controversy surrounding education in America concerns this issue of equality of opportunity. It is likely that a majority of American citizens be-

lieves that the schools do, on the whole, provide equal opportunities. But there is a large minority that views the schools
as highly discriminatory. Exactly how these beliefs are man-
ifested varies widely across the nation. Whether achievement gaps, special education programs, affirmative action, or
busing is the issue, however, a considerable amount of debate, commentary, and open violence has occurred as different segments of the public seek to impose their beliefs about
equality of educational opportunity on others. Thus, the extent to which schools provide equality of opportunity represents one of the enduring dilemmas of American society.

Beliefs in Local Control. It is clear most Americans
strongly believe that the local community should control the
administration of lower-level schools. Such beliefs in local
control reflect the cultural values of freedom and individualism. As these values are applied in local communities, most
people believe that schools should be free from external constraints of the federal government and should administer their
own programs. For example, while racial prejudice is certainly involved, much of the negative and violent reaction to
"court ordered busing" has come from parents who fear the
loss of control over their neighborhood schools. And the recurring controversy over textbook content or prayer in public
schools provides further examples of the degree to which
Americans desire to control the content of primary and secondary school education. This desire confronts the fact that,
increasingly, schools are becoming centralized at the state
level, and that the federal government in recent years has
decreased, through its educational subsidies, the options of
local school districts. As a result, just how much local versus
outside control there should be has become a major dilemma
for Americans.

Basic Versus Progressive Education. Americans disagree over what (and how) the schools should teach. For those
who stress the general value of conformity, children should
learn a strict, standardized, and basic curriculum of reading,

writing, and arithmetic. For other Americans, who place more value on freedom and individualism, a diverse, flexible, and issue-oriented approach to education is desirable. It is hard to know how many Americans fit into these two opposing ideological camps, and how many Americans hold both sets of beliefs. But no issue has generated more controversy in the 1980s than the "quality" of the education in America.

At the level of higher education, this cultural conflict often manifests itself in the form of a debate over vocational (applied) versus liberal arts (pure) education. Throughout most of the history of American higher education, as long as higher education served mostly elite children, the liberal arts view of scholarship, and of the well-rounded student, prevailed. But with the creation of land grant colleges and universities as well as with the extension of higher education to the masses, beliefs in a vocational and "relevant" education became prominent and now pose challenges to traditional beliefs in liberal arts education.

These beliefs reflect what people desire from the educational system. They reflect general values, and as a result, they constitute a moral yardstick by which educational processes are evaluated. But the basic contradictions in American values (see chapter 1) have been translated into contradictory beliefs about education, making easy resolution of the dilemmas virtually impossible, since to deal with an issue in any one way violates the moral evaluations of some segment of the public. And as the centrality of education to people's lives in a credentialed society has become so apparent, the cultural controversy is dramatically exacerbated.

Dilemmas of Lower Education in America

In examining the educational dilemmas of American schools, we must begin by highlighting four basic features of the present system. First, in accordance with beliefs about equal opportunity, lower education is "mass oriented," providing basic education for all school-age children. In the fall of 1981, 1 out of every 4 Americans was directly involved in the educational process—90 percent of the 6 to 13-year-olds, 94 percent of the 14 to 17-year-olds, and 29 percent of the 18 to 24-year-olds. In the fall of 1981, there were approximately 45.4 million Americans attending elementary and secondary schools. At the same time at least 2.4 million people were employed as classroom teachers in public and private elementary and secondary schools.[6] Thus, the size and scope of the task inevitably lead to a bureaucratization of public school organizations. The need for mass schooling can create a "bureaucratic ethic" which stresses the processing of large numbers of students, the maintenance of control, and the appearance of efficiency. With such emphasis the goal of moving masses of students through the system is met, but primarily by stressing the cultural value of conformity. The resulting bureaucratic system, as it is translated into a myriad of rules and procedures, can at times conflict with the value of freedom and beliefs in flexible, individual learning. For it is difficult for students to acquire flexibility, humaneness, and innovation in a system where control, order, and standardization are emphasized.

Second, compared to other modern societies, lower education in America is relatively decentralized, in accordance with beliefs in local control. It is financed and administered primarily at the state and local levels. As a consequence, the United States does not have a clear *national* educational policy and even less capacity to administer one. Although supplemented by federal funds flowing through several agencies, lower public education is financed principally by state and local taxes, and administered primarily by local school officials. Financial and administrative decentralization results in discrepancies in the quality of education in different school districts, cities, states, and regions—which violate widely held beliefs in equality of educational opportunity. Furthermore, dependency on state funds and local property taxes, as well as state and local administrative control, subjects schools to highly uneven but constant social and political pressures, thus creating problems of how schools should be run and by whom. Moreover, the financing of schools through local property taxes works against poor homeowners and renters, since property taxes are even less progressive than income taxes.

Third, because schools are decentralized and are administered locally, the quality of teachers as well as teaching techniques and approaches can vary considerably not only from district to district but also from school to school within a single district. While this situation gives school systems some flexibility in dealing with local variations in the educational needs, it has created a situation where many marginally qualified teachers are employed and where many unproven, ineffective, and even harmful approaches are used. The much publicized fact that student performance on standardized achievement tests continues to drop has led the public to question many of these approaches. The result has been renewed public support for the three Rs beliefs about education and a general dissatisfaction with progressive education. Yet, at the same time, many educators resist this public pressure. They contend that reducing innovation in public schools would impose a rigidity on students that is no longer appropriate for success in a fluid, change-oriented society that must compete in a world system. The issue of innovation versus standardization is now, of course, debated daily in both the national and local political arenas. This debate is inevitable in a society with no centralized policy or administrative structure for implementing policies.

Fourth, the American system places heavy emphasis on individual achievement. Since achievement and individualism are strong cultural values, such emphasis is not considered inappropriate, though it does favor children taught by their parents to be assertive and competitive. But a strong emphasis on achievement can also discriminate against students who do not learn well under conditions of competition and constant evaluation.

These four somewhat contradictory features of schools can generate, for some important segment of the population, a myriad of interrelated social dilemmas. For our purposes, we will narrow these issues to three: (1) control versus freedom of students in the schools; (2) decentralized versus centralized administration; and (3) equality of education.

Control Versus Freedom of Students

Americans value conformity to authority and accepted practices as well as individualism and innovativeness.[7] As we noted earlier, this conflict of cultural values is reflected in educational ideology and practice, since the schools are charged with imparting both the capacity to conform, to do the routine, *and* to be creative. Despite the widespread belief that schools are too permissive, there is much evidence that values of conformity dominate American schools. One historical reason may reside in the fact that American schools grew rapidly in the late 1800s and early 1900s in an effort to assimilate masses of diverse rural migrants and foreign immigrants into the urban American way of life. Thus, conformity to the urban system was the dominant goal of early mass public education. Another reason lies in the nature of the job market for which schools help prepare students, since in industrial systems the job market is dominated by routinized and bureaucratized jobs requiring considerable control of worker activity.

Aside from these two forces, however, the very fact that Americans seek to educate all their young requires mass programs which, in turn, creates extensive school bureaucracies which, like all large bureaucracies, generate their own imperatives for control and regularity. For pursuit of the goals of mass processing of students, of assimilation, and of vocational preparation has increasingly been organized bureaucratically. While the bureaucracy is not so highly centralized at the federal level as in other industrial societies, the large urban areas and populous states have, in order to process the volume of students, been forced to centralize their educational bureaucracy. By itself, such centralization creates pressures for standardized procedures, and hence, an emphasis on routine.

While local control does mitigate, to some extent, bureaucratic pressures for standardization, it creates its own pressures that often emphasize conformity. Since school districts are responsive to public pressure and dependent upon local tax revenues, schools seek to demonstrate their efficiency to local constituents. In seeking to do so, they often stress conformity to rules and procedures, avoiding controversial programs which might antagonize taxpayers. Thus, ironically, state and federal pressures for standardization are often compounded by local pressures. And, since flexible learning and intellectual creativity are hard to document, maintaining an orderly, serene, controlled school environment has become the operational definition of efficiency. In fact, critics have argued that "our schools are hung up on the notion that learning in the classroom is a by-product of order. In fact, it is the other way around. Children will raise hell in a classroom if, as is usually the case there is nothing better to do . . . true learning is not an orderly process to begin with."[8]

Schools operate in many subtle ways to induce conformity.[9] For example, in most American schools there is considerable emphasis on the clock, time, and the schedule. Thus, the school can become a place where the clock and the schedule, rather than the individual needs of students and teachers, determine what should occur. Scheduling can be exacerbated by the lesson plans used by most schools to implement a standardized curriculum. Further, administrative rules can, in some schools, emphasize silence, with a sign of "good teaching" being a quiet classroom. Compounding the concern for silence is the restriction of free movement within the school. By governing the movements of students, much as is done on an assembly line, schools again maintain the appearance of order. The grading system in most American schools, with its emphasis on competitive evaluation, further orders and constrains school activity. Moreover, critics emphasize, the use of standardized IQ and achievement tests, as well as the daily evaluations of teachers and the term grading system of schools, have allowed some schools to prematurely sort out students on the basis of "ability" as established by tests, and to then direct them into achievement tracks from which it can be difficult to escape.

From this perspective, the restrictive atmosphere of schools can become so institutionalized that teaching innovations (for example, team teaching, televised instruction, new types of lesson plans, ungraded learning, and achievement-based rather than age-based groupings of students) are rendered less effective in realizing their goals. One study by Goodlad[10] supports this charge. In summarizing the findings from a study of 100 kindergarten and first grade classrooms in thirteen states, he found little evidence that teaching technique had changed from the past. He and his researchers found that a single teacher tended to lead all instruction, with students passively responding, usually one by one, in a controlled classroom; pupils rarely did individual self-sustaining work; standard textbooks were the most conspicuous learning instruments available; small groups of students studying together were rarely found.[11] This study contradicts the impression many Americans have that schools are engaged in loosely structured programs. The emphasis on conformity, however, does appear to support the schools' desire for order. For example, a Louis Harris poll on parental attitudes conducted for *Life* magazine noted that two-thirds of the parents of high school students believe that " maintaining discipline is more important than student self-inquiry." Are the failings of the schools—poor student performance on standardized tests and lack of creativity—a result of parents' getting what they want? Or, are "loose," unproven educational experiments disrupting the formal educational process? At present, no definitive answer to these questions exists.

The dilemma for American society becomes how to realize the values of conformity through public education as well as the values of freedom and individualism. At the lower-school level, this dilemma becomes one of trying to maintain control while teaching students to feel free to innovate—all within a formal, bureaucratic structure.

Centralization Versus Decentralization

As we have stressed, education is relatively decentralized in America as compared to other industrial nations. The tasks of financing and administering lower education have been given to state governments; and in response to beliefs in local control, they in turn have delegated much funding responsibility to the local community. While some funds flow into the states and communities from various federal agencies, state income and sales taxes, plus local property taxes, provide at least half of the funds which support most lower public education. The consequences of such decentralization are far-reaching.

First, decentralization can generate inequality in school facilities. With the financing of schools tied to state and community taxes, poor states and communities are less able to afford the same physical facilities, or quality of teachers, as schools in more affluent areas. A frequent result is that the people in most need of educational help—the poor and the disadvantaged—are the least likely to get it. In 1971 the California Supreme Court ruled in the *Serrano* decision that the use of local property taxes to finance education "discriminates against the poor . . .[and] makes the quality of the child's education a function of the wealth of his parents and neighbors." This landmark decision has had little effect, to date, on the financing pattern of lower education in other states; and even in California, it is not clear that it has dramatically changed inequalities in school facilities.

Second, the decentralized structure of American lower education reduces the ability of the federal government to improve teaching and to eliminate inequities by implementing nationwide programs, such as school integration. Since schools are more dependent financially on local than on federal funds, they are more responsive to local political leanings and public sentiment. While the federal government has gained some leverage over lower education in recent decades, it does not have as much as either state or local governments. Equally important, the federal government does not have clear administrative linkages to the states and local communities, except through the U.S. Department of Education, which has only vague and shifting fiscal and administrative responsibilities. For example, when President Reagan took office, he proposed abolishing the department as a cabinet-level office; and only when education became a controversial issue in 1983 did he agree to keep it. But even then, its funding and responsibilities were greatly reduced.

Third, with unclear fiscal and administrative linkages to the states and local schools, federal funds flow into the schools from many diverse agencies. While the Department of Education does seek to coordinate these activities, its authority is limited; hence, there is much financial and administrative duplication as money from a variety of sources filters into state and local school jurisdictions.

Fourth, financing schools from local property taxes and state revenues has created a financial crisis in the schools. Each year fewer communities are able to finance adequate schools from local property taxes and increasingly limited state funds. Where parents are trying to provide quality lower education, property taxes have increased to such an extent that taxpayers are now consistently rejecting school and tax override referendums, even in the more affluent suburban districts. In many large American cities, which already have severe financial problems, lack of revenue has caused a dramatic decline in the quality of educational facilities and programs.

Finally, administrative and fiscal decentralization exposes primary and secondary schools to community-level political manipulation and to fads of public opinion. In many American communities public education is a hot political issue, with the result that schools become centers for political battles, only some of which concern the quality of education.

Centralization might seem like the easy solution to most of these problems. The schools could be administratively centralized under the Department of Education and totally financed by increased federal taxes. The increases would be offset by corresponding decreases in state and local taxes. Transforming American lower education in this way would give it a centralized structure similar to that in other modern industrial nations. However, whether such changes are desirable is unclear. Centralization would help resolve one set of problems, but it might create new ones. Experience with large, centralized systems, such as the one in New York, can offer the following clues as to the potential problems of centralization of American education.

First, centralization establishes a long chain of command and system of hierarchical authority that can orient teachers and administrators toward the organization rather than toward the students. Having to work within a long chain of command could, in some circumstances, make teachers and other school employees just as politicized as they sometimes become under local control.

Second, large bureaucratic organizations usually evidence fragmentation of administrative units, resulting in much duplication of effort. Whether such waste of human and other resources would be less than that in the current decentralized system cannot be known, but if previous experience with large federal agencies can serve as a guide, considerable administrative fragmentation, isolation, and duplication might well be expected in a centralized education system.

Third, isolation of administrative units creates a situation in which individual groups of employees spend some of their energies attempting to consolidate their power with respect to other units. In turn, strong informal norms emphasizing self-preservation are likely to emerge within administrative units, further deflecting attention and resources from educational goals. These social processes result in the bureaucracy's increasing insulation from—and ignorance of—students. In such a centralized environment, internal politics and personal career ambitions of bureaucrats could conceivably take precedence over the goals of education and service to the children of a community.

Teacher professionalism and unionization, which are typical of highly centralized school systems, can further compound the trend toward bureaucratic isolation. While professionalism helps keep teacher competence high, it can isolate teachers and administrators from the unique needs of students, because as the national teaching profession assumes prominence, the implementation of its latest fads, techniques, and learning formulas can take precedence over particular needs of diverse groups of students. Similarly, unionism can give teachers political protection and much-needed wage increases, but at the same time it can entrap teachers within one more bureaucracy (the union) and thereby limit their choices in dealing with students, the community, and school administration.

Thus, while centralization could perhaps reduce gross education inequalities, resolve current fiscal problems, allow for more implementation of national policies throughout the schools, and make educators less vulnerable to local political pressures, it can potentially cause a waste of resources, heightened teacher isolation from students, and widespread bureaucratic rigidity. The pros and cons of this issue make centralization versus decentralization another deepening dilemma in American education.

Dilemmas of Educational Inequality

Many early advocates of mass public education saw it as a democratizing influence, increasing the skills, knowledge, and other capacities for personal betterment among all citizens. Public schools, in Thomas Jefferson's words, were to "bring into action that mass of talents which lies buried in poverty in every country for want of means of development." To a great extent, mass education has increased the overall abilities and talents of Americans, but it does not do so for everyone, nor does education do so equally.

This situation is of great importance, since the United States is now a "credentialed society."[12] One's chances for money and occupational prestige are directly related to the possession of educational credentials, and only indirectly to factors like desire, ability, and performance on the job. While credentialing is a convenient and perhaps necessary way to assess qualifications of masses of potential workers, it grants the educational system great power in determining who succeeds, and who fails, in America. Those who conform to the educational system, and who fit in, acquire appropriate credentials; those who cannot conform, for various personal, cultural, and socioeconomic reasons, are likely to find less desirable niches in the economic system.

American education can thus reinforce as much as break down social class, ethnic, and racial boundaries. Such was not always the case, for public schools were not an important path to upward mobility among early immigrant generations. More frequently, mobility was achieved for the whole family by forcing children into the manual work force so that they could contribute to the family's total income. Many early Americans had to sacrifice education for the good of the family. For example, in 1870, for each 100 persons in the American population who were 17 years of age or older, only 2 were high school graduates. Today in 1980, about 24 persons for each 100, in the same age group, have failed to complete high school.[13] Moreover, as education credentials become critical in certifying people's capacities to perform economic roles, achievement gaps among racial and ethnic groups operate to exacerbate broader patterns of discrimination. For example, by most accounts whites outperform blacks in school, regardless of the method of comparison. The "achievement gap" between nonwhites and whites has remained roughly the same in recent years, since absolute gains in years of schooling among blacks and other minority groups have been paralled by similar gains in the white student population, thereby preserving the gap. In credentialed American society, such educational gaps translate into income and other status differentials, thus maintaining societal patterns of ethnic inequality and suppressing much human potential. The failure of American schools to be a greater equalizing force can be attributed to two significant forces: the structure and culture of public education; and the traits that lower-class children—not just minorities and the impoverished but also many in the working classes—bring with them to school.

The Structure of Public Education. Some critics argue that, historically, public schools have long imparted to the lower classes the habits of "obedience and submission necessary for public peace, a docile labor force, and the protection of property."[14] The charge is serious, but it does appear that many of the bureaucratic rigidities of schools have operated, perhaps unintentionally, against intellectually unassertive children and children from non-middle-class backgrounds. Even in the face of a changing American educational ideology and scores of well-intentioned programs emphasizing help for the poor, the structure of our schools has built-in racial, ethnic, and social class biases. Several features of this structured bias need to be emphasized. First, the very formality of the school system, with its emphasis on the clock, scheduling, routine, silence, and restriction of movement can discriminate against many children from some lower-class cultures, especially those in which physical aggressiveness, noise, and spontaneity are valued. Forced to sit quietly and follow routines, many children become alienated from schools where order and control are valued above all else.

Second, teachers who work in public schools are "middle-class." Even though many middle-class teachers have a sincere interest in helping lower-class students, most hold subtle expectations that lower-class students will have "learning problems." Through these expectations, teachers set up self-fulfilling prophecies, for by expecting so little of some students, teachers can inadvertently make it difficult for those students to do well. The effects of flagrant prejudice by teachers are obvious and well-documented, but far more pervasive in American schools is the imposition of a middle-class bias that says, implicitly and subtly, that non-middle-class children will find it difficult to learn. A teacher who responds to students *as if* they should have problems creates learning problems for students. This bias is a stable and constant feature of American education, and it will remain as long as large proportions of teachers—regardless of their intentions—come from middle-class backgrounds.

Third, the testing and grading system used in most primary and secondary schools discriminates against many students, especially those from the lower classes. Whether the instrument is an IQ test, a standardized achievement exam, or an in-class quiz, the very fact that a timed competitive test is being given favors students from middle-class homes where test-taking and competition are stressed. Furthermore, most tests require verbal skills, which again favors students from the middle classes, where children are more likely to be taught how to manipulate words. Doing well on tests is crucial to success in American schools, for it is on the basis of classroom grades, IQ tests, and standardized achievement exams that young students are counseled and otherwise channeled into college preparatory or vocational (terminal) programs. Furthermore, since it is so often school test performance that determines success or failure, a student's educational self-concept as good or mediocre is created on the basis of the examination system. Since one's educational self-concepts not only help determine performance in school but also one's more general educational aspirations, the current system of test-taking discriminates against many children by convincing them, at a very early age, that they cannot survive in the competitive, middle-class world of the American school.

The bias of the lower schools operates against virtually all lower-class children, and against some children from the middle classes, but it is particularly hard on those students who evidence behavior that betrays distinctive cultural patterns that deviate sharply from the middle-class cultural ambience of public schools. It is for this reason that studies of school achievement find family background and neighborhood more closely related to students' test scores than quality of school facilities or teacher qualifications. It cannot be doubted, of course, that certain family and neighborhood characteristics, such as unemployed parents, marital instability, lack of parental education, poor nutrition, and crushing poverty can seriously impair learning potential. But it is also necessary to emphasize that school environments, structured in ways that discriminate against non-middle-class and nonwhite cultural patterns, will inevitably lead to the conclusion that underachievement by lower-class and minority children is caused by the deficient background of the student. To some unknown degree, it may be the cultural and structural environment of the school that is deficient.

The schools need to prepare students for a world that is dominated by expectations for self-control, competitiveness, and verbal skills, and at the same time, to do so in a way that does not decrease the capacity of students to learn. By simply imposing demands in such areas, the schools clearly fail with many students. But by *not* imposing such demands, the schools would surely fail. The dilemma revolves around *how* to create a supportive environment for non-middle-class children and exert pressures for performance. It may be that large bureaucratic systems are, on the whole, incapable of such delicate flexibility, perpetuating inequality and, moreover, the disaffection of a large portion of the population.

The Traits of Schoolchildren. The traits that children bring with them to primary and secondary schools will obviously affect their academic performance. Schools reward some traits and punish others; and schools dominated by middle-class mass culture will, obviously, reward those who can display middle-class characteristics. However, such a portrayal of educational process is too simple. The fact remains that parents in many American families are not helping their children succeed in school. For example, although it is difficult to establish culturally free criteria to use in judging these matters, it is likely that lower-class family backgrounds do not lead to the cultivation of certain motives, attitudes, values, language patterns, and cognitive styles that facilitate learning, and hence, success in any type of school. "Attribute deficiencies" are perhaps not so great as many educators imply, but preschool training may well be necessary for children from *some* lower-class (and also, at times, middle-class) backgrounds.

The dilemma is, once again, how to do so on a large scale and in ways that are nondiscriminatory. Moreover, with shortages in funding and with the inevitable bureaucratization of large-scale programs, the prospects for developing effective preschool programs for large numbers of students with deficient backgrounds are not great. Moreover, as the experience with Operation Head Start documents, the positive effects of preschool programs are often undone as children move through the educational hierarchy in later years. Thus, it may be necessary to have follow-up programs for full-time students. More desirable, of course, would be effective schools for disadvantaged students.

Such schools do exist, but not in the quantities required to meet the magnitude of the problem. In his studies of several "successful" slum schools, Silberman found some of the conditions necessary to success with students from disadvantaged backgrounds: (1) a warm and sympathetic school environment; (2) a school staffed by ordinary teachers who *expect* their students to do well; (3) administrators who will not allow teachers to fail and will hold the teacher rather than the student accountable for failure; (4) schools that also teach parents to help in their children's education.[15] Implementing such changes on a mass scale in a highly bureaucratized school system would be difficult. Moreover, political pressures may operate against such changes. For example, in April 1983 when educational problems became a political issue, President Reagan's National Commission on Excellence in Education recommended stiffer high school graduation requirements, longer school days and years, and merit pay for superior teachers.[16] In response, many school districts stiffened high school graduation requirements by adding another year of English, math, and science to their curriculum. While these changes may be desirable in their own right, the official response to educational mediocrity is likely to revolve around invoking the "back to basics" belief system, while continuing to ignore student backgrounds and the subtle prejudices built into the school system. It is, therefore, most unlikely that America's lower educational dilemmas, especially those revolving around inequality, will be resolved in the near future.

Dilemmas of Higher Education in America

To examine educational dilemmas in colleges and universities, we must begin by reviewing two important sets of facts about American higher education.[17] First, it is young and started small. In 1870, for example, there were only 563 institutions of higher education in the United States. By 1980 this number had grown to 3,150. In 1870 there were 5,553 faculty persons (4,887 of whom were men) employed by institutions of higher education in the United States, but by 1980 this number had grown to 1,127,000 (751,000 of whom are men). In 1870 there were 9,372 degrees conferred by American colleges and universities, and only one of these was at the doctoral level; but in 1980, American colleges and universities conferred 999,548 degrees, including 32,615 doctorates. In 1870, there were 52,286 students (41,160 of whom were male) enrolled in degree programs at American colleges and universities, but in 1980, this number exploded to 11,569,899 students (5,682,877 of whom were male). These figures document the rapid expansion of American higher education during the first three-quarters of the century. Educational expansion was, in large part, due to broader military, political, and economic changes which brought the United States to a place of world dominance.

Second, higher education provides much of the technology, and most of the workers, needed to maintain what John Kenneth Galbraith has called the "American economic techno-structure."[18] Supplying new technology and highly trained workers was not always the goal of American higher education. In fact, well into the last century, higher education existed primarily to help affluent Americans teach their children refinement and to train a few young men for professions like law, medicine, veterinary science, or religion. In those early days of the last century, there was considerably less demand for scientific and other technical skills. But the creation of land grant colleges, coupled with the rapid industrialization and postindustralization of the economy, brought dramatic changes in the twentieth century. The American economy now demands a constant flow of trained employees as well as incessant technological input from colleges and universities. This transformation has increased public interest in higher education as well as economic and political support for its programs.

Yet, while the importance of higher education is clearly recognized, there persist several unresolved dilemmas in American higher education, involving: (1) size and scope, (2) priorities, (3) research versus teaching functions, and (4) the job market.

The Dilemma of Size and Scope

Since World War II, state-supported colleges and universities have grown most rapidly, culminating in today's extensive state college and multiuniversity systems. The growing size of colleges and universities is a reflection of how much the American economy has grown and of how much the United States and other industrial nations have become credentialed societies.[19] For most citizens, to get a good job, extensive formal education credentials are necessary, with the result that over 40 percent of the college-age population at least begins a program of higher education. This percentage is approximately double that of twenty years ago. In the fall of 1981 there were about 12,320,000 students enrolled in American colleges and universities. This was an increase of nearly 2 percent over enrollment figures for fall of the preceding year and was the largest enrollment ever recorded for American higher education.[20]

The growth in enrollments has, obviously, increased the size of college and university campuses. In turn, increases in size have led to even more bureaucratization and consequent alienation of students and employees, for ever-escalating specialization, compartmentalization, and neutralization have become characteristic of American university life. In order to process the masses of students who are now entering American colleges and universities, class size and faculty-to-student ratios have been enlarged; centralized counseling and record keeping have made a simple formality of registration, and other cost-saving and "efficient" ways of processing masses of students have been expanded.

On the positive side, however, far more students than in the past are now exposed to university libraries, laboratory facilities, and concentrations of skilled teachers. Finding better ways to reconcile the advantages of size in higher education with its shortcomings—impersonality, bureaucratization, and the consequences of these for creative learning—represents an enduring dilemma for America's large colleges and universities.

To the extent that the major goals of a college are introducing students to the process of higher learning, helping students use reason in the analysis and resolution of problems, and requiring students to develop both technical competence and intellectual integrity, the current American system of mass higher education is only partially successful. (There are, of course, vocational aspects of college and university life; which we ignore here for the sake of simplicity. However, the points we make about the "pure" side of colleges and universities very often also hold true for their "applied" activities.) The lack of success seems to be largely due to the fact that large multiuniversity systems have come to dominate higher education, since the costs involved in building and maintaining smaller campuses are high. This economic fact now threatens an increasing number of nonelite small and medium-sized colleges and universities, since their tuition costs make them uncompetitive with state systems and their lack of high prestige makes them uncompetitive with elite private schools. Higher education is caught in a trap where the demands for its services are high, but the very size of the task forces homogenization of the system.

The Dilemma of Priorities

Colleges and universities have five principal functions: (1) They are charged with the socialization of general knowledge and skills. (2) In doing so, especially in a society where academic credentials are highly valued, they allocate many people to status hierarchies of the broader society. (3) They store and preserve the culture of a society—its history, lore, technology, and a general fund of knowledge. (4) They expand the cultural storehouse through research and other activities in a wide variety of fields. (5) They are involved in transforming society on a broad front, whether through research and other innovations, criticism of government and economic priorities, policies, and programs, or particular educational programs.

All these are generally believed to be proper functions of universities. However, there is widespread dispute over *which* one(s) should have priority; and this dispute is at the core of many of the problems confronting higher education. Controversies over teaching versus research, over university involvement with industry, military, and other branches of government, over student dissatisfaction with academic bureaucracy, over the failure of universities to help resolve many social problems, and over the creation of an excessively credentialed society all reflect conflict in Amercans' beliefs about the functions of American higher education.

In choosing priorities in the coming decades, a number of critical questions will need to be resolved: First, can America afford to allow colleges and universities to educate a near majority of the population? Are there enough "good" jobs to justify this level of higher education? The education ethic has created a situation where many Americans feel they *must* go to college. Compounding this compulsion is the fact that more and more employers are requiring college credentials as a minimal condition of employment. Is a degree critical for most jobs in American society? As long as the concern with credentials is emphasized by other parts of society, and as long as the education ethic flourishes in American culture, colleges and universities will most likely continue to operate as society's reluctant gatekeepers.

Second, should colleges and universities continue to take large sums of money from industry and government to do applied research which often leads to the production of life-threatening materials or products which only benefit an affluent few? As long as higher education is dependent on these sources of funding it will run the danger of being coopted or of being deflected from its purely educational goals.

Third, can colleges and universities actively transform other parts of societies in lasting and significant ways? Or, are problems such as poverty, racism, urban decay, and inequality only resolvable by changes' in the broader society? Do college and university personnel have a moral obligation to speak out on social, economic, and political issues? Or should they adopt a more neutral public posture befitting employees who are obligated to show students all sides of an issue? Should colleges and universities be staging centers for social protest and other forms of disobedience? Or should campuses of higher education more resemble the "ivory tower" where culture is stored and studied?

For some time now, colleges and universities have been politically tranquil, since they now must concentrate on operating under difficult financial conditions. But higher education is a growing influence in societies dominated by high technology and science. And while the shrillness of protests in the 1960s is gone, questions of priorities persist and pose, for the present at least, quiet dilemmas for higher education.

Research Versus Teaching

In many colleges and universities, there is controversy over the relative places of teaching and research. Research and most other forms of pure scholarship are lonely activities which require faculty to spend long, isolated hours away from students pursuing new ideas. Teaching, of course, requires faculty to spend time with students, transmitting what is already known. It is not surprising that many research-oriented faculty members view teaching and research as somewhat contradictory. Each is time-consuming and requires special training, skills, and interests. And since many lack the energy, time, and aptitude to do well at both, faculty members tend to emphasize one over the other.

This dilemma is a reflection of the dual function of universities: to impart motivation, knowledge, and skills to students; and at the same time, to expand the existing body of knowledge through research and other forms of scholarship. Both are necessary, and yet, to do well at one very often leads to a deemphasis of the other. For example, promotion of high-level research requires the diversion of scarce funds into research facilities, a large pool of graduate students to help with the work, and time off from undergraduate teaching for professors. On the other hand, concentration on undergraduate education requires more "contact" time from professors, less subsidy of graduate students and programs, and large amounts of university funds for a wide variety of undergraduate facilities and programs.

Part of the trouble in reconciling these functions stems from the general expectation that the same faculty must perform both, and do well at both, in order to be any good at either. While such an ideal is realized by a few scholars, the high degree of specialization required within academic disciplines makes it much more likely that exceptional researchers are behind in, or ignorant of, areas where teaching is required. Furthermore, in addition to a breadth of knowledge, good teaching requires that faculty spend a great deal of time with students outside the classroom. Many researchers are not suitably tempered, or socially equipped, for this type of personal contact. It is difficult for any of the faculty to find time for student contact, especially in mass education settings. Excellent researchers can often be exceptional lecturers, but rarely do they have the out-of-class time to spend with large numbers of students. Conversely, teachers who must keep up in several fields, prepare lectures, and spend time with students cannot, except in very rare cases, become overly involved in time-consuming research.

In the abstract, the solution to the dilemma is obvious: a division of labor between research and teaching. But maintaining such a division of labor has proven difficult for three reasons. First, research productivity is more easily measured than is quality of teaching. Since all bureaucracies require evidence of efficiency and employee performance, research will be rewarded more highly than teaching. Second, the reputations of faculty members outside the local school bureaucracy determine their mobility from employer to employer. A reputation as an excellent (or poor) teacher rarely has great influence beyond the local campus. For professors to establish marketable reputations, they must publish. Professional prestige stems from the quantity of publications. Even within most academic departments, prestige is first established by one's nonteaching accomplishments—research, publishing, and consulting. Third, a school's prestige relative to other colleges and universities is rarely established, except for a few elite schools, by the quality of its teachers as teachers, but rather by the quality of its teachers as researchers and scholars. Most college administrators, as well as many students and their parents, are primarily concerned about the reputation of their schools—perhaps unwittingly encouraging the very faculty isolation that can dilute an undergraduate teaching program.

The rewarding of research over teaching also aggravates trends evident with bureaucratization: increasing social and physical distance between faculty and most students, large classes, and a pervasive lack of a general intellectual community. Yet, just how to go about transforming the reward system in higher education so as to encourage good teaching and high-quality research has proven difficult. Some professors are unwilling to give up their prestige and mobility, or to suffer the disapproval of colleagues, in order to become good teachers. Few administrators, parents, or students wish to allow a school's scholarly reputation to decline in the name of improved teaching, especially in a credentialed society where the reputation of the school from which one gets a degree is sometimes more important than one's actual capabilities. For these reasons, then, the dilemma of teaching versus research will endure.

The Dilemma of the Job Market

It is very likely that most college and university faculty value, above all else, "the life of the mind." Thus they are ideologically committed to introducing students to scholarship. That is, their concern is with education for its own sake rather than education for specific jobs and careers. While professional graduate schools, such as law, medicine, business, and social work, are structured along vocational lines, the undergraduate curriculum at most colleges and universities tends to emphasize a more general liberal arts education.

However, all surveys reveal that most students who enter American colleges and universities want to prepare themselves for a good job and to acquire credentials to secure jobs that carry high prestige and income. This situation creates an inevitable conflict between the vocationalism of students and the scholasticism of faculty, even though it can be argued that a broad education facilitates later job performance. The actual knowledge and skills required for most jobs in the United States are not acquired in college but after employment has begun. It is true that some careers require highly technical training—for example, law, medicine, dentistry, engineering, and social work—but critics assert that even much of this training could be done within a much shorter period of time.

These considerations raise questions about the content of higher education. On the one side of this issue are the majority of faculty members who believe an undergraduate degree should involve hard work, discipline, and perseverance in the pursuit of a general fund of knowledge and a broad array of intellectual skills. In spite of their beliefs, students are more likely to ask: how much training do I need for a good job? Is a general education necessary or "relevant"? Many students, then, question the priorities of the university system; but at the same time, they want a degree that certifies them as eligible for certain types of jobs.

This situation poses a serious problem for higher education: is its function to encourage a credentials race among great numbers of anxious students, or should the university opt for its traditional emphasis on liberal arts education, ignoring credential anxiety? In many ways, answers to this dilemma must come from outside the campuses. However, transformations in the criteria for placing people in jobs seem unlikely; the basic conflict between student vocationalism and university scholasticism will remain.

Conclusion

As societies become more complex, education becomes a prominent institution, performing such vital functions as socialization, credentialing for social placement, research for cultural innovation, cultural storage, and social change. It is not surprising that education is the topic of many intensely held cultural beliefs and that its structure and operation are the subject of controversy. Moreover, the scale of the educational system and the broad range of functions it performs makes inevitable a series of dilemmas about what lower and higher education should be, and what they should do. In this chapter, we have portrayed only the more immediate dilemmas, but there are many more. And the centrality of education to modern social life will increase, creating new problems for Americans.

Chapter 7

Wealth
and Poverty

The United States probably reveals a large poverty sector. Juxtaposed to such poverty is a relatively small wealth-holding elite. And between these two extremes is a large grouping of middle Americans who enjoy varying degrees of relative affluence. The existence of concentrated wealth and pauperism is not coincidental. One contributes to the other.

The persistence of poverty in the midst of affluence has posed an enduring dilemma for Americans. This dilemma must, however, be viewed in the more general context of inequality. Indeed, one of the great failings of social science is its tendency to analyze poverty per se without at the same time recognizing that the existence of poverty is tied to the dynamics of inequality in America.[1]

Inequality can be defined as the differential distribution of those resources that members of a society value. The three most basic resources are (1) material wealth, or the money to buy material goods, (2) power, or the capacity to control others, and (3) prestige, or the honor and esteem that one receives from others.[2] In all but the simplest societies, material wealth, power, and prestige are distributed unequally. Some get more of these valued resources than others.

Many of the dynamics of a society are inevitably influenced by how these resources are distributed. Societies that distribute these resources unequally—where relatively few get most of the wealth, power, and prestige—will be very different from societies that distribute these resources more equally—where most everyone enjoys some wealth, power, and prestige. And because much of what occurs in any society is tied to patterns of inequality, we should not be surprised to discover that many of America's most enduring social dilemmas inhere in the distribution of these resources.

The Dynamics of Inequality

Ultimately, the degree of inequality in a society is connected to the level of productivity in its economy.[3] It is difficult to hoard wealth if the economy cannot produce a large surplus of goods and commodities; it is equally difficult to mobilize power unless people can be freed from productive roles and paid to manipulate, coerce, or control others; and if there are few differences in the kinds of economic and political activities, it is hard to make distinctions among individuals in terms of honor and esteem.[4]

This relationship between economic productivty and inequality is intensified by the interrelations among money, power, and prestige. In general, those with money can buy power; those with power can use it to extract and hoard wealth; and those with esteem can—although to a much lesser degree—use their prestige to gain wealth and influence. Thus wealth, power, and prestige become correlated in all societies. In particular, wealth and power become highly correlated, whereas prestige can be held by those without great wealth or power.[5] Naturally, these correlations can never be perfect in complex societies; there is a lot of slippage in any society. In many societies the most powerful are not in every case the most wealthy; many of the wealthy possess little power; and some with high prestige can, on occasion, exert great influence. But the fact that the correlations are not perfect should not dissuade us from recognizing that those with wealth and power tend to be, with some exceptions, the same people, groups, and organizations.

One result of the correlation of power and wealth (and to a lesser extent, prestige) is the creation of social classes. A social class can be defined as a subpopulation whose members' share of resources give them a similar rank in the society and who, as a result, reveal similar attributes—values, beliefs, speech patterns, tastes and desires, and general lifestyles.[6] Such classes result from people's relative shares of material wealth, power, and prestige. That is, the nature of one's job and its income determines, to very great extent, how much power and prestige one will possess in a society. In turn, when people hold similar jobs, derive similar incomes, possess the same sense of power or powerlessness, and enjoy (or feel dismay over) the same level of social honor, then their experiences and views of the world converge. Common world views are reinforced and strengthened by the fact that these people work and live together, and hence, interact frequently with each other. And as people interact, their ways of looking at and behaving in the world converge. Thus, in any society which reveals productivity beyond a subsistence level, we can observe a number of social classes whose members reveal a common perspective and lifestyle by virtue of converging shares of wealth, power, and prestige.

The existence of social classes presents a society with a dynamic source of tension. To some extent, people in a social class accept their fate and take comfort in the fact that others share it with them. But often, people resent their condition, desiring to have more of those resources possessed by members of other social classes. Inequality thus presents any society with the basic dilemma of how the tension-producing effects of inequality are to be mitigated. In all societies, those with money and power tend to impose on others beliefs that legitimate their privileged station and that stigmatize in some way those without privilege, thereby making the system of inequality seem right and proper. Such efforts do not always work, however, as people see through such beliefs and recognize them for what they are. And in their place, the have-nots (or their leaders) articulate a set of opposition beliefs which question the legitimacy of the existing system. At times, as the historical wreckage of societies underscores, opposition beliefs are instrumental in mobilizing people into a revolutionary force.

In sum, then, inequality is tied to economic productivity. Power and wealth are highly correlated, but not perfectly. Esteem is correlated with power and wealth, but not to the same degree as power and wealth are to each other. The unequal distribution of wealth, power, and prestige leads to the creation of social classes, whose members evidence a common perspective and lifestyle by virtue of their similar shares of wealth, power, and prestige. Social classes usually become the arena for an ideological battle, consisting of efforts to impose either legitimating or opposition beliefs.

The Dynamics of American Inequality

With a highly productive economic system, we should expect great inequality in America. The degree of inequality is mitigated by several forces. First, despite its problematic nature (see chapter 3), American society is a political democracy which allows the less wealthy to mobilize proper and to exert some degree of political influence. Second, as the economy has become increasingly dependent upon large numbers of highly educated experts and professionals (see chapter 5), they have been able to convert their "human capital" into high incomes and modest levels of political power. Third, since its inception, America has held values of freedom and equality, and as a result, has been ideologically committed to a series of egalitarian beliefs which, to a limited extent, stigmatize those who seek to hoard *too much* wealth and power.[7] We should not overemphasize these cultural and social forces, but they help explain why there is not more inequality in America.

Inequality in Material Wealth

There are two types of statistical indicators of material inequality: income distribution and wealth distribution. Income distribution refers to how much of the total income in a given year different segments of the population command, while wealth distribution concerns what proportion of all the valuable assets—money, cars, stocks, bonds, homes, and the like—are held by different segments of the population. More is known about income distribution than wealth distribution, primarily because the government has been collecting data on people's income through the Census Bureau and Internal Revenue Service. The government, however, has not collected recent data on how and where wealth has been accumulating; and as a result, we are forced to rely upon data that are two decades old.

In table 7.1, the income distribution of families and unattached individuals by income fifths is reported for recent decades. Income fifths are statistical groupings constructed by rank-ordering every family in America by its total income for a given year—from the highest to lowest—and then dividing this rank-ordered list into five equal categories from the top to the bottom. Each income fifth is equal in size and represents 20 percent of the population, but its share of the total income in a given year will vary. In table 7.1, by reading down the columns for each income fifth, we see that the bottom fifth of the population has derived only about 5 percent of the total income in a given year, while the top fifth has received about 41 percent. The second, third, and fourth income fifths have, respectively, derived around 11 percent, 17 percent, and 24 percent of the total income. Two features of these government figures are noteworthy. First, income distribution has remained constant over the last three decades; there has been

Table 7.1 Income Distribution, Selected Years, 1947 to 1981

	Lowest Fifth	Second Fifth	Middle Fifth	Fourth Fifth	Highest Fifth	Top 5 Percent	Mean Income for All Fifths Combined
1981	5.0%	11.3%	17.4%	24.4%	41.9%	15.4%	$25,838
1979	5.2	11.6	17.5	24.1	41.7	15.8	22,316
1977	5.2	11.6	17.5	24.2	41.5	15.7	18,264
1975	5.4	11.8	17.6	24.1	41.1	15.5	15,546
1974	5.4	12.0	17.6	24.1	41.0	15.3	14,502
1972	5.4	11.9	17.5	23.9	41.4	15.9	12,625
1970	5.4	12.2	17.6	23.8	40.9	15.6	11,106
1968	5.6	12.4	17.7	23.7	40.5	15.6	9,670
1966	5.6	12.4	17.8	23.8	40.5	15.6	8,395
1964	5.1	12.0	17.7	24.0	41.2	15.9	7,336
1962	**5.0**	**12.1**	**17.6**	**24.0**	**41.3**	**15.7**	**6,670**
1960	4.8	12.2	17.8	24.0	41.3	15.9	6,227
1958	5.0	12.5	18.0	23.9	40.6	15.4	5,565
1957	5.1	12.7	18.1	23.8	40.4	15.6	5,443
1955	4.8	12.3	17.8	23.7	41.3	16.4	4,962
1953	4.7	12.5	18.0	23.9	40.9	15.7	4,706
1951	5.0	12.4	17.6	23.4	41.6	16.8	4,194
1949	4.5	11.9	17.3	23.5	42.7	16.9	3,569
1947	5.0	11.9	17.0	23.1	43.0	17.5	3,546

SOURCE: U.S. Bureau of Census, *Current Population Reports,* ser. P-60, no. 137 (Washington, D.C.: Government Printing Office, 1983), p. 47.

virtually no redistribution of income in the United States. Second, over 40 percent of all income goes to only one-fifth of the population, signaling enormous inequality in income for families in America.

In table 7.2, the amount of wealth held in 1962 by in-

Table 7.2 Distribution of Wealth by Income Fifths, 1962

Income Fifths	Percent of Total Wealth Held
Highest fifth	57.2%
Fourth fifth	15.6
Third fifth	11.4
Second fifth	8.6
Lowest fifth	7.2
Total	100.0

SOURCE: Board of Governors of the Federal Reserve System, *Survey of Financial Characteristics of Consumers, 1962* (Washington, D.C.: Government Printing Office, 1962).

come fifths is reported. By referring back to table 7.1 for the year 1962, it is possible to compare the percentage of the income earned in that year and the percentage of total wealth held for comparable statistical groupings.

This fact becomes immediately evident when wealth fifths are computed. Such fifths are computed in the same manner as income fifths, except this time it is wealth—total assets—that is rank-ordered and grouped into five equal categories. Wealth fifths are reported in table 7.3. As can be seen, one-fifth of the families controlled about 76 percent of all assets for the year 1962. Phrased differently, the bottom three-fifths, or 60 percent, of the population held less than 9 percent of all assets in 1962—that is, cars, houses, stocks, bonds, securities, money, or anything that can be converted into money. Such data, despite the fact that they are over two decades old, reveal considerable inequality in America. No comprehensive, systematic data on wealth inequality have been collected by the government since 1962 (a fact which can be attributed to the wealthy's ability to prevent such reporting), but it is evident from these data that considerable wealth is concentrated among a comparatively few families.[8]

In table 7.4 the percentage of total wealth held by the wealthiest 1 percent of the population is reported. These data span a greater period of time and have been collected up to 1969, giving a more complete picture of wealth concentration among the richest people in America. It should be cautioned,

Table 7.3 Distribution of Wealth by Wealth Fifths, 1962

Wealth Fifths	Percentage of Total Wealth Held
Highest fifth	76.0%
Fourth fifth	15.5
Third fifth	6.2
Second fifth	2.1
Lowest fifth	0.2
Total	100.0

SOURCE: Board of Governors of the Federal Reserve System, *Survey of Financial Characteristics of Consumers, 1962* (Washington, D.C.; Government Printing Office, 1962).

Table 7.4 Share of Wealth Held by Richest 1 Percent

Year	Percent of Total Wealth Held
1810	21.0%
1860	24.0
1900	26–31.0
1922	31.6
1929	36.3
1933	28.3
1939	30.6
1945	23.3
1949	20.8
1953	27.5
1956	26.0
1958	26.9
1962	22.0
1965	23.4
1969	20.1
1972	20.7

SOURCES: For 1810, 1860, and 1900, Robert E. Gallman, "Trends in the Size Distribution of Wealth in the Nineteenth Century," in Lee Soltow, ed., *Six Papers on the Size Distribution of Wealth and Income* (New York: National Bureau of Economic Research, 1969), p. 6.

For 1922, 1929, 1933, 1939, 1945, 1949, and 1956, Robert J. Lampman, *The Share of Top Wealth-Holders in National Wealth, 1922–1956* (New York: National Bureau of Economic Research, 1962), p. 204.

For 1958, James D. Smith and Stephen D. Franklin, "The Concentration of Personal Wealth, 1922–1969," *American Economic Review* (May 1974) 64:162–67.

For 1962, 1965, 1969, 1972, U.S. Bureau of the Census, *Statistical Abstracts of the United States, 1982–1983* (Washington, D.C.: Government Printing Office, 1983), p. 449.

however, that these data are not completely comparable from year to year (see note on table). They do give a rough calculation (and only a very rough calculation is possible) of wealth concentrations at the very top. In general, it appears that about 25 percent of all assets in America have been held by 1 percent of the population—another indicator of the degree of inequality in America.

While the data are not complete, they do provide an approximate picture of inequality in America. There is considerable income inequality which has accumulated over time into vast wealth inequalities. The critical question now becomes: what social and cultural forces have caused, and now perpetuate, such a high degree of inequality?

Inequalities in Power

It is difficult to calculate very precisely the distribution of power. Those with power often operate behind the scenes and with subtlety, whereas those without great power can be highly vocal and visible. At best, then, we can only make informed guesses about the distribution of power. Table 7.5 represents one way to visualize the distribution of power in terms of shares possessed by different economic groupings.[9] Reading across the top of the table, the "poor" can be conceptualized here as the bottom income or wealth fifth (official poverty levels will be discussed later in the chapter); the affluent constitute the three middle fifths, plus parts of the top fifth. The wealthy are the upper segment of the highest wealth or income fifth—say, the top 1 percent of income earners and the top 5 percent of wealthholders. Reading down the left side of table 7.5, we have listed those properties of various economic groupings that would be relevant to assessing their power. At the bottom, the cumulative amount of power of these three income groups is estimated (only a rough estimate is possible).

The poor do not fare well on the seven dimensions of power in the table, the affluent do much better, and the wealthy do very well. From dimensions (1) and (2), it might seem that the poor's size and concentration in the cores of cities and in rural areas might help them consolidate power. However, the affluent represent an even larger group who are also concentrated in urban and suburban areas; and as dimensions (3) through (7) reveal, it is the degree of political organization that can be politically decisive. The poor are not organized; they have few financial resources to support organizations; and they have never developed a lobbying tradition or effective channels of political influence. In contrast, the affluent are represented by many organizations such as unions, professional associations, and the corporations in

Table 7.5 Economic Groups and Political Power

	Poor	Affluent	Wealthy
(1) Size	Large	Very large	Small
(2) Distribution	Rural and urban; high concentrations in cores of large cities	Urban; large masses in suburbs	Rural, urban, suburban; much dispersion
(3) Degree of organization	Low; few effective national organizations	High; unions, professional and trade associations; the corporations where they work	High; corporations they own and manage; trade associations of their corporations
(4) Nature of organization	Fragmented; often in conflict; loose organization at national level	Highly centralized, tightly coordinated national confederations with clear goals	Highly organized; covert and overt confederations
(5) Financial resources	Meager	Great	Vast
(6) Lobbying tradition	Short	Long; at least 100 years; most effective since 1940	Long; over 100 years; had always been effective
(7) Tradition of influence	Little	Much, especially since 1940	Much; has always been effective
Total power	Low	High	Very high

SOURCE: Jonathan H. Turner and Charles Starnes, *Inequality: Privilege and Poverty in America* (Santa Monica: Goodyear, 1976), p. 83.

which they work; the resources of these organizations are great; and they have a longer lobbying tradition as well as more developed influence channels. The wealthy reveal all these characteristics and thus can exert enormous political influence.

It is not necessary to assume corruption in government to visualize just how the size, organization, and resources of different income groups create a set of political pressures supporting the present profile of inequality. While illicit practices undoubtedly occur, reform legislation would not necessarily alter the present balance of power. The affluent represent a majority, and their organizations have effectively pursued their interests. Because of their ownership of key industries, the wealthy and government officials usually cooperate to ensure the economic stability necessary to keep the large affluent sector content. While the wealthy's control of income and wealth deprives both the poor and affluent of resources, the middle-income groups' short-run economic interests—economic stability, steady work, and a decent income—drive them to form an uneasy coalition with the wealthy. People rarely want to change a system where they get benefits, especially if change is seen as potentially producing disorder and threatening their affluence.

Inequality in Prestige

In table 7.6, we have reported the data on the prestige rankings for selected occupations for 1963 and 1947. The higher an occupation scores, the more prestigeful it is perceived to be. Although these data are not recent, there is supplemental data from more recent studies to indicate that they still hold for America in the 1980s.[10] As is evident, prestige and honor are given to those occupations revealing skill or expertise, relatively high income, and power. Some prestigious occupations, such as college professor and scientist, do not typically enjoy great income, wealth, or power, but most of the higher-ranking occupations do. Conversely, at the bottom of the prestige hierarchy are occupations that do not involve skill, high income, or the exercise of power. Moreover,

Table 7.6 Occupational Prestige Scores and Rankings in America, 1963 and 1947

Occupational Ranking	1963 Score	1947 Score
Physician	93	93
Scientist	92	89
College professor	90	89
Lawyer	89	86
Minister	87	87
Airline pilot	86	83
Public school teacher	81	78
Author of novels	78	80
Police officer	72	67
Insurance agent	69	68
Plumber	65	63
Machine operator in factory	63	60
Truck driver	59	54
Clerk in store	56	58
Farmhand	48	50
Garbage collector	39	35
Shoe shiner	34	33

SOURCE: Robert L. Hodge, Paul M. Siegel, and Peter H. Rossi, "Occupational Prestige in the United States, 1925–1963," *American Journal of Sociology* (1964), 70:286–302.

there is great inequality in the prestige of different occupations.

Prestige is a most valued resource. To be given esteem is highly rewarding whereas to be stigmatized is highly unpleasant. To do without money or power is one thing, but to be seen as less worthy adds insult to injury. Indeed, it could be argued that it is lack of esteem as much as the poverty or powerlessness that drives people to rebel against a system of inequality. For our purposes, however, the crucial points are that in American and most other industrial systems, there is considerable inequality in prestige and that people at the bottom rungs of the prestige hierarchy are often stigmatized as "less worthy" than those at the middle and upper ranks.

The Creation of Social Classes

The patterns of inequality outlined in tables 7.1 to 7.6 operate to create distinctive social classes in America. People with roughly equivalent job-related incomes, wealth hold-ings, bases of political power, and prestige ranks are likely to converge in attitudes, beliefs, perceptions, and modal behav-iors. The result is a series of social classes which are ranked in terms of their power, income or wealth, and prestige. The exact number of social classes that can be observed in Amer-ica can vary, depending upon how fine-tuned we wish to make our observations. For our purposes, a rough calibration is all that is necessary. Accordingly, we visualize American society as revealing the following class divisions:

The Elite:	High income, high wealthholders who own or manage large corporations or important and strategic firms, who govern major cities and states, or who hold top-level elective and appointive government jobs. These individuals enjoy high prestige and wield consid-erable political power. (Examples: president of DuPont, prominent sena-tor, Chairman of Joint Chiefs, Mayor of New York, Secretary of State, head of Wall Street law firm.)
The Upper Affluent:	High income, sometimes high wealth-holders, who possess highly paid professional skills or who evidence successful entrepreneurial skills. These individuals enjoy relatively high pres-tige and wield some political power through various professional or trade associations. (Examples: successful lawyer and doctor, college president, president of a state university, suc-cessful small business owner.)
The White-Collar Affluent:	Moderate to high income, modest wealth; persons who work as profes-sionals or as middle- to lower-level bu-reaucrats in industry and govern-ment. These individuals possess

	moderate prestige and relatively little power outside the influence of the organization for which they work. (Examples: research chemist, school administrator, insurance salesman, government manager.)
The Lower White Collar:	Moderate to low income, little wealth; persons who work at relatively unskilled white-collar jobs in government and industry. These individuals hold little power outside the organizations (company, unions) to which they belong; and they enjoy only modest prestige. (Examples: secretary, department store sales clerk, file clerk, receptionist.)
The Affluent Blue Collar:	Moderate to sometimes high-income individuals who possess moderate to little wealth and who perform skilled and semiskilled salaried and commission work with their hands (plumbers, carpenters, heavy equipment operators). These individuals have little power and enjoy only modest prestige.
The Lower Blue Collar:	Moderate to low-income individuals who possess little wealth and who perform salaried work with their hands. These individuals have little power outside organizations to which they belong (primarily unions); and they enjoy little prestige.
The Impoverished:	Unemployed, unemployable, or very low-income individuals who must receive public assistance. They have very little power and suffer severe stigma.

The existence of such class divisions can result in conflict. Such conflict in America is reduced by several forces. First, people of different classes generally do not confront one another; they typically live, work, and enjoy recreation in different areas. Second, interaction among members of dramatically different classes is ritualized, so that when interaction is necessary, it is highly predictable and stereotyped. Third, the American economy has been sufficiently productive so that, except for the impoverished, most Americans can purchase symbols of affluence (such as cars) on credit. Fourth, government transfer payments and subsidies give some benefits to not only the impoverished but also to other classes. (Examples include food stamps, free lunches, Medicare, deduction of interest on income tax, relatively inexpensive public education, unemployment benefits, etc.) Rejection of the political system becomes less likely than when the lower classes receive few benefits. Fifth, there is some mobility up the social class system, with the result that individuals of a given class all know someone "who made it" to a higher class. Such a situation may increase people's sense of their own relative deprivation, but it also tends to deflect blame for their situation from the system to themselves or to bad luck. And sixth, and probably most important, a system of beliefs has operated to legitimate patterns of inequality and current class divisions.[11] Such legitimating beliefs so dominate the perceptions of most Americans that opposition beliefs have only sporadically taken hold.

The Culture of Inequality

The tension between beliefs legitimating and opposing inequality not only influences the substantive dynamics of class relations but also the definition of what is "problematic" about American inequality. Indeed, whether a system of inequality is seen as good, bad, or something in between is conditioned both by people's actual class position and by their values and beliefs.[12] If this were not the case, lower social classes would *always* be in revolt. They are not because they frequently do not have the material resources to mobilize power and because they do not see their world accurately through the prism of beliefs that support the interests of the elite.

Thus, before we can enumerate the "dilemmas" inhering in the system of inequality, we must understand the beliefs and underlying values that shape the definitions of what is problematic.[13]

"Trickle-Down" Beliefs. In a capitalist economic system, one of the most dominant beliefs is that wealthy individuals and corporations must be rewarded for investing and that they should be allowed to hoard wealth, which, presumably, they will use to invest in the economy. Such wealth "trickles down" to all sectors of a society because as the wealthy invest their capital, the investment creates jobs which become income to employees at all economic levels. This belief system has been labeled "supply side" economics, and was briefly termed 'Reaganomics" after President Ronald Reagan. It is a belief system that legitimates concentrations of wealth as necessary to economic productivity in two senses: (1) individuals and corporations need to accumulate large amounts of capital in order to invest in expensive and complex productive processes; and (2) individuals and corporations must have profit incentives to accumulate such capital, and hence, it is important to make it highly profitable for those with money to invest (and thereby make even more money).

It is also a belief system that ties the well-being of the less affluent to the privilege of the rich. If the wealthy are rich, and are encouraged to invest their wealth in order to become richer, then the increased production "trickles down" even to the very poor. First, as production increases, the number of available jobs expands, creating economic opportunities for not only the affluent but also the most impoverished. Second, as economic production increases, and as more people are employed, tax revenues to government escalate, making more money available for social programs that assist the least affluent.

Such beliefs in "trickle-down" represent one way that values of activism, achievement, materialism, and progress are used to legitimate the privilege of the wealthy. Those who achieve material wealth must be encouraged to further the progress of the nation by actively reinvesting their wealth in order to achieve increased personal wealth, and at the same time, to stimulate efforts to achieve, to progress, and to acquire material well-being among those who take advantage of the job opportunities created by the investment of wealth and capital.

"Work Ethic" Beliefs. Americans fervently believe that income and wealth should come from work. Income or wealth which does not come from "hard work," "skilled manipulations," or "creative talent" is stigmatized and resented, because it violates values of activism and achievement. Those who "don't work," therefore, are held in contempt in America and are viewed with suspicion.

This belief system operates to legitimate inequality in several ways. First, it forces much of the population to work in any job for very low wages in order to avoid the stigma attached to being unemployed. Because of their low wages, they remain in poverty, and reciprocally, the profits, wealth, and income of those who employ low-wage workers are maintained or increased. Second, it encourages efforts by employers to "keep wages low," and hence profits up, in order to "save jobs." Third, this system of beliefs makes the application of the value of humanitarianism highly conditional. Those who receive public aid must be "deserving" in that they are, at present, unable to achieve in a work setting. And, in order to ensure that those on public assistance be "motivated to work" (lest the values of individualism, activism, and achievement be violated), benefits must be kept low so that people will take any job. The result is that whether or not people take a job, their poverty is maintained. Third, those who employ the poor are subsidized by having a low-wage labor pool from which to draw when they need it and to throw back onto the welfare rolls when they don't. Fourth, since the welfare system will supplement the income of very low-wage labor (indeed, the minimum wage is a below-subsistence wage), consumers are subsidized in that they can purchase goods and services (fruits, vegetables, domestic help, etc.) at prices below the costs of maintaining the worker at a subsistence level.

These two legitimating beliefs—trickle-down and the work ethic—operate to sustain the insitutional processes in the economy and government that create patterns of inequality and class divisions in American society. They also define for most Americans what is problematic about inequality: the unwillingness of the poor to work and the excessive costs of public assistance. And because these beliefs are infused with the tenets of core values, they arouse intense emotions and blind most Americans to other realities: the extensive subsidies to the affluent that far exceed those to the impoverished. For while privilege and wealth are at times considered a problem in America (people, for example, get mad about "tax loopholes" and wealthy people who don't work), most public attention focuses on the poor. It is the poor who are a problem, not the highly affluent. As a result, members of the elite and the upper affluent (and to a lesser extent, the white-collar affluent) enjoy privilege without extensive scrutiny or stigma, whereas members of the impoverished are subject to constant monitoring by a highly suspicious public which questions the moral worth of those "who do not work" for their income.

There are, however, some opposition beliefs that challenge these legitimating beliefs. At times, these are dismissed as radical diatribes, but at other times, they strike a responsive chord in the public, because they, also, invoke the values of activism and achievement and use them to question the morality of the affluent. These beliefs call into question the *wealth*fare system"[14] where the rich are seen as getting too much subsidy from government to maintain their privilege. Such beliefs question trickle-down policies, asking questions such as: why do oil corporations pay *so little* in taxes? Why do the wealthy get *so favorable* tax treatment? Yet, next to the chorus of questions about the moral worth of the poor who do not work, these and related questions about the wealthy are not frequently asked. But even with their suspicions about the poor, the public in America does want "to do something" about poverty. It is indeed a source of national embarrassment that wealth and poverty should be so juxtaposed. Thus, one of the most enduring set of problems confronting American society revolves around the coexistence of vast wealth and poverty.

Privilege and Poverty in America

The Political Economy of Poverty

No dilemma can persist in a society unless political and economic processes operate in systematic ways to perpetuate it. Nowhere is this fact more evident than in the case of poverty. Guided by cultural beliefs that the poor's motivation to work must be left intact and that subsidies to the wealthy will trickle down to the poor, government policies and economic processes have sustained a persistently large proportion of the population in poverty. It is our task to understand just how this can be so.

The Politics of Defining the Poor. Just what constitutes "poverty" is an arbitrary question whose answer is greatly influenced by people's beliefs and by political acts. What level of subsistence, short of starvation, is to be defined as "poverty"? Different societies have varying definitions of what it means to be poor, as a comparison of "poverty" in the United States, India, Java, Latin America, or Africa would quickly reveal. Poverty in America might well seem to be a decent life for a Latin American peasant or an inhabitant of a shanty town outside Mexico City. Moreover, varying political systems develop different responses to the impoverished. Some can do little about the impoverished; others make a concerted effort and fail; and still others have virtually eliminated poverty.

In the United States, poverty has persisted and been the topic of much moral agonizing and political maneuvering. This becomes immediately evident in the attempts at defini-

tion. Table 7.7 reports the percentage of the population defined as poor from 1959 to 1980; and in table 7.8, the official
income figures for what constitutes poverty for different categories of people are listed for 1980.

The existence of a poverty level, stated in terms of dollar incomes, would seem to settle matters. But the goal of
counting the poor assumes that political efforts are to be directed at doing something about poverty.[15] In order to initiate political action, however, the public must be sympathetic
and willing to commit its tax resources to special programs
and to public welfare. Thus the counting of the poor poses a
political problem: if there are too few poor, it is difficult to
mobilize public sentiment to do something; conversely, if the
number of poor is too great, serious questions will be raised
about the accuracy of the count. And since public sentiment
changes from sympathy to antipathy toward the poor, there
is always a political problem in generating an "acceptable"
head count.[16]

The current poverty figures reflect a standard initially
set in 1969, when the Bureau of the Census added a count of
the poor into its annual series of publications. The count was
extrapolated back to 1959 in order to get the trend series
presented in table 7.7. As the data reveal, the number of poor
dropped steadily until around the mid-1970s.

This drop is politically acceptable in that the public
would probably not tolerate an increase in poverty in light of

Table 7.7 Percentage of the Population Defined as Poor, 1959–1980

Year	Number (in millions)	Percent of Total Population
1959	39	22%
1960	40	22
1964	36	19
1968	25	13
1972	25	12
1976	25	12
1980	29	13

SOURCE: Leonard Beeghley, *Living Poorly in America* (New York: Praeger, 1983).

Table 7.8 Official Poverty Levels by Selected Characteristics, 1980

Size of Household	Poverty Level
1 person	$ 4,184
15–64 years	4,286
65 years and over	3,941
2 persons	5,338
head, 15–64 years	5,518
head, 65 years and over	4,954
3 persons	6,539
4 persons	8,385
5 persons	9,923
6 persons	11,215
7 persons or more	13,883
Location of Residence and Type of Four-Person Household	
Nonfarm household	8,414
two adults	8,418
female head with no male present	8,382
Farm household	7,170
two adults	7,170
female head with no male present	7,152

SOURCE: U.S. Bureau of the Census, *Statistical Abstracts of the United States, 1981* (Washington, D.C.: Government Printing Office, 1982).

its inaccurate perception (greatly biased by beliefs in the work ethic and trickle down as these are fueled by core values) that a great deal of money and effort has been spent on the poor. Yet, the data are somewhat illusory, for several reasons. First, the poverty line is based on the amount of money spent by families of varying size and location "to purchase a nutritionally adequate diet on the assumption that no more than a third of the family income is used for food."[17] Such a criterion works so long as food prices bear a stable relation to other costs— housing, clothing, transportation, medical care, etc. Thus, in times when food prices remain stable or increase at a slower rate than housing, clothing, transportation, and other necessities, the number of poor will be underestimated. The use of food costs, multiplied by three, to arrive at the poverty level is based upon a 1955 consumer survey which found that the *average American family* spent one-third of its budget on food. It can be questioned whether this one-third figure applies to *poor* families and if a ratio established in 1955 is still relevant thirty years later.

Second, the poverty line is established in terms of absolute costs (of food), and thus, it will tend to fall behind prevailing standards of living. During the late 1960s and early 1970s, standards of living in America escalated; people lived better and expected to live better in the future. Thus, relative to the subjective expectations of the more affluent, the poverty line increased the relative distance between the poor and nonpoor and did not count those just above the poverty line who were, no doubt, worse off relative to the rising living standards of the affluent.

Third, one justification for keeping the poverty line low is that over the last decades income-in-kind, which is *not* counted in income figures for the poor, has greatly increased. Thus, the argument goes, if the in-kind cash benefits of free school lunches, food stamps, Medicare, and the like were computed in the poverty figures, the poor would be much better off. This is, no doubt, true if the poverty line is to represent an absolute minimum standard of living for people in America. It is an inadequate argument, however, if a relative poverty line is to be established, since the nonpoor receive many in-kind benefits that are not counted as income (as we will see shortly, most of these are "tax expenditures" for the affluent and represent hidden subsidies that are much more expensive than all forms of public assistance to the poor).

In sum, then, the creation of the cut-off line for poverty (as presented in table 7.8 for 1980) is a difficult task. The fact that the cost of food for families of varying sizes, multiplied by three, has remained the basic way to calculate the poverty line is more than a methodological convenience. It is a political and moral act. It is justified by the belief that in-kind, noncash benefits compensate for any deficiencies in the definition. And the line is kept very low, relative to standards of living for the affluent, because the public believes that incentives for work must be maintained and that people should not be encouraged to become permanent wards of the state. This latter belief is fostered by Americans' commitment to the work ethic, but a simple accounting of just who the poor are can help us examine the accuracy and relevance of this belief.

Composition of the Poor. A number of studies clearly document that the public believes that most poor "could work if they wanted to,"[18] that most poor "misrepresent their need," and that the "poor have babies to increase their level of public assistance." These perceptions are, on the whole, inaccurate. They are biased by Americans' belief in the work ethic and by their misperception that economic opportunities do indeed trickle down to the poor who refuse to take advantage of them. While the data vary somewhat from year to year, depending primarily on economic conditions, the categories of those below the poverty line are reported in table 7.9.

From this table we can see that half of the poor families are female-headed and that well over half of the poor are under fifteen or over sixty years of age. In addition, one-half of all poor family heads worked full time or part time. It is clear that a good many poor cannot work, because they are

Table 7.9 Composition of the Poor, 1980

Selected Characteristics of Those Living in Poverty	Number of Persons [a] (in millions)
Race	
White	19.7
Black	8.6
Hispanic	3.5
Family Type	
Married couple	3.3
Female headed	3.3
Age	
Under 15	9.7
15–24	5.6
24–60	8.8
Over 60	5.0
Work Experience in 1980 of Families	
Did not work	3.1
Worked full time	1.2
Worked part of year	1.9

[a]Note: numbers are slightly higher than in table 7.7 because a somewhat more realistic definition of poverty is used.
SOURCE: U.S. Bureau of Census, "Money Income and Poverty Status of Families and Persons in the United States, 1980," *Current Population Reports,* ser. P-60, no. 127 (Washington, D.C.: Government Printing Office, August 1980.)

too young or too old or because they must be at home with young children. And among those who did work, their incomes were inadequate and/or the jobs were temporary. Thus, many of the stereotypes of the poor are simply inaccurate. Most cannot work, or should not; and among those who do, they are victims of an economic system that does not sustain full employment or high enough wages for many workers. The dilemma of poverty, then, does not reside so much in the moral shortcomings of the poor[19] but in their demographic profile and in the nature of the economic system.

The Economics of Poverty. As the United States has moved toward a postindustrial profile, an increasing premium has been placed upon nonmanual job skills;[20] and for manual work, demand is for skilled labor. These trends have been aggravated by involvement of the American economy in the world system in several senses (see chapter 11). First, many assembly line jobs have simply been exported to foreign countries where labor costs are cheaper than in the United States, with the result that many jobs which could employ the poor have been lost. Second, the declining productivity of the American economy in relation to the productivity of other industrial nations has caused a decline in basic industries which have in the past served as a starting point for the unskilled labor. The sum consequence of these forces is for unskilled labor to be in oversupply in postindustrial America; and thus, the poor must compete intensely for unskilled, manual jobs—a fact which assures that, in accordance with the dynamics of supply and demand in the labor market, their wages will be low. And, for many who lose in this competition, only a temporary job with no future is available, or in even more cases, no job at all can be found.

This situation is further exacerbated by the business cycle inherent in all capitalist economies (see chapter 2). As the economy moves into a period of recession, unskilled labor is typically the first to be laid off, forcing these workers into poverty categories as soon as their unemployment benefits (if they have any) run out. Skilled white-collar workers and union workers of all kinds enjoy considerably more protection from recessions and can resist efforts to lay them off, because they can mobilize government subsidies of their workplace, because they have savings to tide them over, or because they are entitled to generous unemployment benefits. In contrast, part-time workers, workers in the underground economy (for example, illegal aliens, or off-the-books maids, gardeners, etc), or unskilled, nonunion workers are highly vulnerable and have little capacity to insulate themselves from the vicissitudes of the business cycle.

It should not be surprising, therefore, that half of the poor worked full or part time during the year in which they were counted as poor. Contrary to dominant beliefs, the economic opportunities that trickle down to the poor are not great, and despite public perceptions, studies[21] consistently show that the poor are quite willing to work but cannot find jobs at all or cannot find ones that pay sufficiently well to keep their incomes consistently above the poverty level. Thus, the existence of a poverty sector is, to a large extent, built into the structure of the American economy. Unfortunately, as we will see next, government policies have done relatively little to remedy the situation, despite the seeming decline in the percentage of impoverished reported.

The Politics of Poverty. There are two basic kinds of government programs for the poor: those that are designed to eliminate poverty and those that maintain the poor. Antipoverty programs were expanded in the 1960s under President Lyndon Johnson's Great Society initiative, and are now recessive.[22] In contrast, income maintenance programs now constitute the principal source of aid to the poor in America. Both types of programs will be analyzed in more detail shortly, but first, we need to recognize some of the cultural and structural constraints imposed on all efforts to assist the poor.

Cultural beliefs in trickle-down and the work ethic have greatly influenced social scientists' as well as the public's view of the impoverished. One set of beliefs concerns the hypothesized existence of a "culture of poverty," where it is pre-

sumed that generation after generation of the poor are socialized in ways that prevent acquisition of those core values,
motivational dispositions, work skills, self-definitions, and
cultural orientations that allow people to be active participants in the schools and the work force.[23] Such beliefs implicitly argue that the "solution" to poverty is to change the
values and personalities of the poor rather than the structure of economic organization or the system of public aid. Another cluster of beliefs concerns the necessity that government programs maintain the "sanctity of the free enterprise
system." These beliefs stress that government should not
compete with private businesses in providing jobs and that
work aid to the poor must be "channelled through the private
sector." Yet another system of beliefs emphasizes that public
assistance must not undermine "the incentive to work" and
that aid must always be kept sufficiently low in order to induce (force) people off the welfare rolls and into the job market. A final cluster of beliefs, which were given added impetus under President Ronald Reagan, stresses that aid should
be locally funded and administered, since the federal bureaucracy cannot know the needs of individuals in diverse states
and communities.

The structural limitations on how aid to the poor can
be delivered in America include: first, the structure of the
federal government, which makes providing services of any
kind difficult. Programs tend to be created and implemented
through separate and competing executive branches—Commerce, Housing and Urban Development, Education, Labor,
Health, for example—and as a result are often fragmentary,
piecemeal, and overlapping. Second, the nature of federalism
with ascending layers of local, state, and federal powers creates additional administrative problems, conflicts, and
squabbles over which level of government is to finance and
administer aid—city, municipality, county, state, or federal.
Third, because the morals and desire to work of the poor are
held in suspicion by the more affluent, all aid programs must
reveal an elaborate administrative system for establishing
eligibility to receive benefits and for monitoring the use of

benefits. The result is for a considerable portion of the costs of any program to be devoted to administrative overhead.

These structural and cultural forces circumscribe the implementation of governmental aid to the poor. This fact can best be appreciated by examining in more detail programs designed to eliminate poverty and those established to maintain the poor.

1. *Eliminating poverty.* Virtually all programs designed to eliminate poverty have operated under a belief in "culture of poverty." Hence, most have been directed at youth and their resocialization. The names of the programs best communicate their intent: Operation Head Start (preschool education), Operation Follow Through (special education in schools), Neighborhood Youth Corp (summer job experiences so that the work ethic can be appreciated), Job Corps (job training for the unskilled), or Volunteers in Service to America (affluent help the poor "learn how" to work and participate in society). These and other antipoverty programs also accepted, at least implicity, trickle down beliefs: the poor need to be resocialized into core values and can, thereby, take advantage of job opportunities that trickle down to them. Antipoverty programs also held the work motivations of the poor in question and thus accepted beliefs in the work ethic and the presumption that the poor are motivationally flawed.

These programs also suffered from a variety of structural problems. In addition to being underfinanced, they were highly disjointed and often overlapped, since different agencies had their own programs. Moreover, each program became embroiled in controversy over who and which level of government was to administer any given program. The end result was a series of controversies that made the public and Congress in the late 1960s and early 1970s unwilling to support special antipoverty programs. And so, at present, the commitment to antipoverty programs is minimal.

Probably the great flaw in most antipoverty programs is that they do not directly address the issue of job creation. And when they do, they operate under the constraints that government cannot compete with private industry. Thus, the now virtually defunct CETA program subsidized employers who hired and trained the poor. While this program enjoyed some success, many employers simply took the money and did little to upgrade the work skills of the poor. As abuses in the program were exposed, its funding was, like other antipoverty programs, cut back.

At present under the Reagan Administration, there is little effort to eradicate poverty in America, partly under the presumption that it has already been substantially eliminated. But more fundamentally, the public and government are more committed to implement trickle down policies which, as we will come to see later, subsidize the affluent far more than they help the poor. And with federal budgetary priorities directed toward defense spending (see chapter 3), there is little ability to fund any type of povery program. At best, the government is only willing to maintain a scaled-down version of public welfare.

2. *Welfare and maintenance of the poor.* In table 7.10, the costs to the federal government of cash and in-kind public assistance programs are presented. State and local costs vary too much for easy computation, but on the whole, the federal government pays about 70 percent of the costs for all public assistance.[24] As is evident from table 7.10, the two large cash programs are Aid to Families with Dependent Children

Table 7.10 Federal Cash and In-Kind Expenditures for Public Assistance, 1982 (in billions of dollars)

Cash Programs	Expenditure
Aid to Families with Dependent Children	8.3
Supplementary Security Income	8.0
Earned income tax credit	1.3
Low income energy assistance	1.9
Refugee assistance	0.8
Other	0.2
In-Kind Programs	
Medicaid	17.9
Food stamps	11.5
Other nutrition	4.3
Housing subsidies	8.2
Total	62.4

SOURCE: Executive Office of the President, *Budget of the United States Government* (Washington, D.C.: Government Printing Office, 1983).

and Supplementary Security Income, whereas the two large in-kind programs are Medicaid and food stamps. As the bottom figures underscore, the total costs of all public assistance were less than 8 percent of the total federal budget in 1982.[25] These subsidies, we should emphasize again, are maintenance programs. They do little to eliminate poverty; they simply allow people to survive.

Most of these programs are entitlement programs: if individuals or families can meet the eligibility standards, they are "entitled" to benefits. Thus, to cut the costs of these programs, it is necessary to change the eligibility requirements. Moreover, to reduce the impact of inflation, many programs are indexed, with benefits rising in relation to the Consumer Price Index. All these programs are highly constrained by cultural premises and structural limitations. Each cash program is designed to keep the work ethic and faith in trickle down intact. In-kind programs keep cash out of people's hands in order to prevent them from "squandering" their money and to force them to work at those jobs that trickle down to the poor. Cash programs are highly restrictive in their eligibility requirements, and at the same time, usually structured to keep benefits below prevailing wages in the private job market. Aid to Families with Dependent Children, for example, operates to restrict benefits when a father (who is presumed to be a potential breadwinner) is present.

Structurally, these programs are in flux. General guidelines on minimum benefit levels are set by the federal government, but the implementation of more specific guidelines and the administration of the programs take place at the state and local levels. As a consequence, benefits vary enormously from state to state, and even within a state. The result is inequalities in the administration of federal welfare to the poor. Moreover, with funding and administration divided in this way, there are many jurisdictional disputes among federal, state, and local branches of government that consume a great deal of time and money. In addition to the funds lost in jurisdictional disputes, a considerable portion of all welfare is devoted to maintaining the administrative bur-

eaucracies that seek to monitor eligibility of welfare recipients and to catch "welfare cheaters."

More recently, there have been political initiatives to
turn some welfare programs over to the states; and while the
full implications of such efforts cannot yet be assessed, structural problems will, no doubt, intensify. It is likely, for example, that benefit levels would be dramatically cut or eliminated in some states. And without federal constraints, it is
also likely that there would be considerable abuse of the poor
in many local jurisdictions. As a result, the current inequities within as well as between states would increase.

In looking at the political economy of poverty, then, it
is clear that the economic system cannot maintain full employment, especially for the unskilled. Without federal commitments to create jobs, a permanent poverty sector is inevitable. Efforts to eliminate this sector have been ineffectual,
primarily because they have focused on the motivational and
cultural deficiencies of the poor rather than on the structural
problems inhering in postindustrial capitalism. Public assistance programs have simply maintained the poor; and while
they are designed to encourage people to work, they are often
counterproductive and almost always ineffective, since the
economy cannot provide enough low-skill jobs that pay a living wage. These problems signal that poverty, and what to
do about it, will remain a continuing dilemma in American
society, especially in the context of those processes that sustain privilege in America.

The Political Economy of Privilege

In capitalist economic systems (and other types of
economies as well), the creation of wealth for investment in
economic activities is necessary to sustain the system. The
incentive for investment is to make a profit and hence increase one's capital or monetary wealth. Those without wealth
must seek income through their "human capital," or job skills
that they sell in a labor market. It is not necessary to be a
Marxist to recognize that such a system will inevitably pro-

duce inequality. Those with wealth use their resources to invest in the economy for a profit and to exert political influence so as to gain favorable treatment from government. Those without wealth, but with high levels of skill (human capital), can typically derive a relatively high income in selling their services; and hence, they usually support the efforts of the wealthy to gain a return on their investment and to extract favorable political treatment. The less affluent, without high levels of human capital, are more vulnerable in the labor market; only when they organize collectively can they influence government to recognize their right to force corporations to negotiate over wage levels. Since the poor have little human or material capital, they are typically in no position to organize collectively and exert political influence. Only when they became violent, or when elites take up their cause, does government begin to respond to the needs of the poor.

The differential political influence of individuals and organizations at various economic levels is inevitable in all types of societies. And in a political democracy like the United States, where party organization is weak and where political candidates must rely on private campaign contributions, those with resources to invest in the political process can exert a disproportionate influence. Moreover, those with resources can organize lobbying efforts that sustain political pressure on legislators. The overall result is political decisions that, on the whole, benefit the more affluent sectors of a society. But as we will see, these benefits are less direct or visible than those given to the poor, and so are not typically defined as "public relief" to the affluent. But in fact, the subsidies to the elite and the upper affluent classes cost much more than those to the poor. Other classes derive some benefits from public assistance to the rich, although the benefits represent only a trickle. But other social classes receive *just enough* in the way of benefits to keep them from protesting welfare to the rich (actually, we might term it "wealthfare"). When this is coupled with the general ignorance of the public about the sums of money involved and their highly charged feelings about the moral deficiencies of the poor, it is not surprising that the wealthfare system has remained intact.

Whether these dynamics are good or bad depends upon one's beliefs. Our point is that they are inevitable in capitalist economic systems, and America is no exception. The task before us is to understand more clearly the ways that the wealthy (and their affluent allies) have created a political economy that gives them favorable treatment, especially when compared to the benefits received by the poor through the welfare system.

Government Budget Expenditures. The most visible forms of government subsidies to the wealthy and affluent come from direct expenditures. One kind of direct expenditure is the "government contract" in which private corporations and businesses are paid to provide goods and services. Such contracts benefit the owners, managers, and workers of government contractors. The contracts do not appear, on the surface, to be a subsidy, but as we will see in chapter 11, over the years they have involved a suspension of competitive bidding requirements and the selective bestowal of profits, jobs, and income on favored industries. Since many industries could not survive without these government contracts, they represent maintenance programs for the more affluent.

Another kind of subsidy is government control of prices for many commodities. The actual mechanisms for regulation of prices are complex, but they revolve around efforts to directly set or indirectly influence prices by manipulating the supply and demand dynamics of the market. Price supports, government purchases of surplus foods, and manipulation of export-import policies are prominent examples of how the government works to maintain the profits and salaries in selected industries, and hence, the privilege of the more affluent (and at times the less affluent blue and white-collar worker).

Government Tax Expenditures. The largest portion of government subsidy to the more affluent does not come as a direct budget expenditure. Rather, it comes as a tax expenditure, which is defined by the Budget Act of 1974 as "those revenue losses attributable to provisions of the Federal tax laws which allow special exclusion, exemption, or deduction or which provide a special credit, a preferential rate of tax, or a deferal of tax liability." The general public knows of these expenditures as "tax loopholes," but they represent a much more pervasive pattern of subsidy than the term "loophole" connotes.

A tax expenditure occurs when the government refrains from collecting taxes from individuals or corporations that would be due except for a special provision in the tax law. These expenditures do not appear as a line item in the federal budget. They are hidden in an increasingly complex tax code whose progressivity (that is, the higher the income, the higher the tax rate) has been eroded under the constant political pressure of wealthy individuals and large corporations. Recognition that these tax expenditures deny the government vast sums of money, while at the same time subsidizing the more affluent, led to the passage of the 1974 Budget Act which mandates the creation of a "tax expenditure budget." This budget attempts to calculate the total cost of not collecting all taxes and to determine just where the uncol-

Table 7.11 Tax Expenditures, 1967–1986 (in billions of dollars)

Fiscal Year	Expenditure	Fiscal Year	Expenditure
1967	36.5	1977	113.5
1968	44.1	1978	123.5
1969	46.6	1979	149.8
1970	43.9	1980	181.5
1971	51.7	1981[a]	228.6
1972	59.8	1982[a]	266.3
1973	65.4	1983[a]	306.4
1974	82.0	1984[a]	350.5
1975	92.9	1985[a]	403.7
1976	97.4	1986[a]	465.3

[a]Figures for 1981–1986 represent estimates and do not take into account President Reagan's tax reform acts, which substantially increased these expenditures.

SOURCE: Congressional Budget Office, *Tax Expenditures: Current Issues and Five Year Budget Projections for Fiscal Years 1982–1986* (Washington, D.C.: Government Printing Office, September 1981)

lected tax money is going.[26] One way to visualize the tax expenditure budget is to ask: what if the government collected all taxes in accordance with the progressivity of the tax code, and then, wrote "wealthfare checks" to various individuals and corporations? The budget thus tries to convert tax expenditures into direct budgetary expenditures.

Table 7.11 gives the total amount of tax expenditures for the years 1967 through 1980. The figures for 1981 to 1986 represent estimates that will need to be revised upward when the impact of President Reagan's tax cuts and revisions are calculated. In table 7.12 the largest items in the tax expenditures budget for 1981 are presented; as can be seen, those

Table 7.12 Tax Expenditures Exceeding $5 Billion for Fiscal Year 1981 (in millions of dollars)

Investment tax credit, other than on TRASOPs (employee stock ownership plans) and rehabilitated structures	19,975
Deductibility of nonbusiness state and local taxes (other than on owner-occupied homes or gasoline)	17,305
Capital gains (other than for farming, iron ore, timber, and coal)	15,695
Exclusion of employer contributions for medical insurance premiums and medical care	15,215
Deductibility of interest on owner-occupied homes	14,760
Net exclusion of pension contributions and earnings—employer plans	14,740
Deductibility of property tax on owner-occupied homes	8,975
Reduced rates on first $100,000 of corporate homes	7,510
Exclusion of OASI benefits for retired workers	8,695
Deductibility of charitable contributions other than education and health	7,095
Exclusion of interest on general-purpose state and local debt	6,525
Capital gains at death	5,085

SOURCE: Congressional Budget Office, *Tax Expenditures: Current Issues and Five Year Budget Projections for Fiscal Years 1982–1986* (Washington, D.C.: Government Printing Office, September 1981)

expenditures are the kinds most likely to benefit the wealthy and the affluent. Most wage-earners and the poor do not, for example, have investment tax credits, stock ownership, or capital gains income. However, many "middle Americans" enjoy some tax expenditure benefits—interest deductions, exclusion of employer contributions to medical programs, exclusion of employer pension contributions, for example—and thus are likely to support continuance of the tax expenditure system, even though this system gives disproportionately favorable treatment to the wealthy.

In reviewing the tax expenditure budget, we can observe five basic ways that the tax codes operate to subsidize the more affluent: (1) exclusions from income, (2) deductions from income, (3) tax credits, (4) special tax rates, and (5) tax sheltering.[27] Each of these is briefly discussed below.

1. Much income does not count for tax purposes and is excluded from net income. Income from an expense account, income earned abroad, sick pay, welfare payments, exercise of stock options, employer contributions to medical insurance, the first returns on stock dividends, the interest on life insurance savings, and the interest on some local and state bonds are but conspicuous examples of a general practice to exclude certain forms of income from taxation. Some of these exclusions are helpful to the poor, such as welfare payments, but most favor the affluent who own stocks, bonds, and large life insurance policies, and who work in jobs where expense accounts, medical insurance, and stock options are fringe benefits. While many of these tax policies are for good purposes, they violate the progressivity of the federal income tax structure because they prevent higher tax rates for the wealthier sectors of society. They are in reality, tax expenditures for the affluent.

2. Individuals and corporations are allowed to deduct their expenses. Deductions can be quite appropriate when the expenses are directly involved in earning an income, since only net income—that is, income less the cost of earning it—is supposed to be taxed. But some individuals and all corporations are allowed to deduct much more than their actual ex-

penses, signaling another form of subsidy. The deduction of 50 percent of all capital gains income (the major source of income for the wealthy), the accelerated depreciation allowed for real estate, oil wells, cattle, or orchards, and the deduction of depletion allowances are conspicuous ways the wealthy and corporations protect income by amassing deductions that bear little relationship to costs incurred in making money. For the less affluent and poor, interest on home mortgages and other purchases can be deducted, as can state income, sales, and gasoline taxes. These latter, however, are small subsidies when compared to those available to the highly affluent and wealthy.

3. Some forms of income are given tax credits in that certain types of expenditures can be deducted from taxes (rather than from income). For example, tax credits are given to those who install solar equipment or engage in other energy savings. These credits allow a certain percentage of the costs to be deducted from one's tax liability; and as such, they represent a subsidy to the txapayer (the affluent) as well as to the provider of the service who has the demand for solar products increased by the tax credit. Similar and much more costly tax credits are allowed to corporations for the purchase of capital equipment, and hence, represent a subsidy to the purchaser and provider of the equipment.

4. Some kinds of income are taxed a special rate that is lower than the rate for ordinary income. For example, capital gains income—profits from the buying and selling of assets such as stocks, some bonds, real estate, etc.—is taxed at a rate that is about half that of ordinary income. Since only the wealthy and affluent receive a large proportion of their income in the form of capital gains, this special rate represents an enormous subsidy to them.

5. Tax sheltering is a general process of using the tax codes allowing for credits, deductions, depreciations, and exclusions as a means for protecting potentially taxable income. For example, by taking a large tax credit in a given year, an individual or a company can protect their income. Or, if the depreciation of a property is accelerated, this de-

preciation can become a deduction against ordinary income, reducing tax liability. Tax sheltering is only possible for the wealthy who have high incomes that need to be sheltered and who can use their income to invest in those activities that offer credits, depreciations, and exclusions. Thus, a tax code that permits tax sheltering subsidizes the affluent.

Beliefs Legitimating Privilege. Any persisting social pattern is legitimated by cultural beliefs. To some extent, the indirect, hidden nature of tax and budget expenditures operates to prevent accurate assessment of subsidies to the affluent. The public is suspicious of tax loopholes, leading some to propose a flat tax rate system instead of the loophole-ridden progressive system that we now have. But even with the public's suspicion, much subsidy remains hidden and not subject to assessment by the public in terms of dominant beliefs. Moreover, since the less affluent derive some benefits from the system, they develop beliefs making it seem their right and privilege to deduct such things as interest payments and medical expenses and to receive favorable treatment on employer contributions to their benefits package. In so doing, they legitimate the privilege of those who derive even more from government subsidies: wealthy individuals and large corporations.

The more general beliefs in trickle down and the work ethic also operate to condition people's perception of government subsidies. The belief in trickle down in its more extreme formulation as supply side economics makes tax subsidies to the wealthy seem necessary to stimulate economic growth. By subsidizing those with capital, the argument runs, the affluent and poor are both given opportunities to realize the tenets of the work ethic. Thus, rather than maintaining the dependence of the poor on public welfare, where they are discouraged from following the dictates of core values, it is necessary to subsidize those sectors of the society that can create jobs (and hence, it should be noted, maintain the affluent's dependence on the public dole). Such beliefs perpetuate inequality by making it seem right and proper to subsidize those who are productive and can stimulate the economy, whereas they further stigmatize the poor who are seen as violating the work ethic with their dependence on public welfare.

Wealth and Poverty: Prospects for the Future

The future prospects for eliminating poverty and curtailing vast privilege are not bright—assuming that such is considered a desirable goal. The most likely scenario is for the progressive tax structure to continue to erode through tax expenditures and for the system of public welfare to be continually restructured in an effort to reduce costs. If such proves to be the case, the problem of wealth and poverty will become severe.

As the progressivity of the tax system is eroded, several problems will surface. First, the tax burden will shift increasingly from corporations to individuals and from the more to the less affluent. Second, as the essential unfairness of this process becomes evident, people will cheat, become active participants in the underground, off-the-books economy. Third, the revenue available to government will decrease as a proportion of the GNP, and as a result, budget dilemmas will escalate. And fourth, unfair tax systems cause people to withdraw legitimacy from not only the tax codes but also from broader institutional arrangements.

As budget problems accelerate as a result of tax expenditures, public assistance programs will be cut back. Yet, as we have seen in table 7.9, the poor will have few options. As the effects of cuts push the poor, relative to the affluent, deeper into pauperism, revolt and violence become increasingly likely.

Is there another choice than this gloomy scenario? Several options have been proposed, and while they may prove politically infeasible, they offer alternatives to the present situation and the unhappy future. They all involve revision of the tax codes in a way that eliminates both tax expenditures and public assistance in its present form. We close this chapter with a discussion of these.

A Progressive, No-Loophole Tax System

Probably the most politically infeasible alternative to the present tax system is a no-deduction progressive tax code. That is, for any given level of income, there would be an established tax rate which could not be lowered by deductions, credits, sheltering, or any of the current procedure. Such a system would eliminate the elaborate tax code and the awkward tax reporting system. In exchange for eliminating deductions, or any procedure that would violate the integrity of the progressivity of the tax rate, the tax rate itself would be dramatically lowered. A progressive rate, ranging from zero to 25 percent on the highest income, would probably yield as much revenue as the current system; and at the same time, it would dramatically cut costs. This system would also eliminate inequities in the present system by forcing large corporations and wealthy individuals to assume a fairer share of the total tax burden. Moreover, if the government wished to subsidize a particular activity, it could do so in the direct expenditure budget (as opposed to the tax expenditure budget) so that an accurate accounting of the subsidy could be maintained.

This proposal is, of course, utopian. Too many powerful sectors of the society have a vested interest in the complex tax codes that allow tax expenditures. Such expenditures are justified by trickle down beliefs. In addition, the middle classes who derive some tax expenditure benefits would also oppose the no-deduction alternative.

The Flat Rate, No Loophole System

More politically viable is a flat-rate, no-deduction system. For example, one proposal would tax all income at one rate of 14 percent, while allowing no deductions, credits, depreciations, special rates, or sheltering. This system has the same advantages as the progressive no-deduction proposal, but it tends to be regressive. It allows millionaires and average-income citizens to pay the same tax; and as a result, it does not shift the tax burden away from middle-income citizens. Moreover, a flat-rate system would not generate sufficient revenue to finance the federal budget.

This proposal, however, appeals to many wealthy individuals and large corporations—a clear signal that it is a regressive tax. Given the general public's view that a flat rate is "fair," it is possible that in the next several decades such a proposal could be enacted.

A Negative Income Tax System

In 1962, the conservative economist Milton Friedman proposed a "negative income tax" which would replace the current welfare system.[28] This proposal has been discussed extensively, and renamed the "guaranteed annual income," but despite support by both conservative and liberal elements, it has never seriously challenged the present system. The basic idea of a guaranteed annual income is for the government to pay cash to individuals as their total income drops below an established poverty line.

There are several advantages to the negative income tax. It would eliminate the present administrative problems and reduce overhead costs built into the current public aid system by using the Internal Revenue Service rather than the social work establishment and federal bureaucracy. It would reduce inequities by establishing nationwide rates for all states. And it would still preserve commitments to the work ethic by keeping the benefit levels sufficiently low so as to encourage people to work.

There are potential problems in the system. The most obvious is that in the effort to keep work incentives intact, benefit levels would be too low, with the result that recipients could be in even more desperate straits than before. Another, related problem is that the public might too readily assume that the "problem of poverty" has been eliminated, and hence, not make any real commitment to eliminate poverty, and hence, the need for the negative tax.

The great fear by the public and politicians alike of a negative tax is that it would undermine the incentive for people to work. In an effort to see if this was indeed the case, a number of income maintenance experiments were undertaken.[29] Unfortunately, since the experiments were so horribly flawed methodologically, it is difficult to draw any clear conclusions. Our best guess in reading the evidence is that a negative income does not discourage work any more than the present system, and from the somewhat distorted data, it may even encourage work by enabling people to have income while they seek more permanent and better-paying jobs. Probably the best result of the experiments is that many of the administrative details of how to run a negative tax system have been worked out. And should Congress and the President ever move to implement a negative tax, the transition to a new administrative system would be less troublesome.

Conclusion

Our sense is that the best possible solution to the dilemma of inequality in America would be to restructure the tax system. This restructuring would not eliminate wealth, but it could reduce poverty. Nor could the proposed changes create jobs for an economy that cannot sustain full employment or a wage structure that does not allow the poor to make a living wage. But a no-deduction progressive tax system with a maximum rate of 25 percent, coupled with a negative income tax, would greatly alleviate the problems inhering in the coexistence of wealth and poverty. This proposal seems, at present, unrealistic. But in the face of enduring economic problems (see chapters 2 and 11) and the potentially disruptive effects of poverty in the midst of affluence, a proposal like this one may be more appealing in the future. Until that time, inequality will remain an enduring dilemma and will be the root cause of considerable tension in America.

Chapter 8

Racial
and Ethnic
Antagonism

The Dynamics of Race and Ethnicity

As human populations have adapted to different ecological regions, they have over long historical stretches of time developed distinctive differences in superficial aspects of their anatomy—skin tones, facial features, eye color and shape, average height, and similar characteristics that facilitate adjustment to an ecological area. Less superficial physiological processes, which cannot be easily altered by environmental pressures, remain comparatively invariant across populations of humans.[1] Yet, these superficial differences in populations have enormous consequences for social relations within and between societies, for they become associated with the identification of individuals as belonging to a particular "race." Such identification dramatically affects the patterns of interaction and the forms of social relations among individuals. And as we will discuss shortly, the perception of "racial differences" is one of the most interesting dynamics of any society.

Compounding perceived biological differences among subpopulations of humans are cultural, organizational, and behavioral variations. Sometimes, variations in people's values, beliefs, language, kinship and friendship networks, and modal behavioral responses are highly correlated with "their race." As people are treated differently on the basis of race, they tend to develop unique cultural, organizational, and behavioral patterns which further highlight their distinctiveness. Variations in culture, organization, and behavior are also associated with social forces revolving around geographic region, social class, and national origin. Such variations are denoted by the term "ethnicity," but since "ethnicity" and "race" are often highly correlated—that is, racial groups usually exhibit a distinctive ethnicity—the distinction between race and ethnicity is often hard to draw. Indeed, ethnic differences are perceived to create a "race"—as is the case with those who label "Jews" as a distinctive race. Moreover, it is hard in terms of biological criteria to demark where one race ends and another begins, signaling again that "racial differences" are often social constructions based upon perceptions of ethnic variation. These considerations might tempt us to abandon the concept of "race" since it is difficult to define. Yet, the *perception*—however inaccurate and inappropriate in purely biological terms—of race is a critical force in human affairs. For as we shall come to appreciate, it makes a great deal of difference for the dynamics of a society if people are perceived to be different for racial (biological) as opposed to ethnic (cultural, social) reasons.

The most pervasive dynamic that results from perceptions of racial and ethnic variations is discriminatory treatment of those who are defined as "different." Discrimination can be defined as the process in which members of one identifiable population engage in actions which deny members of another identifiable population access to valued resources—money, power, prestige, citizenship, neighborhoods, churches, jobs, and other resources which humans value. We can term discrimination as "racial" or "ethnic" when perceived differences in a population's biological makeup and/or in their cultural, organizational, or behavioral patterns are the basis for discriminatory acts.

In all of the world's societies, and in all those of the past, racial and/or ethnic discrimination has been prominent when diverse populations have sought to live together. In most cases, those that discriminate are the numerical majority, but at times, they are a powerful numerical minority, as is the case in South Africa today. Yet, whether as a minority or majority, the discriminators and their victims set into motion some of the most interesting dynamics in a society.

Figure 8.1 presents the mutually reinforcing processes of (1) racial/ethnic distinctiveness, (2) perceptions of threat by the majority or powerful minority, (3) negative stereotyping, (4) institutionalized discrimination, (5) inequalities in the distribution of power and other valued resources, and (6) the respective resources of identifiable subpopulations. These forces have a variety of direct, indirect, and feedback effects on each other; and this mutually reinforcing quality makes established patterns of race and ethnic discrimination particularly difficult to change.[2]

Identifiable Subpopulations

To be a target of discrimination, a subpopulation in a society must be identifiable in terms of racial and/or ethnic

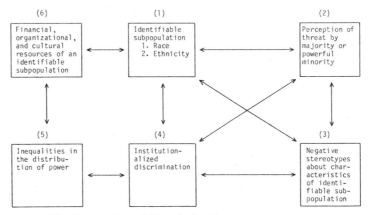

Figure 8.1 The Dynamics of Discrimination

characteristics. And the more distinctive these characteristics, then the more focused, consistent, and persistent can acts of discrimination be. In particular, readily identifiable "racial characteristics," such as dark skin color in a light-skinned population, can assure high levels of discrimination, since these traits cannot be eliminated by mere acculturation. They can only disappear with interracial breeding—an unlikely event once the processes outlined in figure 8.1 begin. When high racial visibility is coupled with (1) a very distinct set of cultural values and beliefs, (2) unique patterns of kinship, economic, community, or religious organization, and (3) distinctive behavior responses such as language, nonverbal gestures, and interpersonal style, then discriminatory patterns are even more difficult to alter.

The other forces involved in discrimination reinforce a subpopulation's distinctiveness. For as people's sense of threat translates into hostility which, in turn, creates negative stereotypes about the character flaws of the targeted subpopulation that legitimate extreme discrimination, the victims of such discrimination are forced to maintain high rates of internal interaction and intermarriage (and hence, interbreeding) and they typically maintain or develop distinctive values, beliefs, doctrines, organizations, and personal styles as a result of their own interactions and as a defensive response in a hostile environment. And as members of a subpopulation become more alike, their level of identifiability is sustained or increased. The longer distinct patterns are maintained, the greater will be other people's sense of threat, the more codified will negative stereotypes become, and the more institutionalized in law and informal practice will discriminatory acts be. Conversely, the more a subpopulation is seen as a threat, is the subject of stereotypes, and is the victim of discrimination, the more they will be isolated and distinctive. Thus the dynamics are cyclical and reinforcing.

Perceptions of Threat

When a majority population, or a powerful minority, perceives an identifiable subpopulation as either an economic or a political threat, then negative stereotyping and discrimination are particularly likely. Several conditions increase the perception of threat, including: the size and growth rate of the targeted subpopulation; the degree of contraction in labor markets, coupled with the extent to which members of the minority subpopulation are willing to work for less than the majority population;[3] the concentration of a population in a given region so that they constitute close to a numerical majority over those with power in the region; the extent to which the targeted population possesses economic advantages, such as pooled kin labor or self-help organizations,[4] over those with whom they compete for jobs or against whom they compete in business enterprises; the degree of political instability in a society, coupled with scapegoating by economic and political elites of identifiable populations as the cause of economic and social ills; and the extent to which cultural beliefs emphasize national purity and a distinct ethnic/racial tradition.

Under these and perhaps other general conditions, an ethnic or racial population will be seen as a threat to the balance of political power, the economic security of some segments of the population, and the traditional way of life of many. When threatened, people will initiate both informal and formal means of discrimination. They will seek to keep the targeted subpopulation out of certain jobs; they will erect barriers to the political arena; and they will attempt to segregate them into ghettos and housing enclaves. Such discrimination is made easier and more legitimate by the codification of negative stereotypes about the character, lifestyle, and purposes of the minority subpopulation. Conversely, once a subpopulation is viewed as a threat and is subject to negative stereotypes and discrimination, it is likely to maintain its identifying characteristics; and as a consequence, its "menacing character" is likely to persist, increasing the sense of threat, the negative stereotypes, and the discriminatory practices. Thus, the very sense of threat that generates discrimination is self-reinforcing, for as a subpopulation is victimized, its visibility is retained—thereby setting into motion a renewed cycle of threat, stereotyping, and discrimination.

Negative Stereotyping

The greater the degree of discrimination, the more negative are the stereotypes about the victims of discrimination. Such stereotypes are used to legitimate discrimination, but they also have the consequence of codifying in the extreme negative people's perception of a population's identifying characteristics—which, in turn, increases the sense of threat. And, as people are threatened, they portray the source of threat in negative terms and use the emotions thereby aroused to discriminate. Thus, the codification of negative beliefs initiates a self-fulfilling prophecy in which such beliefs increase people's sense of threat which, as a result, further codifies the very beliefs intensifying the perception of threat. And as people respond to the greater threat by increasing the level of discrimination, they maintain the identifying features of the subpopulation, and hence, the source of their threat.

In societies which value freedom and equality, this cycle poses a particularly severe moral dilemma. For as negative beliefs are used to legitimate discrimination, both the beliefs and the acts of discrimination that these beliefs justify contradict core values. The "cognitive dissonance"[5] inhering in this contradiction usually generates turmoil in a society, for some segments of the population resolve the dissonance by decrying in highly moralistic terms the persistence of the contradiction, whereas others reduce the dissonance by hardening their negative beliefs in ways that make the core values not applicable to people with such negative features.[6] As a result, the conflict among these two factions—and all those in between the extremes—ebbs and flows, often erupting into episodes of violence, as was the case in the American Civil War where moralizing by Northern Abolitionists came against the increasing moral intractability of the proslavery South.

Institutionalized Discrimination

When members of a population can be identified, when they are perceived to present a threat, and when they are the subject of negative stereotyping, then high levels of discrimination are likely. Discrimination can be informal and simply practiced as a matter of implicit agreement, or it can be formal and written into laws while being enforced by the police and courts. Usually, discrimination is a mixture of formal and informal sanctions against selected subpopulations. In societies valuing freedom and equality, formal sanctions are the first to recede as the ebb and flow of conflicts over core values, on the one hand, and discriminatory beliefs and practices, on the other, gradually erode legal barriers for selected subpopulations. Yet, even as formal practices recede, informal practices persist and, at times, lead to a temporary reestablishment of formal sanctions. Of course, in societies where equality and freedom are not highly valued nor extended to all, then formal and informal discrimination operate in concert. In such societies, violence, guerrilla warfare, and revolution by the targets of discrimination are typically the only ways that discriminatory practices can be eliminated or reduced.

Discrimination results in several interrelated outcomes: (1) exclusion of the minority from the society, (2) forced inclusion in a limited range of economic and political roles, and (3) social segregation from the other members of a society. The extent to which each is evident in a society is related to the relative power of the victims, the level of perceived threat, the intensity of beliefs, and the correlation between informal discriminatory practices and formal legal processes.

1. *Exclusion* involves denying access by an identifiable population to a society through immigration policies. At times, such efforts can be effective if a society can monitor its borders, if the migrating subpopulation is highly identifiable, if there is consensus among the indigenous population that exclusion is appropriate, and if there are no economic interests that profit from immigration. Since all the conditions are difficult to meet simultaneously and over time, other "solutions" become prevalent.

2. *Forced inclusion* usually involves the creation of

economic and political castes where both informal and formal policies directly restrict the range of economic, social, and political roles that members of a subpopulation can play. Such politics are particularly effective if the subpopulation is readily identified, if a large portion of the workforce is economically threatened by the subpopulation, if the political influence of these threatened segments is greater than that of economic interests which would want to include members of the subpopulation (as, for example, "strike breakers" or "lowerwage labor"), and if such policies do not conflict with core values of freedom and equality. These last two conditions are, over the long haul, difficult to sustain in capitalist societies where values of freedom and individualism prevail and where economic interests seek the lowest-priced labor. Yet, because threatened sectors of the society resist the breakdown of the caste, the rates of mobility among ethnic or racial subpopulations out of their caste are low. But when efforts to be upwardly mobile increase, then violence between the subpopulation and its oppressors usually accompanies the distintegration of forced inclusion.

3. *Social segregation* is the process—both formal and informal—by which members of identifiable populations are forced to reside and carry out many of their daily activities in areas, districts, or regions that are separated from the rest of the society. Segregation often accompanies forced inclusion, but is often a de facto mechanism for maintaining a castelike situation by keeping people residentially remote from mainstream jobs, from good schools, and from participation in the political process. In societies where values of equality prevail, and where transportation and communication technologies are well developed, segregation becomes less and less effective, since residential isolation violates core values and can be overcome through rapid movement to jobs outside segregated areas. Yet, social segregation can be sustained for long periods of time through informal acts of discrimination, especially when the targeted population reveals distinct biological features and when the discriminators have a high sense of threat.

Two other forms of discrimination, in addition to the three discussed above, can also occur: (1) genocide and (2) assimilation. At times, members of subpopulations are simply killed, whereas at the other extreme, they are fully incorporated into the society. Genocide is most likely when the targeted population is viewed as an extreme threat by the general population, and when there is a political need by elites to find scapegoats for social and economic ills. Assimilation is most likely when the differences between subpopulations are purely ethnic and do not involve perceived racial differences and when there are educational and economic channels for social mobility. Both genocide and full assimilation are comparatively rare, for in most societies exclusion, forced inclusion, or social segregation are more typical resolutions to racial and ethnic diversity.

Inequalities in Power

The capacity to discriminate is dependent upon the possession of power. Thus, discrimination against a targeted subpopulation is not effective unless there are large differences in the relative power of those who discriminate and those who are subject to this discrimination. Typically, the numerical superiority of the majority, and their resulting influence on political and economic decisions, is sufficient to institutionalize discrimination. At times, it is a comparatively small minority that holds power and uses this power to institutionalize discrimination against the majority. Such is the case, for example, in South Africa and was, until recently, the prevailing situation in Zimbabwe.

Discrimination tends to solidify the existing distribution of power, for when a subpopulation is denied access to resources, its power is likewise reduced. Conversely, the power of those who discriminate is sustained and often augmented. More invidiously, political elites often seek to maintain their power and privilege by deflecting the majority's attention to the "menace" and other "ills" posed by a minority. The history of Jews in Europe is perhaps the best example of this strategy, but it has, to lesser degrees, been practiced on almost all minority populations. Thus, the dynamics of discrimination are intimately connected to the dynamics of power.

Financial, Organizational, and Cultural Resources

Inequalities in power influence, in a general way, the level of other resources possessed by a subpopulation, but the reverse is also true: the financial, organizational, and cultural resources of a subpopulation affect its capacity to exert power, and hence alter patterns of discrimination. One of the ironies of discrimination that sustains the identity of a subpopulation is that it also forces a subpopulation to develop its own financial, organizational, and cultural resources which can subsequently be used to change the balance of power and patterns of institutionalized discrimination. Yet, counteracting this process is the fact that as a subpopulation develops its own unique resources, it increases its identifiability, thereby initiating again the cycle of threat, stereotyping, and discrimination outlined in figure 8.1.

Thus, as minority populations (or majority subpopulations in a system dominated by a minority) experience discrimination, they develop their own forms of mutual financial aid, their own familial, economic, political, community, educational, and religious organizations, and their own system of unifying cultural beliefs. Those who discriminate often recognize the potential for such mobilization of resources, and as a consequence, they intervene and attempt to disrupt a minority's efforts at mobilization. Indeed, the more organized a minority or oppressed majority, the greater will be the attempted intervention, which often has the ironical result of furthering the mobilization of resources to ward off intervention.

The relative level of resources possessed by a minority subpopulation in a society greatly influences its economic position and the form that discrimination takes. Minorities subject to discrimination tend to fall into three general categories: (1) "lower class" minorities, (2) "oppressed majorities," and (3) "middleman minorities." Each of these is discussed below.

1. *Lower-class minorities* are identifiable by their low socioeconomic standing, their confinement to a limited range of low-paying economic roles, and their social segregation. When subpopulations are in a numerical minority, isolated, and poor, members possess few resources with which to redress their situation. Kinship and religion often provide emotional support for individuals but little power to alter socioeconomic hardships. If members are not racially distinctive, then assimilation is possible, although difficult in light of cultural, organizational, and behavioral deviations from the mainstream. In political democracies, a lower-class minority that is numerous and concentrated can exert some political influence, but more effective in securing some benefits from the majority are moral appeals to powerful elites for redressing inequities and/or the threat of sporadic civil disorder.

2. *Oppressed majorities* typically suffer a great deal because their numerical superiority poses a constant threat to the powerful minority which (a) engages in harsh measures of social control, (b) seeks to keep the majority confined to low-paying economic roles, and (c) maintains considerable social segregation. Because the minority's relation to the majorities is often one of economic exploitation, the majority typically has few resources with which to counter the actions of the powerful minority. Yet, over time, such exploitive arrangements give rise to opposition factions which can initiate revolt, especially if outside resources (armaments, leadership, money) can be secured.

3. *Middleman minorities* tend to occupy entrepreneurial economic positions which are neither upper nor lower class. Such minorities typically pool kin labor, develop systems of self-help and rotating credit, have strong religious beliefs, evidence extended kindship networks, and confine themselves in areas or ghettos within a community. By using these internal resources, they come to dominate a limited range of labor and service markets in which they provide goods and services for each other and for the numerical majority. At

times, they become very prosperous and even wealthy, but they typically do not enter the larger political process, except to place pressure on elites to protect their limited range of activities from persecution by a majority that views them with suspicion.

In sum, then, race and ethnic relations are one of the most conspicuous dynamics in human societies. Our goal thus far has been to outline the crucial processes underlying these dynamics. It is the mutual effects among these processes that make patterns of discrimination difficult to alter, once they are institutionalized. Thus, any society with identifiable subpopulations will evidence these dynamics; and as one of the most ethnically diverse societies in the world, the United States should present us with a conspicuous example of how these dynamics operate.

Race and Ethnic Relations in America

Cultural Contradictions in Majority-Minority Relations

Widespread and long-term discrimination has typified relations between the majority and a variety of minority subpopulations in America. Such discrimination has violated core values of freedom, equality, and individualism as well as pervasive beliefs in "equality of opportunity" and "fair and humane treatment of others." To legitimate discrimination in the face of these values and beliefs has, at times, required severe negative stereotyping. For example, labels like "sambo," "redman," "wop," "polack," "buddha head," "chink," "jap," "chinaman," "nigger," "bean," "spick," "spook," "nazi," and "kraut" denote more pervasive sets of negative beliefs. The existence of such epithets and the more elaborate stereotypes that they signal represents a severe cultural contradiction in America.

The cognitive dissonance created over this contradiction is resolved in several, often conflicting ways. First, people intensify their negative stereotyping in order to remove a minority population from the purview of dominant values and beliefs. For example, if "Jews are ruthless," then they do not "deserve fair treatment"; if slaves are "childlike," they cannot be given "adult freedoms"; if Mexicans are "here illegally," they do not deserve "equal treatment with citizens"; and so on. Second, a smaller but vocal portion of the population resolves the dissonance by decrying the contradiction and by advocating its elimination. From Northern Abolitionists to contemporary "civil rights" groups, there has always been some effort in America to expose racism and to lobby for the passage of antidiscrimination laws.[7] Third, often the majority simply separates cognitively the contradiction between core values and negative stereotypes. Most Americans fervently adhere to core values *and,* at the same time, hold some negative stereotypes; and most simply ignore or repress the contradiction. Fourth, a number of reconciling beliefs have emerged to mediate the contradiction between core values and negative stereotypes. Beliefs in "the right to choose your neighbors," "people want to live with their own kind," and "integration lowers property values" have been used to legitimate housing discrimination and neighborhood segregation[8] in ways that sustain core values and mitigate the contradiction between these values and discrimination. Beliefs in the desirability of ethnic diversity and "pluralism" are also used to justify the segregated position of minorities in ways that do not contradict core values. And, beliefs like "there is opportunity to integrate" and "if people don't take advantage of these opportunities, it's their own fault" have operated to shift the blame for ethnic inequalities from the discriminators to their victims.

The interplay among these resolutions is one of the more interesting dynamics in American society, and it poses a constant cultural dilemma. Reaffirmation of the negative stereotypes eventually arouses civil rights activities; cognitive segregation of the contradictions is hard to maintain when either civil rights or reaffirmation processes are prevalent; and reconciliation of beliefs is difficult to sustain when civil rights activity exposes their discriminatory intent. Thus, historically race and ethnic relations in America have been intensified by the cultural contradictions between values of equality and freedom, on the one side, and severely negative beliefs justifying discrimination, on the other. In turn, these cultural processes have both influenced and been influenced by the contradictions between democratic organization of the broader society and the way discrimination has been institutionalized.

Structural Contradictions in Majority-Minority Relations

The persistence of discriminatory patterns of exclusion, forced inclusion, and segregation contradicts some of the basic structural trends in America. Most prominent among these are (1) historically high rates of immigration, (2) high rates of geographical mobility, (3) moderate rates of vertical mobility, and (4) high levels of structural heterogeneity.

1. There have been contradictory dynamics in the patterns of immigration in American society. The United States is a land of immigrants, but immigration has come in waves in that distinct subpopulations have tended to immigrate successively during a relatively delimited period. Thus, the respective immigrations of English colonists, black slaves, Germans, Irish, Scandinavians, Poles, Italians, Chinese, Japanese, Koreans, Vietnamese, Mexicans, Cubans, Puerto Ricans, Haitians, Samoans, Philipinos, and other subpopulations have occurred during a particular period in American history. Such high levels of immigration over a long period of time would, on the one hand, create pressures for assimilation of each successive wave. But on the other hand, each new cohort of immigrants has presented a threat to the previous immigrant population, for new immigrants were typically willing to work for less and were viewed as a disruptive force which could negate hard-won political and social gains. As a result, the cycles diagramed in figure 8.1 began for each new wave of immigrants, resulting in their social segregation and

caste confinement to certain economic roles. And in some cases, pressures were sufficient to cause serious efforts at exclusion of certain categories of immigrants.

One of the ironies, then, of a society populated by immigrants is that, despite core values and dominant beliefs to the contrary, successive immigration generates hostilities and antagonisms among ethnic groups rather than tolerance and rapid assimilation. Yet, at the same time, immigration constantly disrupts the demographic, economic, and political balance; and it sets into motion changes in the relative economic, social, and political position of each ethnic subpopulation. Such changes often aggravate the cyclical processes in the short run, but they also prevent caste and segregation from becoming completely ossified in the long run. Thus, short-run antagonisms may be the price to be paid for long-run stability among diverse ethnic and racial populations.

2. Internal geographical mobility has operated in the same contradictory ways as immigration. On the one hand, migration to new cities and regions occurs in response to perceived opportunities to better one's situation; on the other hand, it often is viewed as a threat by current inhabitants. Yet, as with immigration, the movement of people breaks down older patterns of discrimination, alters balances of economic and political power, and forces new patterns of majority-minority accommodation. The long-run result is to erode discrimination, although this erosion is very slow for highly identifiable subpopulations who can become targets of discrimination wherever they go. Blacks, American Indians, Hispanics, and many categories of Asians have had difficulty breaking the cycles delineated in figure 8.1 even as they have radiated all across the nation.

3. As with most industrial nations, the expanding economy has provided economic opportunities, as has the consequent growth of educational and governmental bureaucracies (see chapters 2, 3, and 5). Moreover, the "structural" alterations in the economy from primary to secondary and tertiary production[9] have provided many new white-collar opportunities for ethnic subpopulations. And as geographical

mobility to new positions occurs, and people move up the socioeconomic ladder, ethnic barriers and antagonisms decrease. Yet, for those who are racially or culturally distinct, barriers can be erected to prevent vertical mobility and keep a subpopulation ghettoized and confined to lower-class or middleman minority economic positions. For instance, blacks and most classes of Hispanics have been blocked from vertical mobility at the same rate as white ethnics, whereas most recent Asian migrants have been confined to middleman minority roles (although there are numerous exceptions to this generalization).

The irony of moderate rates of vertical mobility for the majority and relative stagnation for selected minorities is to increase the "relative deprivation" of those left behind.[10] The intensity of ethnic and racial tensions and their potential for violence can actually escalate at a time when there are increased opportunities for many ethnics to break the cycles of discrimination.

4. Social systems which reveal high degrees of structural heterogeneity—that is, those that reveal many different groups and organizations which are open to diverse individuals—evidence higher rates of interaction across subpopulations.[11] Frequent interactions can break down the inaccurate stereotypes of ethnic populations toward each other, and as a long-run outcome, they can undermine the justification for discrimination. In America, there are wide varieties of voluntary organizations, clubs, and activities that are open to most. Moreover, there are numerous economic and political organizations (trade unions; parties, lobbying groups) which members of many different ethnic/racial subpopulations can join. The existence of these many different kinds of organizations represents a powerful force for breaking the discrimination cycles. Yet, in the short run, subpopulations which do not have access to these organizations because of social segregation and/or forced inclusion are likely to feel particularly deprived. Moreover, their lack of opportunity to participate in these organizational activities maintains their rates of interaction "with their own kind," sustaining their

identifiability. The consequence is to maintain the cyclical dynamics outlined in figure 8.1. Despite some modest gains in recent decades, participation of many subpopulations such as blacks, Hispanics, Native Americans, Chinese, Koreans, and Vietnamese in the diverse organizations of American society is very low; and their exclusion from the "organizational society" only works to intensify antagonistic attitudes toward the majority and participating minorities.

The Process of Discrimination in America

In table 8.1, the six forces delineated in figure 8.1 are presented as they have operated for selected subpopulations. Obviously, many racial and ethnic groupings have been omitted, including: all the white ethnics except Jews; the large and growing Southeast Asian populations such as the Vietnamese; the significant South Seas populations like Philipinos and Samoans; and the cuban portion of the Hispanic population. Table 8.1 should be seen as only a rough and imprecise way illustrational of the more general discussion below on the dynamics of discrimination in America.

As the table reveals, discrimination has involved all the basic patterns outlined earlier: genocide, forced exclusion, forced inclusion (caste), segregation, and assimilation. The "Indian Wars" and their aftermath are the closest Americans have come to genocide. Restrictions on immigration—from the banning of the slave trade to the efforts to limit categories of immigrants such as Asians, Southeast Asians, Southern Europeans, and most prominently today, Mexicans—have been effective when the populations' point of emigration has been distant. But efforts to restrict various Hispanic and Caribbean immigrations have been less successful because there is a ready set of entrepreneurs who, for relatively low costs, can smuggle illegal immigrants into the country. Forced inclusion into an economic caste has been the most frequently practiced form of discrimination. All immigrants have endured restrictions on the jobs made available to them, but if their physical features have not deviated significantly from the "Anglo stock" of America, then caste solutions have not been fully effective. As a result, a large proportion of white ethnics—Irish, Italians, Poles, Swedes, Germans, and other Europeans—have been able to move into a wide range of economic roles. In contrast, readily identified populations, such as blacks, Hispanics, Native Americans, and Asians, have had much more difficulty breaking out of caste positions, whether as low-class workers or middleman minorities. When coupled with high identifiability *and* social segregation, particularly ghettoization into residential districts, caste discrimination has been particularly effective. To some extent, the dispersion of Japanese in rural communities prevented their ghettoization in urban areas, as has been the case for Chinese and other Asians; hence, despite their visibility, some assimilation has been possible. Other rural minorities, such as Mexicans and blacks, have been less fortunate, since as they move from rural to urban areas, white violence, realtor practices, traditional mortgage policies of the Federal Housing Authority (which until 1962 would not insure the mortgages in integrated neighborhoods), and conservative policies of banks (which, until forced, would not extend home improvement loans to integrated neighborhoods) all operated to isolate these populations from the housing, job, and educational opportunities available to other classes of ethnics. While federal civil rights legislation has greatly diminished formal and legally sanctioned discrimination, informal practices still operate in jobs, education, and housing to limit the options of existing and new immigrants, such as the Vietnamese, Mexicans, Haitians, and Puerto Ricans.

These discriminatory practices have prevailed to this day even in the face of beliefs in freedom and equality—a fact which signals that the majority perceived these populations to represent a threat. Each successive wave of white immigrants posed a threat to the previous wave, and since their language, religion, and traditional customs made them initially visible, they experienced enormous discrimination. But with each generation, such discrimination becomes increasingly difficult to maintain. Blacks, Chinese, Japanese, and

Table 8.1 General Patterns of Institutionalized Discrimination for Prominent Ethnic/Racial Subpopulations

(1) *Identifiable Subpopulations*	*(2)* *Perceptions of Threat*	*(3)* *Negative Stereotypes*
Blacks	Will flood job markets with low-wage labor and take jobs from whites; disrupt the lifestyle of whites; marry with white females; control local politics; lower property values	Have varied historically, from portrayals as "slave animals" to "childlike sambos" to "sexually aggressive" to "culturally deprived"
Hispanics Mexican-Americans	Will flood job markets with low-wage labor and take jobs away from Anglos; will overbreed and burden public facilities, from schools to welfare system	Have varied from: simple peasants who cannot participate in economic and political mainstream to aggressive "urban Chicanos" who threaten Anglo-dominated economic, educational, political, and housing patterns. High birth rates produce large families that tax-paying Anglos must support.
Puerto-Ricans	Will flood job market with low-wage labor; will overburden public facilities, especially New York City welfare system	Are unacculturated to American system, and have too many kids that are destroying the New York City public service system
Asians Chinese	Early belief that they represented a "yellow peril" on domestic job market. More recent perceptions of threat revolve around (a) entrepreneurial ac-	Have varied from: "clanish" foreigners who care little about the American ways to cliquish clans that are standoffish from American ways

(4) Forms of Discrimination	(5) Consequences for Inequality in Power	(6) Consequences for Resource Mobilization of Subpopulation
(1) Slavery and denial of citizenship; (2) Residential segregation maintained by: (a) white violence (b) restrictive covenants (c) realtor conspiracies (d) FHA politics (e) realigning (3) Political gerrymandering of black ghettos (4) Literacy tests for voters (5) Inequality in school facilities (6) Exclusion from jobs (7) Exclusion from craft unions (8) Restricted inclusion in industrial unions (9) Restrictions on immigration	Inability to mobilize power, create effective political organizations, achieve proportionate representation in Legislative bodies. Generally low voter turnout	Early reliance on moral contradictions and some political lobbying; urban violence and civil disorder in twentieth century; coalitions of civil rights activists, 1930–1970; established black organizations, 1950–1980. Church has been primary organizational resource until recent years
(1) Denial of citizenship (2) Harassment by Border Patrol, Texas Rangers, Immigration and Naturalization (3) Deportation and restriction on immigration (4) Poll taxes/literacy tests for voters (5) Political gerrymandering of barrios (6) School discrimination (7) Confinement to agriculture and certain classes of industrial jobs (8) Residential segregation in barrios	Inability to mobilize politically and create effective organizations. Have not achieved proportional representation in legislative bodies. Low voter turn-out	Church and family structure have been major organizational resources. Moral suasion, violence, and alliance with Anglo civil rights groups have yet to be highly effective
(1) Maintenance of ambiguous citizenship status (2) Political gerrymandering of Puerto Rican districts	Politically, a weak force, even in New York City. Few effective political organizations. Low voter turn-out	Few indigenous resources. Maintenance of kin-ties to the island district of Puerto Rico inhibits mobilization of mainland economic and organizational resources
(1) Job exclusion (2) Forced residence in "Chinatowns" (3) Discrimination in schools (4) Religious persecution	Politically not well organized to exert influence in city, state, or national politics. Low voter turn-out	Indigenous organizations— kin groups, religious cults, economic syndicates, community organizations— operate to sustain viabil-

Table 8.1 General Patterns of Institutionalized Discrimination for Prominent Ethnic/Racial Subpopulations *(cont.)*

(1) *Identifiable Subpopulations*	*(2)* *Perceptions of Threat*	*(3)* *Negative Stereotypes*
Chinese *(cont.)*	tivities that take business away from small white businesses, (b) organized criminal syndicates, and (c) youth gang violence	
Japanese	Early belief that they represented a threat to nonagricultural work force. More recently, relatively little threat perceived because of assimilation	Have varied from: foreigner. who have little loyalty to America to relatively few stereotypes. In fact, are of portrayed in positive term
Koreans	Pooled kin-labor in entrepreneurial activity seen as threat to small business. Willingness to do any work, for a low wage, seen as threat to wage labor force	Are viewed as "aggressive" a "pushy," with little apprec tion for "American ways"
Jews	From early views as business operators who pose a threat to domestic economic and political processes to ideas about disproportionate influence on American foreign policy	Non-Christians who do not care about American religious institutions; ruthles and clanish business oper tors who quietly control t much monetary activity
Native Americans	From early perceptions as a threat to white man's ways and domestic tranquility to more recent views as unacculturated and not capable of full participation in mainstream institutions. Even more recent sense that control of vast tracts of land and natural resources poses a threat to economic vitality of certain regions and to the nation	From violent "redman" to u stable and untrustworthy peoples with severe behav ioral problems, such as hi rates of suicide, alcoholis and welfare dependency

(4) Forms of Discrimination	(5) Consequences for Inequality in Power	(6) Consequences for Resource Mobilization of Subpopulation
(5) Restrictions on immigration		ity of Chinatowns and their isolation
(1) Deportation or internment during World War II and confiscation of property (2) Early confinement to "truck farms" and other limited-range economic roles (3) Early ghettoization, which has now broken down (4) Restrictions on immigration	Politically not organized to exert influence, but high voter turn-out	Use of kin, religious, economic, and community resources to assume professional and entrepreneurial roles. High rates of mobility out of ghettos and up the economic ladder
(1) Some housing segregation (2) Informal discrimination in community	Politically not active in mainstream arena. Low voter turn-out	Use of kin labor to pursue entrepreneurial activity. Pooling of resources to further individuals and kin units in economic pursuits
(1) Informal exclusion from clubs and organizations (2) Some housing segregation (3) Some categories of jobs have, until recently, been informally closed	Politically well organized. High voter turn-out. Active participation in political organizations, often in low-visibility roles	Use of religious, kin, financial organizations to promote family and individual well-being, success in entrepreneurial activities and professions
(1) Defeat and genocide in "Indian Wars" (2) Confinement to federally controlled reservations (3) Land and resource "grabs" by local, state, and federal government and by private business (4) Destruction of Indian culture as well as economic and kin, religious, and community patterns (5) Confinement to separate and unequal "Indian Schools" (6) Informal disrespect, hostility, and violence in local communities near reservations	Politically not well organized. Some leaders are able to exert moral suasion and mobilize public support for certain, limited goals. Virtual isolation from mainstream political processes	Destruction of indigenous organizational resources of Indian tribes and nations resulted in confinement to reservations and excessive dependence on federal government. New organizational base has yet to prove economically or politically viable

Mexicans were brought to America to perform inexpensive labor; but once here, the existence of this large, identifiable, concentrated, exploited, and low-wage (non-wage in the case of blacks) labor pool increasingly was seen as a threat. This was particularly the case as the economic functions for which they were imported—the plantation system, the labor-intensive, nonmechanized agricultural system of the Southwest, the railroad construction boom—began to decrease. The "release" of this pool into the labor market was seen as a threat to workers whose wages would be undercut as profit-making and cost-conscious owners/managers sought the cheapest labor available. Ethnic labor was also viewed as a political threat as they congregated in urban areas or in strategic rural communities where their votes could potentially swing elections away from the prevailing power structure. Today, Mexicans in the Southwest, Puerto Ricans in New York City, Cubans in Miami, and Vietnamese in Los Angeles and Orange counties of California are all viewed suspiciously.

Perceptions of economic and political threat, which typically have had at least a partial basis in reality, have been greatly magnified by unrealistic and often fanciful images of how ethnics posed a threat to a "way of life." Fears of "godless Asians," "sexually aggressive blacks," "hordes of Catholic Mexicans" in Protestant communities or "aggressive and entrepreneurial Vietnamese" have fueled the diffuse sense of threat posed by an ethnic subpopulation. Diffuse fears were sometimes deliberately implanted by economic and political interests; at other times, they simply emerged to legitimate existing discriminatory practices.

The need to legitimate discrimination in a society valuing equality leads to negative stereotyping which is relatively easy as long as a subpopulation remains distinctive. Blacks have historically been the most subject to such stereotypes because they are easily identified, because their oppression was the most severe, and because their numbers have posed the greatest sense of threat to white Americans. All white ethnics, Asians in the West, Puerto Ricans and Cubans in the east, Mexicans in the Southwest, and Native

Americans in the West and Midwest have had to endure stereotyping, but never so severe as that experienced by black Americans, whose sexual aptitudes, family structure, morals, and intelligence have all been codified into viciously inaccurate beliefs. In general, then, the darker the skin in America, the more severe the stereotyping, and the more stereotypes legitimate forced inclusion into a caste.

The overall consequence of these processes has been to maintain the identity of some ethnic subpopulations. Blacks remain highly identified because their isolation maintains low rates of intermarriage with whites. Similar processes operate for Chinese, Vietnamese, Koreans, Cubans, Puerto Ricans, and Native Americans, but not so severely (although Native Americans' isolation on reservations perhaps represents an exception). Discrimination has kept these subpopulations distinctive and comparatively powerless. Blacks are just beginning to gain power in the cities where they constitute a majority; Mexican-Americans have power disporportionately low for their numbers, even in areas where their concentration is high. Ethnics with a large proportion of their members operating as middleman minorities, such as the Chinese, Koreans, and Vietnamese, remain politically isolated, focusing their energy on maintaining a limited range of economic roles. Only the white ethnics, who have experienced high rates of assimilation, exert high degrees of political power.

Without power, it is difficult to mobilize other resources—jobs, access to education, housing, health care, or social prestige. Conversely, without jobs and education, it is difficult to mobilize power. Thus, those ethnic minorities that have been historically denied power and jobs have had great difficulty mobilizing other resources to redress their situation. Middleman minorities have been able to generate some resources because of their unique pattern of financial self-help and strong and extended kin bonds, whereas lower-class minorities have tended to use their resources, such as religion and kinship, as a way to make more bearable their suffering. Only in recent decades, for example, has the church in black America become an active political force; and only in alliance with powerful white organizations has it been effective in changing national policies. But even as these policies have changed, there is no evidence that black Americans are better off economically relative to whites than they were a decade ago. Such is also the case for Native Americans, and to a lesser extent, for Hispanics.[12]

Resolving "The American Dilemma"

In some ways, America represents a unique experiment. Nowhere in the present world, or in the past, is there such ethnic diversity. All societies reveal ethnic subpopulations and antagonisms, but American society evidences an incredibly diverse set of large subpopulations—making it a truly unique system in the history of the world. We should expect high rates of tension in this sytem, because it would be inconceivable that so many different ethnic traditions could mesh and blend smoothly. But more fundamentally, a capitalist economic system assures competition for economic resources and for educational credentials that lead to jobs; as subpopulations have entered this competitive situation, it is not surprising that they have clashed. Moreover, the fact that many subpopulations were imported in servitude for specific economic tasks adds yet another source of potential antagonism. A democratic political system is also based upon competition for influence and control; and hence, economic competition among ethnic populations is simply magnified by the political facts of American life.

Why, then, is the inevitable viewed as a dilemma?[13] The answer resides in the core values and beliefs that are often used to evaluate ethnic and racial diversity, inequality, and antagonism. In essence, it is argued that a society which values freedom, equality, and justice should never have oppressed selected subpopulations and should not continue to do so. The persistence of this line of argument has gradually changed the legal system in ways that, formally at least, are supposed to inhibit discrimination. But the accumulated legacy of past discrimination—segregation, economic inequality, cultural deprivation, powerlessness, personal pathology, isolation and despair, alienation, anger, and resentment—is hard to eliminate without truly massive alterations in urban living patterns, public educational systems, welfare and health systems, political processes, and economic patterns. These changes are unlikely to come; and in fact, efforts to bring them about are likely to increase the ethnic and racial competition that leads to antagonism and the cyclical processes outlined in figure 8.1.

The real American dilemma, then, is not the contradiction between cultural ideals and actual practice. Rather, the true dilemma is that efforts to resolve the contradiction often aggravate conflict. And yet, to do nothing about the problem allows it to escalate in ways that also insure conflict. American society has fitfully vacillated between an active and a passive approach to the problem; and such will continue to be the case in the future. But the realities of ethnic and racial tension are with us for as far as is prudent to look into the future. Perhaps "the American dilemma" will always be a crucial force in the dynamics of American society.

Chapter 9

Sexual
Inequality

The Dynamics
of Sexual Differentiation
and Discrimination

In all human populations, people are defined as either male or female. Such definitions are initially made on the basis of clear physiological differences between males and females. Yet, in all societies, these biological differences are elaborated upon by cultural beliefs which are used to legitimate sex-typing in the roles that males and females play and the positions that they hold. That is, males and females are differentiated in terms of their activities in society; and these patterns of differentiation seem right and proper because of cultural beliefs about differences between males and females.

There is no necessary reason for sexual differentiation to involve inequality. Yet, in most societies that exist and that have existed in the past, sexual differentiation has been associated with some degree of sexual discrimination, creating varying levels of inequality between the sexes. Historically, for most of human history when humans were hunters and gatherers, great inequality of resources did not exist, although there was a clear sexual division of labor, with women doing most of the work. But the historical trend since hunting and gathering has been toward increasing discrimination against women, so that in most any society men hold a disproportionate amount of the power, wealth, and prestige. It is only with postindustrialization that a serious attack on the social and cultural processes that have perpetuated this discrimination has been made—setting into bold relief the tensions created by sexual discrimination and the resulting sexual inequality.

The dynamics of this process are much the same as those outlined in the last chapter on racial and ethnic antagonism. And hence, we can adopt this model in analyzing the dynamics of sexual discrimination, differentiation, and inequality. In figure 9.1, the critical elements are outlined.

Just where one begins in the model presented in figure 9.1 is less important than the realization that these processes are interconnected and mutually reinforcing. The "ultimate cause" of the processes denoted in the model can never be known, but it is reasonable to assume that the superior physical strength of males over females has been decisive. For our purposes, it is more important that discrimination reinforces sex differentiation, existing patterns of inequality, and the respective resources (money, organization, skills, contacts) that males and females can mobilize. We can see the

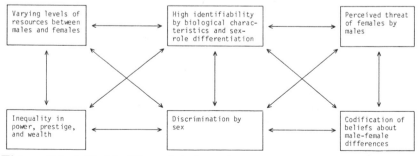

Figure 9.1 A Model of Sexual Antagonism

mutually reinforcing nature of these dynamics by looking at the left side of the model. If men force women into roles that deny them power and wealth, then this reinforces patterns of societal inequality, increases the identifiability of women as "different" from men, and at the same time, denies them the organization, financial, interpersonal, and other resources that they could use to fight discrimination. This self-perpetuating cycle is supported by the mutually reinforcing processes presented on the right side of the model. If females are identifiable and distinctive by virtue of discrimination, they can potentially pose a threat to males, since they represent at least one-half of the population and since demands for equality would require that men give up many of their privileges. And it seems reasonable to infer that men are unlikely to give up the access to better-paying jobs, prestige, and power easily. Under the conditions of threat, sometimes only implicitly perceived, men have used their power to create cultural beliefs that both men and women come to accept about the "differences" between the sexes. These beliefs are then used to make discrimination seem appropriate and the resulting differentiation of the sexes as in "the natural order of things."

Such are the underlying dynamics of sexual antagonism. At times this antagonism becomes manifest, and overt protest by females is evident, as it has been over the last decades in America. At other times, the antagonism is implicit; both males and females accept their respective stations in society. In most industrial and postindustrial societies, there are overt signs of sexual antagonism, as females (and male supporters) have mobilized resources to challenge cultural beliefs, political and economic arrangements, and sex categories that operate to deny women equal access to power, wealth, and prestige. Such protests increase the sense of threat of others—both males and females—who have accepted the system of sexual inequality. As a consequence, an overt conflict between those who want to maintain the status quo and those who seek change exacerbates sexual antagonism. Such is currently the case in the United States.

The Dynamics of Sexual Antagonism in America

Cultural Contradictions and the Emerging Dilemmas

Americans value freedom and equality, especially as these values apply to people's ability to be active, to achieve, to progress, and to acquire material well-being. As we saw for racial and ethnic populations in the last chapter, the existence of discrimination creates a true cultural dilemma for Americans. Similarly, the denial to women of equality and freedom to be active, to achieve, to progress, and to acquire material wealth represents an emerging moral dilemma.

As in any structural situation that contradicts cultural core values, pressures to change structural conditions mount, at least in the long run. But in the short run, those who have a vested interest in present arrangements can resist structural transformations. Their cause is facilitated by a series of cultural beliefs that have been used to reconcile, at least temporarily, the contradiction between core values and the existence of widespread sexual discrimination. These beliefs have legitimated past discrimination and sexual categorization, thereby denying women the resources to realize parity with males.[1]

One belief emphasizes that females are "naturally" more expressive, emotional, and affectionate than males, and hence, they are naturally attracted to, and suited for, homemaker roles or feminine occupations—teaching, nursing, social work, and other jobs where their expressiveness and affection can be put to good use. Thus, women are to be active and achieve within the constraints of their emotionalism.

Another belief stresses that women are "naturally" less aggressive, and hence, more submissive and dependent than men. Thus, it is natural for females to remain dependent upon their breadwinning husbands, to subordinate their activities to male careers, and to avoid pressure-producing positions where they have to compete with males.

These beliefs have been under intense attack in the last

decade; and as a result, they are no longer so widely held as they were twenty years ago. But a substantial portion of the male and female population does hold these beliefs, setting into motion intense cultural conflict. Moreover, as these beliefs are challenged, and as consensus over them decreases, the contradiction between core values and the facts of sex discrimination is no longer reconciled and mitigated. Hence, the conflict over beliefs is further exacerbated by the moral dilemma resulting from the violation of core values. These conflicting forces operate in a wide variety of structural contexts, the most critical of which are the familial, educational, economic, political, and legal arenas.

Family Processes and Sexual Discrimination

As we saw in Chapter 5 on the family, the relatively isolated nuclear unit is the dominant pattern, although high divorce rates and other forms of dissolution have created over nine million female-headed families and almost two million headed by an unattached male. In intact families where the wife does not work outside the home, there is a clear division of labor between males and females; several facets of which involve discrimination. First, on the average, women work longer than men in their jobs, as is revealed in table 9.1. Second, housework is undervalued and not given high prestige in American society, where occupational position is the major

Table 9.1 The Division of Household Labor: Average Time Each Week Males and Females Spend on Work

Activity	Husbands	Non-Wage-Earning Wives
Housework	2 hrs., 13 min.	33 hrs., 6 min.
Child care	1 hr., 57 min.	17 hrs., 10 min.
Shopping	2 hrs., 55 min.	5 hrs., 12 min.
Labor force	40 hrs.	0
	47 hrs., 5 min.	55 hrs., 28 min.

SOURCE: J. Vanek, "Keeping Busy: Time Spent in Housework, U.S., 1920–1970," in M. Richmond-Abbott, *Masculine and Feminine: Sex Roles Over the Life Cycle* (Reading, Mass.: Addison-Wesley, 1983), p. 226.

source of prestige. Third, where men make the money, they have control of the key resource for any family; and as a result, they can use their earning power to extract other concessions. Fourth, once children leave the home, the most gratifying aspect of mother-homemaker is lost, whereas males continue to achieve in their spheres outside the home.

Increasingly, however, this traditional breadwinner-homemaker division of the sexes is changing, but discriminatory processes are still evident. In the 1960s, over 50 percent of all U.S. women were full-time housekeepers, and about 37 percent were in the labor force. In contrast, by 1982, at least 53 percent of all U.S. women were working outside the home or actively looking for work, and approximately 35 percent were full-time housekeepers. In 1982, in 52 percent of all families husbands and wives *both* worked outside the home for a wage, and almost 55 percent of all American children were cared for by wage-earning mothers. In 1982, there were still 32,000,000 full-time female American homemakers, but 60 percent of them were 45 years or older and many faced outside jobs in the future.[2] Wives are less likely to work full-time and year round than are other working women, but 45 percent of all wage-earning wives have full-time jobs, and this proportion is rising. In over 7 out of 10 cases, wives with no children under 18 work full-time outside the home. Of those with underage children 44 percent still work full-time outside the home.[3]

The division of household labor by sex tends to discriminate heavily against these wives who work outside the home for a wage. For example, Vanek reports that wives who work outside the home spend about one-half as much time doing household chores as do non-wage-earning wives, but when their outside work and travel time is added to the time other domestic duties take, a typical working wife might easily approach the 95–100 hour work week. On the other hand, Vanek's data indicate that husbands of wage-earning wives work no more at home than do their counterparts who are married to non-wage-earning women.[4]

Among career-oriented women, as opposed to those who

are simply forced to find a job, there are additional pressures in trying to reconcile career, parenting, wife, and household roles. One study, for example, revealed that wives who sought to have full-fledged careers while at the same time raising a family were under enormous physical and emotional strain.[5] Another study of women practicing law or medicine and those teaching at the college level revealed that they tended to sacrifice their careers in order to avoid emotional strain caused by the demands of their "home work." By emphasizing family, these women achieved more short-term emotional tranquillity at the expense of their career aspirations.[6] Another study reported that working women developed a "tolerance for domestication," meaning that they kept their occupational sights low, while seeking minimal career training and not becoming too involved. Through this mechanism most women studied sacrificed their chances for a satisfying, fully developed career to the demands of a family life.[7] In another study of twenty dual-career professionals, a considerable degree of compromise between husbands and wives was observed. To some degree, the woman's career influenced the man's career decisions, but in almost all cases, the woman made the career sacrifices when decisions about where to live were made.[8] In yet another study of career women, it was observed that women tend to choose careers which will allow them to be mobile, and to accommodate themselves to their husband's career plans. Careers in fields like teaching, nursing, social work, psychological testing, accounting, or real estate sales, for example, can usually be "picked up" in the new city by the wife whose husband moves her in pursuit of his career. For example, the occupations most dominated by females—secretaries, nurses, telephone operators, key punch operators, servants, retail clerks, and bank tellers—are all of this "pick-up" variety and generally do not have opportunities for career development.[9]

Thus, from the available data, family processes operate to place working women under overwhelming child rearing, domestic, wage-earning, and wife obligations. Women and men are socialized to accept such conditions as natural, even though they require women (1) to lower their career aspirations and (2) to channel their energies into limited careers that can be "picked up" at the next stop on the male-dominated corporate or organizational ladder.

These structural features are often made to seem "right and proper" by several dominant cultural beliefs which reflect those discussed earlier. One such belief emphasizes the "glory and creativity" of childbirth and stresses that it is one of a woman's more valuable acts. However, acceptance of this belief can also communicate to women that, since this is one of the female's most noble tasks, she need not seek further security and gratification outside the mother–household worker role. A related American belief emphasizes that only the mother can provide the love, care, and nurturance so necessary in raising healthy children. From this perspective, it is the mother's love that is most important in child rearing. Thus, women should make job and career sacrifices in order to parent children, whereas men are largely excused from this obligation. These sacrifices are necessary from women, especially during their children's "formative years," so that America's youth may be provided with the emotional support that only a mother can give. Such beliefs enable males to maintain their advantageous position as breadwinners, while decreasing the external resources—money, prestige, skills—that the female can bring to family relations.

Educational Processes and Sexual Discrimination

Many of the discriminatory practices used against women are learned and reinforced in the educational system. In school, students have been exposed to a formal curriculum which channels girls into homemaking classes and courses where "feminine" occupational skills are taught. Boys are imparted skills that will lead to higher salaries and more prestigious work. While these formal practices have decreased in recent years, the informal curriculum still discriminates. Consequently, as students move through the educational hierarchy, curriculum sex-typing and channeling of males and females into different roles occur.[10] By the time most American females become adolescents and young adults, many "masculine" career options have been closed off. Below, we examine this process, as females move through the American educational hierarchy, from primary through high school to college and graduate studies.

Numerous studies of teacher-student interaction in primary schools document a consistent pattern: on the average teachers direct more attention to boys, in terms of formal instruction, encouragement, and praise.[11] Moreover, teachers are more likely to encourage independence among boys, while encouraging docility among girls. One study of New York City school teachers revealed that many teachers wanted boys to be dominant, assertive, and independent, while they voiced clear preferences for unassertive and submissive girls who were concerned about their appearance.[12] Thus, in terms of those personal qualities most valued in American society—activism, achievement and individualism—teachers place expectations on male students that these traits will develop, while encouraging more "feminine" patterns among girls. Such teacher-student interaction in primary schools better prepares boys for higher forms of education and for advantaged occupations.

There are also several studies of the content of elementary school textbooks, all of which reveal similar findings: women and girls are depicted in major roles less frequently than men and boys; few females are cast into professional roles; and girls are usually depicted as dependent and passive.[13] Other data on textbook discrimination come from the American Library Association's list of notable books, that calls attention to two books about boys to each one about girls. More important, content analysis of such books shows that boys are, on the average, portrayed as independent, competent, and engaged in exciting tasks; girls are pictured as domestically inclined, or as "watching" boys.[14] Even animal characters in children's books put males and females into stereotyped roles.[15] Sometimes the sexism is more subtle, as was the case in a study of arithmetic books, where boys were pictured in photographs, examples, and problems as making money, while girls were portrayed as buying supplies or cooking.[16] Recent changes in federal law are forcing textbook makers and school systems to reduce much of the blatant sexism that exists in required reading materials, but it is too early to tell how effective these new laws will be in changing patterns of sex discrimination. Laws without enforcement have little meaning. Today, as most American children read in public schools, a sex-typing of their "appropriate" feminine and masculine roles still occurs.

Research on the formal curriculum of elementary schools reveals similar patterns of sexual bias. Girls are expected to like reading, while boys are supposed to excel in math and science. Such discriminatory expectations constitute pressures which well-meaning teachers use to "make life easier for children" by channeling male and female intellectual activities. It is perhaps in American sports and physical education that sex-typing is most evident, even today with the tremendous expansion of athletics for females. In school most boys and girls are segregated during athletics, even though elementary school girls are, on the average, as big and strong as boys. It is still the rare elementary school girl who ventures into organized boys' athletics.

In informal classroom activities, sex-typing can also occur in primary schools. For example, boys are asked to move furniture and desks, while girls set tables and put out refreshments.[17] Once again, at elementary school ages girls are, on the average, stronger than boys, and thus, they could easily lift furniture, but girls are typically encouraged to stay away from such "masculine" activities, including the ones that even a frail boy must attempt. Moreover, many activities, involving competition like spelling bees, foot races, math games, and the like are segregated into girl's and boy's events, thereby communicating to girls that they should not compete with boys, even when they have an advantage. In terms of noise levels, boys are assumed to be noisier in their required activities than girls, and thus boys are given more freedom. In extra-classroom activities, girls still become nurses, boys traffic monitors; girls are elected class secretaries, boys class presidents; girls cheer, jump and watch, while boys block, tackle, and make the points. Thus, recurring sex-typing of boys' and girls' public school activities often works against girls, who are on the average kept less active and quieter and who, as a result, are subtly prevented from acquiring as much experience in individual and team competition with (and against) boys. Sex discrimination in elementary schools thus deprives many girls of the practice in competition and in other interpersonal skills that they will need later in life, should they try to participate equally with men.

These forms of sex-typing in elementary schools continue in secondary schools. Many junior high schools still offer separate programs for boys and girls; and in high schools sex-segregated vocational training is emphasized.[18] But, because of the close proximity of high school to decisions males and females must make about work or college, patterns of school sex discrimination begin to have direct consequences for the placement of males and females in the broader society. Girls are encouraged to take homemaking, secretarial skills, or cosmetology courses; boys are encouraged to compete in interscholastic or intramural sports, against other boys.

As students leave the secondary system, men seek work and women seek husbands, or if they must work, a job. But even among working females, they do not have a chance at the same jobs as males. Table 9.2 describes the kinds of jobs that males and females who have recently dropped out of, or graduated from, high school find. Job placement involves clear sex-typing, with males achieving work that, even in these low prestige categories, will offer more pay and more career opportunities.

In higher education, clear changes are evident in the roles of men and women. Table 9.3 reveals the large increase in female enrollment in colleges, signaling perhaps a desire to improve their options in life. In 1963, for example, male students dominated college and university campuses, but today, women seek higher education in equal numbers with men

Table 9.2 Major Occupation Groups of Employed 1980 High School Graduates Who Are Not in College, and of 1979 School Dropouts, By Sex (in percent)

Major Occupational Group	1979 Dropouts [a]		1980 Graduates [b]	
	Males (N = 194,000)	*Females* (N = 113,000)	*Males* (N = 580,000)	*Females* (N = 498,000)
White collar workers	10.8	25.0	13.4	54.0
Professional, technical, and kindred	1.7	1.5	2.0	1.1
Managers and administrators	1.4	1.0	2.0	3.2
Sales workers	2.6	3.3	3.0	9.8
Clerical workers	5.1	19.3	6.5	39.8
Blue collar workers	71.1	23.9	59.1	14.1
Craft and kindred	18.7	1.8	15.9	1.8
Operatives except transport	30.8	19.1	13.8	8.9
Transport equipment operatives	3.1	—	3.9	0.4
Laborers, except farm and mine	18.5	25.6		3.0
Service workers	11.6	50.7	20.7	31.1
Farm workers	6.4	0.4	6.8	0.7

[a] Persons who dropped out between January 1, 1979 and December 31, 1979.
[b] Persons who graduated between January 1, 1980 and October 18, 1980.
SOURCE: National Center for Education Statistics, *Digest of Education Statistics: 1982* (Washington, D.C.: Government Printing Office, May 1982), p. 184.

and could dominate, in terms of numbers, in the future. However, a number of discriminatory practices prevail against American women who seek a college education, especially in postgraduate degree programs. To some extent, admissions policies still favor men, since it is still widely believed that they are the most likely to be family "heads" and "breadwinners," but equally important, women self-select away from high

Table 9.3 Enrollments by Sex in Institutions of Higher Education: Fall 1963, 1970 and 1979

Year	Total Enrollment	Men	Women	Women as Percent of Total	Men as Percent of Total
1979	11,707,126	5,740,551	5,966,575	51.0	49.0
1970	8,580,887	5,043,642	3,537,245	41.2	58.8
1963	4,765,867	2,955,217	1,810,650	38.0	62.0

SOURCE: U.S. Department of Labor, *Equal Employment Opportunity for Women: U.S. Policies* (Washington, D.C.: Government Printing Office, 1982), p. 34.

income-prestige graduate programs such as medicine and law.[19]

Even though women have reached parity with men in their higher educational participation, there is still a considerable degree of sex-typing in the jobs that males and females receive, or seek, after graduation. Table 9.4 documents the kinds of jobs found by graduates with B.A.'s and M.A.'s who received their terminal degrees between July 1976 and June 1977. A majority of well-educated males moves into a wide range of professional careers, and many of their choices seem to be closed to equal proportions of women. For example, well-educated men dominate entry-level managerial positions, except, of course, for clerical work. In fact, even when we look at the bottom of the occupational ladder, men can still be seen entering the labor force in larger portions than similarly educated women.

Table 9.4 Employed U.S. Bachelor's and Master's Degree Recipients, by Sex, February 1978[a] (in percent)

Major Occupation Group	Males (N = 553,000)		Females (N = 471,000)	
Professional and technical workers	55.0		69.2	
Engineers		8.8		0.6
Life and physical scientists		1.5		0.8
Health occupations		1.3		2.0
Social scientists		2.3		1.4
Teachers, college and university		3.1		3.6
Teachers, except college		10.7		33.7
Engineering and science technicians		2.5		1.2
Others		24.8		25.9
Managers and administrators, except farm	15.6		7.7	
Sales workers	7.4		3.3	
Clerical and kindred workers	7.4		14.4	
Secretaries		0.1		4.2
Others		7.3		10.2
Service workers	5.3		3.6	
All other workers	8.7		1.4	

[a] Data are for persons in the civilian noninstitutional population in February, 1978 who received B.A.'s and M.A.'s between July 1976 and June 1977.
SOURCE: National Center for Education Statistics, *Digest of Education Statistics: 1982* (Washington, D.C.: Governnment Printing Office, May 1982), p. 185.

Economic Processes and Sexual Discrimination

In 1920, 23 percent of working-age American women participated in the labor force; in 1940, approximately 28 percent; and even as late as 1950, fewer than 30 percent of American women participated in the paid labor force. But, from 1950 to the present, as table 9.5 shows, more and more women have been moving out of the home and into a wage-paying job. By 1983, for example, approximately 46 percent of all U.S. workers were women. And it is expected that women will represent around 60 percent of the employed work force before the end of the century. The trend in America is thus very clear: a greater number of women, many of whom are married and have young children, are entering the labor force. From the data in table 9.6 we get some indication of the pat-

Table 9.5 Women As a Proportion of U.S. Labor Force, 1950, 1960, 1970, and 1981

Year	Total Women Working in U.S.	Women as Percent of Total Labor Force	Men as Percent of Total Labor Force
1981	45,760,000	43.0	57.0
1970	31,520,000	38.1	61.9
1960	23,240,000	33.4	66.6
1950	18,389,000	29.6	70.4

SOURCE: U.S. Department of Labor, *Equal Employment Opportunity for Women: U.S. Policies* (Washington, D.C.: Government Printing Office, 1982), p. 20.

Table 9.6 Female Labor Force Participation Rates, by Age Group, 1950, 1960, 1970, and 1981

Year	All Women 16 Years and Over	16 and 17 Years	18 and 19 Years	20 to 24 Years	25 to 34 Years	35 to 44 Years	45 to 54 Years	55 to 64 Years	65 Years and Over
1981	52.2	42.6	61.1	69.7	66.7	66.8	61.1	41.5	8.1
1970	43.3	34.9	53.6	57.7	45.0	51.1	54.4	43.0	9.7
1960	37.7	29.1	50.9	46.1	36.0	43.4	49.8	37.2	10.8
1950	33.8	30.1	51.3	46.0	34.0	39.1	37.9	27.0	9.7

SOURCE: U.S. Department of Labor, *Equal Employment Opportunity for Women: U.S. Policies* Washington, D.C.: Government Printing Office, 1982), p. 21.

tern of this movement. We see that, for example, the female labor force is coming to resemble the general composition of the female population.[20] In the 1980s, women will fill 7 out of 10 new jobs; as a result, in 1982, 55 percent of all children had a mother who worked at home *and* in the labor force.[21] However, most American women remain stratified in "feminine" jobs. For example, in 1982, 99 percent of secretaries, 96 percent of nurses, and 82 percent of elementary school teachers were women. In 1982 over 50 percent of all female wage earners still held clerical or sales jobs.[22]

More recent data on the distribution of jobs in the U.S. between men and women are portrayed in table 9.7. Here we see the distribution of American men and women into major occupational categories and their subtypes. From this data, it is clear that women are excluded from some occupations. For example, in farming, forestry, and fishing, women are far

Table 9.7 Distribution of Employed Civilian Males and Females in Major Occupation Categories, May 1983 (in percent)

Occupation Category	Total (N = 99,543,000)		Males (N = 56,175,000)		Females (N = 43,368,000)
Managerial and professional	23.7		24.7		22.4
Executive, administrative, and managerial		10.6		12.8	7.8
Professional (includes teachers)		13.1		11.9	14.6
Technical sales and administrative support	31.0		19.7		45.6
Technicians		3.1		3.0	3.2
Sales		11.6		11.0	12.4
Clerical and administrative support		16.3		5.7	29.9
Service occupations	13.5		9.6		18.7
Private household		0.9		0.1	2.1
Protective service		1.6		2.5	0.4
Other service		11.0		7.0	16.2
Precision production, craft, and repair	11.8		19.3		2.1
Operators, fabricators, and laborers	16.0		20.7		9.8
Machine operators, assemblers, and inspector		7.6		7.7	7.5
Transportation and material moving occupations		4.3		6.9	0.8
Handlers, equipment cleaners, helpers, and laborers		4.1		6.0	1.6
Farming, forestry, and fishing	4.0		6.0		1.4

SOURCE: U.S. Department of Labor, *Employment and Earnings* (Washington, D.C.: Governmer Printing Office, June 1983), 30(6):44.

less likely to hold jobs. Precision production and craft work continue to be all but closed to women. Even executive, administrative, and managerial positions continue to be filled by larger proportions of men. Where, then, do women work in the modern economy? For the most part, the answer remains the same as in the past: in 1983, 73 percent of all American working women were employed as clerical help, sales personnel, elementary school teachers, and servants. In contrast, only 5.7 percent of the male labor force does clerical work, 7.0 percent low-level service, 11.9 percent elementary school teaching, and 11.0 percent sales, totaling 35.6 percent of all working males. This suggests that sexual selection in the American work force is still very common. Moreover, women work in those areas that pay the least. All industries with "low average hourly earnings" employ large percentages of females.[23] This leaves a majority of the high-paying jobs, which lead to increased power and prestige, for men.

The monetary impact of occupational sex stratification and inequality is shown in table 9.8, where the median income levels of adult males and females for periods covering the last thirty years are reported. We can see that in recent history, men have made more money for working outside the home than women. Yet, since 1960, women have made gains

Table 9.8 Median Income of Male and Female U.S. Workers, 14 Years Old and Over, 1950, 1960, 1970, 1980

Year	Males	Females	Income Gap[a]	Female Income[b] as Percent of Male Income
1980	$12,530	$4,920	$7,610	65%
1970	14,154	4,747	9,407	50
1960	11,353	3,509	7,844	45
1950	8,797	3,262	5,535	37

[a] Defined as the difference in median income between males and females.

[b] These figures are for full-time workers. If the large number of part-time workers is also considered, then female wages as a proportion of male's wages in 1980 decline back to the 1960 level.

SOURCE: U.S. Bureau of the Census, "Money Income of Households, Families, and Persons in the United States: 1980," *Current Population Reports,* ser. P-60, no. 132 (Washington, D.C.: Government Printing Office, 1982), pp. 138–39.

which in 1980 meant that the average wage-earning woman made 65¢ for each dollar brought home by a working male. Thus, the data indicate that the earnings picture is changing, but women still have a long way to go to reach parity with men.

When women do enter traditionally male-dominated professions, several studies indicate that they are likely to be employed at the lower end of the salary, retention, and prestige scale. In college professions, for example, women are more likely than men to be at lower academic levels; they tend to locate at smaller, less prestigious schools, and they hold less prestigious research (versus professorial) positions.[24] In medicine, women are found more often to specialize in pediatrics, psychiatry, and public health than surgery.[25] Women practicing law tend to be excluded from judicial appointments and are overrepresented in less prestigious forms of practice such as legal aid and family law. In contrast, women are highly underrepresented in high-paying and prestigious tax, corporate, and real estate law.[26] Another indication of sex discrimination in the professions is the fact that men dominate most of the top-level positions. This is the case among deans and directors of social work schools, in elementary school administration, and among college library personnel, even though females, in terms of numbers, dominate these fields.[27]

Thus, from the available data on female participation in the American economy, it is clear that most women receive less income and prestige than men. Most women continue to be segregated away from the better-paying and more prestigious occupations; and even in those professions where they work in large numbers, men control the top-level positions. More women are working for a wage now than ever before, but sex-based economic discrimination nevertheless prevails. This situation is the result of several discriminating forces which we need to examine in more detail.

One discriminating force is the use of women as a reserve labor pool. Well over one-half of all American working women hold clerical, service, or low-level sales jobs; this fact alone reveals much about women's place in economic arrangements. Many argue that most women are seen as primarily marginal employees who, during times of recession and cutbacks, for example, can be easily laid off. Such critics point out that women are confined to relatively few occupations and that women traditionally suffer from high unemployment. Using this information they argue that American women represent a reserve labor pool that is called upon to work when needed and discharged when no longer needed. Because women have fewer job opportunities than men, they must often accept this situation and make their peace in a "man's world."[28]

Today many sectors of the American economy depend upon low-paid service and clerical workers. This means that, should service and clerical salaries increase and working conditions improve, then costs and prices of American consumer items would abruptly rise. As more women acquire educational credentials and enter what used to be male-dominated occupations, competition for high-pay, high-status jobs will increase and become more intense. This process, in the long run, might hurt men and women by oversupplying well-educated workers, thereby decreasing pressures for high wages and job stability. Thus, to create new opportunities for women and to raise their salaries will require considerable displacement of male workers, adjustments in costs of consumer items, and changes in labor-management relations. For most sectors of the American economy, these facts represent strong incentives for avoiding changes in the use of women in the economy.

Another discriminatory force revolves around women's disproportionate child bearing and child rearing responsibilities. Dominant cultural beliefs still hold that the mother should take the lead in raising her young children—a belief that places the wage-earning working mother in personal conflict over her career and her children's well-being. Equally significant is the interruption of a career that child bearing requires of women, a process that can take a minimum of weeks, but more likely months, from a job or career. At present, there are few ways for women to overcome these impediments to equality. Few employers are willing, or required, to give women time off from work to have a baby if she intends to spend an extended period of time after birth with her child. Child-care facilities for the wage-earning working mother are expensive, particularly for the care of very young children, and not always available. Thus, the economic system discriminates against women by not adjusting, to a sufficient degree, to the child bearing/rearing cycles of wage-earning women. Since child bearing and child rearing come at the same period when careers are begun, women are placed at a severe disadvantage in the work force. And, if they stay unemployed while they raise their children, reentrance (or late entrance) into the labor market will be difficult as prejudices against "older" employees begin to operate.

Yet another discriminatory force revolves around the simple fact that men dominate most positions of economic power in American society, and as a consequence, women are at a disadvantage in their competition with men. Much of the resulting sex discrimination is subtle and goes unnoticed, but it has profound implications for women. For example, many employees invoke "white male" norms about how a job is to be conducted; and even though there may be acceptable alternatives for doing a job effectively, employees are forced to adopt the white male style of performance—a situation that obviously places women at a disadvantage when they are competing for jobs with white males. To illustrate further the subtlety of these processes, much information about the availability of jobs and about ways to win recognition and approval on the job is acquired informally in social activities outside offices and other work places, where men tend to congregate together. Since women are likely to be excluded or held on the periphery of such activities, they are also systematically denied valuable job and career information. Finally, because many men in the American economy continue to hold traditional views of appropriate "man's work" and "woman's work," they are likely to be hostile—often in unconscious ways—toward career-oriented women. Many male employees, decision-makers, and power-brokers will both overtly and covertly resent women working as equals around them, especially since successful women must often be exceptional workers in order to overcome discriminatory barriers. Employers are likely to avoid male-female ego conflicts by excluding or devaluing women, since male workers still constitute a powerful interest group.

Still another discriminatory force is the by-product of women's socialization experiences. To a large degree, American women still select themselves out of male-dominated occupations, feeling "that they cannot compete with men," or "handle the pressure" of a well-paying, prestigious job, partly because many families fail to encourage girls to think about an occupation or career for themselves. Instead, girls are left to play house, even though they may see their mothers in household *and* wage-earner roles. Girls are discouraged from being "aggressive" and "masculine" by their families and then at school. Media still portray women in domestic roles. Thus, most American women were, as girls, discouraged from having high occupational aspirations; and as a consequence, they do not receive the socialization experiences that could give them the confidence as well as the critical interpersonal skills necessary to enter male-dominated occupations.

A final discriminatory force is cultural. Two dominant American cultural beliefs are currently used to justify confining women to "feminine" occupations, and paying females comparatively low wages.[29] First, many people still believe that women should get less pay than men for equal work, because female workers require additional facilities and because employers incur extra costs due to their higher rates of absenteeism, turnover, and the likelihood that they will marry, quit the labor force, and raise a family. Second, many Americans still believe women should get less pay because they are not the principal breadwinners of their households and because they are merely working for family "extras." Neither of these common beliefs corresponds to the facts of life for the typical wage-earning working woman. Yet, such beliefs are constantly used to justify employment discrimination against women. We should examine, then, the actual facts to see if they support these beliefs.

Are women more costly to employ? There is no reliable

evidence that women are less productive wage earners than men, but there is some evidence that they perform better than men at some types of production and assembly work.[30] Moreover, a U.S. Public Health Department survey showed roughly comparable rates of "annual worker absenteeism" for men and women, 5.6 days for women, 5.3 days for men. The small differences between men and women disappeared when the researchers looked at men and women in comparable jobs. They found the highest rates of "absence due to illness" among *all* workers in the lowest salary levels (where women, of course, are most likely to find employment). With respect to employee turnover rates, 2.6 percent of the female workers quit each year, 2.2 percent of the men; another 2.6 percent of the women were laid off, as were another 2.2 percent of the men. From one year to the next 10 percent of the men changed jobs, whereas 7 percent of the women did so. This study suggests that there is little evidence to support beliefs that women are more costly employees; and if women were not, on the average, employed in lower-status and lower-paying jobs than men, where larger numbers of all types of employees feel dissatisfaction and experience absentee and health problems, the small differences between male and female workers would disappear.

Do American women need to work? Roughly 25 percent of all married women have husbands with incomes only just above the poverty level. It is obvious these women must work to support the basic needs of themselves and their families. Many other married women whose husbands make considerably more must now work for a wage in order to buy a home and educate their children in the manner to which Americans have grown accustomed. In addition, in 1980, there were 11,683,000 single women maintaining households in the U.S. Single women obviously need to support themselves, and they do so on an average annual income, in 1980, of $8,891, compared with $14,347 for single men. Many widows and other female householders whose husbands are gone must earn income in order to survive; in 1980, there were 9,082,000 such women in American society. These women earned, on the average, $13,480 per year, compared with $21,743 for males whose wives were absent. Thus, it is clear that the vast majority of working women must work in order to survive, but they must work for a smaller wage than men facing similar circumstances.

In sum, then, one's place in the economy determines, in large part, access to money, power, and prestige. And most women continue to be denied access to these scarce resources. In a society which values "activism" and "achievement," especially in the occupational sphere, many women are forced to endure fewer financial rewards than men and to bear the stigma of being seen as less "active" and less "achieving." Despite changes in the level of female participation in the labor force, women must still exist, to a greater degree than men, at variance with dominant American cultural values. At the very best, many American women can realize these values only within a highly delimited set of options, such as low-status family and wage work. Such are the consequences of recurring economic discrimination against women in the United States.

Legal Processes and Sexual Discrimination

As with minority groups, women have suffered because the law has explicitly denied them certain rights and privileges enjoyed by men. A good example of legal sex discrimination is found in the denial of American women the right to vote in federal elections until 1920. In being denied the right to vote, women were reminded that they were less than full-fledged citizens; and more important, they were excluded from equal participation in politics.

After 1920, when the Nineteenth Amendment was passed granting women the right to vote, the lesser legal status of women did not significantly change again until the 1960s and early 1970s. In 1964, the biggest change occurred when Congress passed the Civil Rights Act. While the act was aimed principally at lessening the plight of ethnic and racial minorities, Title VII prohibits discrimination on the basis of sex. In

1965 this was followed by an Executive Order from the President of the United States, extending to women the provisions of the Equal Pay Act. These changes in the law make it illegal to discriminate against employees on the basis of sex, in job hiring and in pay scales. Moreover, some provisions of Title VII require of employers "affirmative action" to recruit women for a full range of job classifications. These recent laws, for the first time in American history, provide women and women's organizations with a sound legal basis for challenging discriminatory employment practices of employers. These changes help us understand why seven out of every ten new jobs created in the 1980s will go to a woman. However, the law places much of the burden on individual women to "prove" discrimination—a time-consuming, expensive, and arduous task. Today, because legally acceptable proof is difficult to establish, many informal discriminatory practices of the past are allowed to continue.

In the context of education, Title IX of the Education Amendments Act of 1972 represented an important legal step:

> No person in the United States shall, on the basis of sex, be excluded from participation in, be denied the benefits of, or be subjected to discrimination under any educational program or activity receiving federal financial assistance.

Shortly after passage of the Education Amendments Act, the Department of Health, Education, and Welfare issued guidelines stipulating that all programs within any educational institution receiving federal financial aid must meet the requirements of Title IX. If these laws were enforced, it would mean, for example, the end of sexually biased curricula, reading materials, and classrooms; the demise of dress codes and behavioral rules that apply only to girls; the suspension of discriminatory college admission quotas and standards; the cessation of favoritism in financial aid, promotion procedures, and tenure decisions. However, presently in the mid-1980s, we are in a period of political conservatism, and thus, legal agencies are backing away from enforcement of new laws. If the legal system does not require compliance to the law, and if the legal system does not actively seek out and punish violators, then educational sex discrimination will continue on a wide scale.

Many informally practiced forms of sex discrimination could be outlawed with full passage of federal legislation such as the Equal Rights Amendment. A form of this amendment, which simply states, "Equality of rights under the law shall not be denied or abridged by the United States or by any state on account of sex," has been introduced into Congress every year since 1923. The Equal Rights Amendment finally passed both houses of Congress in 1972, but it was allowed to die short of ratification by state legislatures. As a result, women's rights must be addressed at lower levels of government and the courts on an issue-by-issue basis; and it will, no doubt, take women far more time and energy to overcome discrimination than would be the case if the Equal Rights Amendment were in place. The failure of the Equal Rights Amendment underscores the fact that, even though women can now vote, they are less than equal participants in the political process.

Political Processes and Sexual Discrimination

Changes in established patterns of sexual discrimination are likely to occur through two related processes: (1) the raising of both male and female consciousness about overt and subtle forms of discrimination and (2) the use of political power by women to change discriminatory practices. The first of these processes is still in its infancy, as women's organizations seek to educate the populace and politicians as to the extensiveness of sex discrimination in the United States. However, the second of these processes has faltered, since many women self-select themselves out of professions that might lead to political power and since most women are excluded from political decision-making. Below, we describe these two processes in greater detail.

As a voting block, American women potentially possess considerable political power. For example, in federal elections, and most others, women cast well over 50 percent of the votes—a pattern that reflects their greater numbers in the general population. However, to date, women in the United States have not used their voting power to elect large numbers of female candidates. The result is that few American women hold positions of political power. For example, there has never been a female President, or Vice-President, and only one woman has been appointed to the U.S. Supreme Court. The Senate and the House are over 95 percent male in composition, and there have been only a handful of female cabinet appointments. In fact, before 1975, there had been only two female mayors of a large U.S. city; only four female governors had been elected, less than fifteen female foreign ambassadors appointed, and fewer than twelve female federal judges could be counted. In other words, until 1975, women were, for the most part, disfranchised from high-level U.S. politics. Thus, for most of the twentieth century most women have been allowed to vote but discouraged from holding public office.

More recently women are beginning to make inroads into male political strongholds. But the data in table 9.9 suggest that progress is slow. The table shows the numbers of appointments to political office made by two recent U.S. Presidents, covering a period from 1976 to 1983. Women are filling more and more powerful political offices. For example, between 1976 and 1980 there were four times as many female federal judges appointed than had ever sat before on the federal bench in all of U.S. history. Similar improvements in female participation can be seen for each branch of the federal government represented in the table. However, for each woman appointed to a high office by the last two U.S. Presidents, nine men were appointed to similar positions. This suggests an extreme pattern of inequality and discrimination in recent presidential appointments, especially if we look at the last few years. These data also suggest that many qualified women might today be finding their way into political office by serving as "tokens" to draw public attention away from

Table 9.9 Unequal Opportunity in Presidential Appointments, 1976–1980 and 1981–1983

| | 1976–80 | | | | | | 1981–83 | | | | | |
| | | Male | | Female | | | | Male | | Female | | |
Type of Appointment	Total No.	No.	Percent of Total	No.	Percent of Total	Total No.	No.	Percent of Total	No.	Percent of Total
Total appointments[a]	1,182	1,039	87.9	143	12.1	980	902	92.0	78	8.0
Federal departments	233	196	84.1	37	15.9	287	263	91.6	24	8.4
Federal judiciary	298	253	84.9	45	15.1	121	111	91.7	10	8.3
U.S. Attorneys	87	83	95.4	4	4.6	93	91	97.8	2	2.2
U.S. Marshalls	87	87	100	0	0	81	80	98.8	1	1.2
Ambassadorial	159	147	92.5	12	7.5	125	118	94.4	7	5.6

[a]Includes types of presidential appointments that are not listed below

SOURCE: U.S. Commission on Civil Rights, *Equal Opportunity in Presidential Appointments* (Washington, D.C.: Government Printing Office, June 1983), pp. 5–6, 8–9, 12–17, 19–20.

more general, and lasting, patterns of male political dominance.

Women are not suddenly becoming political; on the
contrary, women have long been active in U.S. politics. But
female participation in politics has, in many ways, been shaped
into an extension of the traditional female household role. Most
women enter politics as volunteers, where they tend to be assigned the office work—mailing, licking envelopes, duplicat-
ing materials, typing, doing telephone work, and the like.[31]
Men, on the other hand, tend to fill the top positions as organizers, managers, and, of course, candidates. Why are most
women assigned routine, menial political roles? Why do so few
women become organizers, managers, and political candidates? And why do women not elect great numbers of female
candidates when they do run? There are no simple answers
to these questions. But, we suspect organized sexual discrimination, and popular women's definitions of their own place
in politics, play a part in maintaining the status quo.

Several researchers have found that most men *and*
women feel it is not "right" and "proper" for women to enter
a "competitive, dirty, and difficult world as politics."[32] Patsy
Mink, a rare female long-term Representative, affirmed this
situation when she observed that "politics may be the last and
most difficult area of breakthrough for women . . . the barriers . . . are mainly based upon custom which no court can
eradicate." Thus, because of custom and discriminatory cultural beliefs about women, many women are likely to prefer
being passive and "feminine"—disqualifying women as successful political candidates. Most females in America, moreover, have already grown accustomed to dominance by males
in their families, schools, and jobs. Similarly, women have had
fewer opportunities to hold leadership positions in equally
discriminatory educational and occupational systems. Finally, household, wife, and child-rearing roles also preclude
much female political activity.

Thus, the same barriers which operate to inhibit wom-
en's participation in other spheres also operate to suppress

political ambitions. We suspect that many women do not vote for women candidates because they have been conditioned to exclude women from all but familial and traditional sex-typed work roles. This suspicion is supported by a number of studies which report, for example, that women vote much like their husbands. Too few American women today possess a high degree of consciousness about their situation and about the barriers which still exist to their achieving fulfillment in politics and other worlds outside the home.

Between 1920, when the Nineteenth Amendment was passed, and the 1960s, little organized political activity by and for women was visible. But in the late 1960s with the formation of the National Organization for Women (NOW), the American feminist movement was reborn. Throughout the 1960s and 1970s its membership remained small, but NOW chapters received considerable publicity and its ranks have begun to grow. The first goal of NOW was to work within the existing male-dominated political and economic system and to break down discriminatory barriers operating to oppress women. Pursuing this goal, NOW created a traditional organization: NOW has a central national office with local chapters spread throughout the United States. It is staffed by a national president and officers, paralleled by local chapter offices, which collect dues and use the revenues to lobby for women's causes. And in the wake of ERA's defeat, NOW's membership and lobbying activity have increased, ensuring that sexual discrimination causes will remain at the center of American politics. As a result of the activities of NOW and other feminist groups, all American women now appear to have more awareness of their common political goals. And a majority may now share such general goals as (1) the consolidation of female political power; (2) the elimination of negative sex stereotypes; (3) the creation of alternatives equal to those available for men; and (4) the development of a sense of solidarity. The critical issue is: can these general goals be translated into effective political action to redress discrimination in other institutional spheres?

Conclusion

Until this political response to discrimination occurs, the dynamics outlined in figure 9.1 will continue to operate, creating ongoing sources of tension and conflict in American society. And even as this political response mounts and grows, conflict over the issue of sexual inequality will be evident. In turn, as this conflict persists, the cultural contradiction between the facts of sex-typing and discrimination, on the one side, and core values emphasizing equality, freedom, activism, and achievement, on the other, will pose a dilemma for the society.

Chapter 10

The Chaotic
Metropolis

The Dynamics of Urbanization

$\mathbf{I}$t is not difficult, yet essential nonetheless, to recognize that people must live and carry out basic social activities—economic, political, religious, familial, recreational, and educational—in physical space. "Community" is the generic term to denote just how humans organize themselves in geographical space; and when we refer to urban communities and to the process of urbanization, we are isolating a particular form of community organization.[1] Since Americans live primarily in urban areas,[2] it is necessary to understand the general dynamics of urbanization, for in these dynamics some of America's most pressing dilemmas can be found.

Urbanization is the process whereby relatively large numbers of individuals and families are organized in a comparatively concentrated area. The process of urbanization began some 8,000 years ago[3] under the impact of demographic, economic, military, and religious forces. It is difficult to know exactly which force was most critical in causing urbanization. Indeed, in different areas, somewhat varying forces were no doubt at work, and the interaction among factors is sometimes difficult to discern. Yet, we might construct the following general scenario and not deviate dramatically from the actual historical record: demographically, at some point in human prehistory, some populations must have begun to grow to a point where a nomadic existence was no longer possible. It is still a point of historical debate whether the development of agriculture caused the population increase or the reverse, but the two clearly reinforced each other. Once people settled, they needed to cultivate food; and as agricultural production techniques improved, a larger immobile population could be supported.

Cities then grew as trading centers for both nomadic and settled peoples who used established communities as a place for exchanging valued commodities. And as trading and other distributive processes improved, a larger population could be supported, since goods and commodities could be imported from far away, freeing a population from its local resource base. Trade also created traveling routes, a critical infrastructure for migration into the emerging city. Cities may also have been created for military defense and offense as political elites sought to protect their base for launching armies. In addition, religion may have been a vital factor in the emergence of urban centers, as most early cities reveal elaborate temples and other religious structures that signal well-organized religious activity.

The operation of these historical processes was dramatically changed with industrialization and postindustrialization. With industrialization, the economy becomes paramount in shaping the nature of urbanization. Military, religious, and demographic forces begin to reflect the dramatic transformation of the economic processes that, in chapter 2, we described as gathering, producing, and distributing. Sometimes these new economic forces were superimposed upon preexisting urban forms, and at other times, they were the impetus behind the creation of new cities and urban patterns. As we will see shortly, urbanization in America reveals a somewhat distinctive pattern because urban growth occurred only with industrialization and did not involve the superimposition of a new economic base on preindustrial urban forms.

Whether stimulating new urban growth or transforming old patterns, industrialization increases the rate of urbanization and the scale of human communities. In its early stages, industrialization revolves around the factory system where inanimate sources of energy, such as coal, are harnessed to large concentrations of machine capital that are run by a large, unskilled labor force. The factory system represents a truly revolutionary mode of production, in several senses.[4] First, it encourages mass migrations from rural agricultural areas to the concentrated cities that are built around factories. Second, it creates a large labor market of unskilled and semiskilled workers who exchange their work for wages which they use to purchase life-sustaining goods and services. Third, the creation of a wage-earning population (as opposed to one that produces most of what it needs on farms) expands the system of markets in a society, since now basic goods and services must be bought (rather than produced) by the labor force.

These processes are mutually reinforcing in their effects. As a mobile industrial labor force is assured, production can expand and be constantly improved with new technologies (especially in capitalist systems, where markets are competitive). Another force encouraging expanded production is the escalated demand in markets for goods and services needed by the wage-earning labor force. And as ever more goods and sevices are desired by the urban population, and as production expands, distribution processes are further transformed. Many distribution structures—business centers, shopping malls, retail chains, credit cards, standardized pricing, etc.—are in fact fairly recent inventions that have been created to facilitate the flow of goods and services. In turn, the existence of expanded production and ever more efficient systems of marketing encourages even more migration to cities as people seek new opportunities for "the good life."

Industrialization thus accelerates urbanization, but it

also changes its form. The preindustrial city was relatively concentrated in space and was often a walled-in enclosure surrounded by temporary and transitory structures.[5] But as industrialization lures ever more people into the city, the larger population extends the boundaries of the city, creating patterns of living outside the city's center. These patterns can vary dramatically, as is evident when the affluent suburbs of America are compared with the huge shantytowns surrounding the cities of Latin America and most of the Third World. In more prosperous industrial nations, the extension of the urban boundaries is facilitated by (1) new production technologies that require more space; (2) improved roads, rails, and other transportation facilities; (3) new modes of housing construction and financing; and (4) new and varied telecommunications. The process of suburbanization—where new cities or districts emerge around a large, core industrial or preindustrial city—is self-reinforcing. As people move out of the core cities, so do retail businesses, production facilities, and service industries, with the result that increasing numbers of people are pulled out of the core city into the suburbs. At times, suburbs of cities become so extensive that they merge, creating a giant urban region of contiguous suburban communities that link larger core cities together in a vast urban corridor.[6]

As urbanization expands, it greatly alters patterns of economic organization. Increasingly, a higher proportion of the economy in mature industrial societies becomes organized around providing services—banking, insuring, acounting, advertising, etc.—and distributing both the commodities of industrial production and its many services. This servicing and marketing revolution shifts the composition of the work force from a blue- to a white-collar profile, but it also alters urban patterns. Once many jobs are no longer tied to actual production facilities, and once much of the work force is involved in servicing and marketing, mobility out of the city is greatly escalated. People can, in essence, provide services for each other and import from manufacturing centers necessary hard goods. Coupled with the revolutions in communications and transportation that accompany industrialization, these processes enable people to live and work in areas ever more remote from large cities, and yet at the same time, be proximate to them in that they can maintain communication with the city (cities) as well as travel rapidly to any urban area.

It is in the context of these dynamic processes that we must view the American community system, for many of the problems of America's cities, suburbs, and urban regions have been caused by the specific ways that these dynamics have operated in America over the last 150 years.

The Dynamics of American Urbanization

The Growth of American Cities

In 1800 only a few cities in the United States had a population over 25,000; none exceeded 100,000.[7] Compared with older preindustrial European cities, such as London with 800,000 or Paris with 500,000 residents, Philadelphia and New York were little more than towns with, respectively, 70,000 and 80,000 residents. By 1860, however, New York had a population of more than 800,000 inhabitants (not including Brooklyn) and was the third largest city in the Western world, behind London and Paris. Philadelphia, with over 500,000, had surpassed Berlin in size, and six other American cities had swelled to over 100,000 inhabitats.[8] By 1880, with the vast immigrations from southeastern Europe only beginning, twenty American cities exceeded the 100,000 mark in population.[9]

The spectacular emergence of large American cities can be attributed to several interrelated dynamics: (1) industrialization and the creation of urban jobs, (2) the resulting massive internal rural-to-urban migrations of people in search of these jobs in industry, (3) the immigration of peasants from rural Europe into the cities in search of a prosperous life, and

(4) the natural increase of urban residents stemming from the high birthrates of migrants and immigrants.

Industrialization was thus a critical force in the growth of the American urban system. Yet, the first large cities in the American colonies (New York, Boston, Baltimore, Philadelphia, Charleston, and Newport), were commercial seaports that marketed goods from Europe while distributing indigenous agricultural goods from their own hinterlands. Migrations westward from these cities resulted in new cities beyond the Appalachians, and at the same time, changed the nature of early eastern cities. The new cities were populated not so much by rural migrants as by sons of city residents on the eastern seaboard. The westward expansion of urban communities altered the commercial profile of eastern cities to one centered around the manufacture of goods for the new territories. At the same time, industrialists began to establish factory towns along the banks of rivers which were easily exploited sources of power. From 1815 to 1850 industrial towns grew and greatly extended urban industrial communities into the interior of the nation along major waterways—a pattern that persists to the present day. As the factories on the seaboard and river cities grew in number and size, farmers from the surrounding areas moved into them in search of opportunities not available in the increasingly unprosperous hinterland. This rural peasantry was rapidly transformed into an urban proletariat and became crowded into the tenements surrounding the factories. In the 1850s the railroad allowed further urban development in the West, most notably in Chicago and Toledo, and stimulated increased industrial manufacturing in the East, thereby initiating new manufacturing in the Midwest.

By the 1850s the urban-industrial profile of American communities was becoming clear. With further industrialization, the demand for unskilled factory labor began to exceed the supply available from rural migrations and natural population increases in the city. Fleeing from impoverished conditions in Europe in search of these job opportunities, waves of immigrants began to pour into the cities, resulting in a new and persistent pattern of urban organization: the ethnic ghetto or enclave. The influx of foreign immigrants was so great that the cities were overrun, creating incredibly crowded and unsanitary living conditions. Housing was scarce, and rents soared as buildings became increasingly crowded and deteriorated. Thus, by 1850 the ethnic slum and its absentee slumlord had become permanent fixtures of the American city.

Concomitant to the development of urban slums was the emergence of middle-class residential areas of white-collar workers who managed the factories and provided the services necessary to keep them running. Also, extensive downtown shopping and commercial areas developed to service both the factory and the white-collar worker, as well as to market many of the products of the industrializing economy. Within a comparatively small geographical region, working-class tenements, impoverished ethnic slums, middle-class neighborhoods, factories, and an extensive downtown commercial center typified most urban-industrial cities by the turn of the century.

While the ethnic and cultural diversity, as well as the concentration of so much human activity around a prospering central business district, gives, in retrospect, an image of a vibrant polis, today's cities, with all the problems imputed to them, are much safer and more sanitary places to live in *in absolute terms* than they were at the turn of the century. By 1910, with the development of the automobile, cities became highly congested, since the streets were not designed for the use of cars and trucks. Furthermore, as industrial production increased, as the sewage facilities of the city were overtaxed by the urban masses, and as the concentration of cars and trucks into the narrow city streets worsened, the air and water began to be polluted—although at that time few considered pollution a serious social problem.

Partially because cities in America developed so rapidly and spontaneously, they were largely unplanned and went unregulated by the federal government, which, in accordance with beliefs in local autonomy, did not think it appropriate to intervene extensively in the internal affairs of cities. Hence the dangers, unsanitary facilities, grievances of the urban peasants from Europe, and deteriorating conditions of the inner city were viewed as outside the province of the federal government. Furthermore, the vast capital needed to plan cities more rationally was unavailable to the federal government in an era when there was no federal income tax. Thus, from their outset, cities were politically decentralized and autonomous from the federal government. This tradition of local autonomy—buttressed by a laissez-faire ideology in economic activities (see chapter 2)—makes federal involvement in city problems difficult and often ineffective, even today.

The lack of national policy for cities created a pattern of urban city politics that dominates many large eastern and midwestern cities to this day. The immigrants from rural areas in Europe and the outskirts of urban areas encountered many problems of adjustment that were partially resolved by the local ward heeler of the big-city political machines—Tammany Hall in New York, Crump in Memphis, Hague in Jersey City, Curley in Boston, and Pendergast in Kansas City. Ward heelers provided help, comfort, and vital services to the new city residents who were poor and insecure in the new urban-industrial complex. They became intermediaries between the slumlord and resident (usually at a price unknown to the resident), and eliminated the bureaucratic entanglements—residency requirements, red tape, and delays—in securing assistance for families requiring aid. The big-city machine was thus established on the principle of a personal relationship between its local representative and the new urbanite, but for a great price: the urbanite agreed to vote for the machine's candidate in elections and, hence, to perpetuate the machine and its capacity to make great profits for its leaders. While most of the big political machines in large urban areas have diminished, a *pattern* of political control was established and persists today. Widespread political corruption and patronage, as well as control of a city's resources by a few elites, have persisted and often inhibited federal involvement in a city's internal affairs. When such involvement has been allowed, as in urban renewal, local corruption has often been the result. What is important for our present purposes is to emphasize that big-city politics had been *built into* the structure of American communities by the early decades of this century.

From 1910 to 1930 a new form of internal immigration from rural America became conspicuous: the rural, southern black began to migrate to northern cities in search of work. For decades rural conditions in the South had deteriorated, and with the boll weevil's devastation of the cotton industry, along with the industrial expansion and changes in immigration policies accompanying World War I, blacks began to pour into northern cities in search of job opportunities. Because of their poverty and because of racial discrimination, black migrants were forced into the most dilapidated and crowded tenements, so that the black ghetto was born. From these conditions, exacerbated by white attacks on black residents, came the first urban race riots and interracial conflicts. Between 1915 and 1919, Allen and Adair conclude,[10] eighteen major race riots occurred. For example, between May 28 and July 2, 1917, 39 blacks were killed in East St. Louis, Illinois, because they had been used as strikebreakers. Reports indicate that the intense violence, burning, and disruption were subdued only by the use of the National Guard and increased police activity. By 1920 urban segregation and exploitation of blacks and their resulting racial tensions were clearly built into the structure of major cities in the United States.

We have presented this brief historical scenario to emphasize that many of the dilemmas that presently confront America's large cities inhere in the dynamics of rapid urbanization per se, and in the particular historical circumstances of American society. For unlike European societies, urbanization in America involved rapid expansion into vast tracts of open land, importation in a very short period of large numbers of foreign immigrants, redistribution of a large, formerly slave population and persistence of a Revolutionary ideology in local control and decentralized federalism that prevented the creation of a strong central government. These ideological beliefs had added weight because they represented application of such core values as individualism and freedom.

By the end of the second decade of this century, then, a number of present-day dilemmas confronted most American cities:

1. Overcrowded and impoverished slums with substandard housing and unsafe sanitary facilities;
2. Ethnic and racial segregation of neighborhoods;
3. Industrial pollution of the air and water;
4. Community pollution of waters stemming from inadequate sewage facilities;
5. Extreme congestion from trucks and automobiles;
6. Corrupt big-city politics;
7. Racial tensions and riots.

European cities evidenced some of these problems, especially (1), (3), (4), and (5), whereas (2), (6), and (7) were more typical of American cities.

The Emergence of the American Metropolis

These cities and their attendant problems were perhaps inevitable in light of the industrial technology of the late nineteenth century as it was adapted to American conditions. The technology of early industrial societies did not allow for the flexible movement of energy over long distances by electrical cables. Factories had to be located near sources of energy or at least near railroads or major waterways, from which coal and oil could easily be supplied. Since work was concentrated in cities, so was the work force, which, because of limited transportation facilities, had to remain close to the factories. The markets for industrial goods were in the central cities; therefore, commerce and trade also became tied to cities in the central business districts.

Just as the imperatives of early industrial technology stimulated the growth of large cities, changes in that technology and the resulting changes in the economy created a new form of urbanism in the twentieth century: metropolitan areas composed of large decaying cities inhabited by the poor and surrounded by suburbs inhabited by the white and the more affluent. For shortly after the turn of the century a technological revolution occurred. In 1915 there were 2.5 million automobiles, but twenty years later assembly-line production had increased the number of cars exponentially. Cars made it possible to adapt transportation facilities to where people wanted to live, rather than the reverse. Heretofore, residential areas had to be adjusted to the existing fixed trolley and rail transport systems, but with the increasing development of roads and highways, more flexible living patterns outside the city limits could be enjoyed by those who could afford a car and the costs of commuting to work from the suburbs.[11]

There were other technological forces contributing to the outward growth of urban areas.[12] Mechanical refrigerators, wide varieties of canned foods, and high-voltage electrical transmission cables allowed people to have the amenities in the suburbs that previously were available only in the central city. Furthermore, the communications revolution involving first the radio, then television, enabled suburban residents to remain psychologically tied to cities while being geographically separated from them.

Technological changes also allowed, and in some cases forced, industry to follow residents out of the central city. The development of extensive assembly-line production techniques required more space than was economically feasible to buy in the central city. The rapid proliferation of a road and highway system and the emergence of a trucking industry allowed producers to disperse their production facilities without losing access to raw materials and markets. These and other kinds of technological change had a profound impact on the way the American economy in the twentieth century became organized. In turn, as we noted earlier, these changes in the economy facilitated suburbanization.

As people began to move into the suburbs, marketing and service organizations also relocated to serve the affluent suburbanites. This movement created jobs for white-collar workers, with the result that even more white-collar residents migrated out of the city to take advantage of new jobs and better services. As ever more white-collar, middle-class residents relocated to suburbia, so did more marketing and servicing enterprises in search of a more lucrative market. In this way, a cycle of suburbanization of economically prosperous residents and skilled, white-collar industries was begun and perpetuated.

As the buyers for many industrial goods located in the suburbs, manufacturing corporations also began to relocate near these affluent markets, where land was cheap and taxes were low. One result of the movement of servicing, marketing, and manufacturing enterprises was to drain the central city of its skilled and affluent work force, as well as some of its major enterprises in the central business district.

While America's early industrial cities emerged unfettered by the federal government, the pattern of American suburbanization was profoundly influenced by federal policies. For during World War I, and then in the Great Depression of the 1930s, the federal government had greatly expanded and exerted considerable, though often indirect, control over internal affairs. Nowhere is this more evident than in federal housing policies. During the 1930s the Federal Housing Administration (FHA), and in the 1940s the Veterans Administration (VA), encouraged the construction of single-family dwellings in the suburbs by insuring mortgages. This policy overcame traditionally conservative banking practices and enabled people who had a little economic surplus to purchase their own homes in the suburbs. The FHA thus kept the urban exodus alive, even during the depression years. During World War II, the government established stricter housing, building, and rent controls, and many industries in the older central cities were revived, resulting in migrations back into the cities. After the war, however, with the help of the VA home loan guarantee and FHA guarantees, movement out of the city accelerated and led to the dramatic transformation of American cities.

State and local governments also contributed to the emergence of suburbia. Initially the central city annexed the new residential areas along its borders, but eventually short-sighted city leaders began to feel that the suburbs were a liability because the taxes they yielded did not pay for the services the city had to supply (police, fire prevention, sanitation, streets, etc.). By the time large city governments began to realize that their tax base had vanished to the suburbs, suburban communities had begun to incorporate in order to determine their own fate, patterns of land use, allocation of tax monies, and just who their neighbors were to be. In state after state legislators from suburban areas, who craved self-government, joined forces with rural legislators, who saw the growth of large cities as a threat to rural power, to enact legislation that made the annexation of the suburbs by central cities very difficult. By the end of the 1920s the delineation between suburb and central city was well established in American metropolitan regions.[13]

It is in the context of these historical processes, then, that we must view current urban problems. For the dilemmas of America's metropolitan areas inhere in the particular way that the general dynamics of urbanization interacted with the unique conditions present in the United States in the last and current century.

Enduring Dilemmas of American Communities

Cultural Contradictions in Community Processes

The dilemmas of American urban communities are, to some extent, conditioned by core values as these have become translated into dominant beliefs. These beliefs have operated historically to circumscribe the pattern of urbanization in America, and now influence people's perceptions about what is right, proper, and possible. The most dominant of these beliefs can be labeled "local autonomy," which is an application of the values of activism, individualism, and freedom to community patterns. This belief system is not uniquely American, but the way in which it operates to influence responses to the problems of metropolitan regions is typically American. The basic tenet of this complex belief system can be stated simply: communities, through their active efforts, should be free to determine the shape of basic living patterns in accordance with their individual preferences—their zoning laws, roads, schools, form of government, public works, and community services. Federal control of such matters is considered inappropriate and undesirable.

Contradicting these beliefs is the fact of federal intervention in the affairs of American communities. Indeed, there is another application of the value of activism which, in essence, asserts that the federal government "should do something" about various problems. In accordance with this belief and the need for societywide planning, along with the human needs of many residents, the federal government has increasingly become involved in community life. But the *pattern* of intervention has been influenced by widely held beliefs in local control. Federal assistance to cities has tended to be indirect and piecemeal. Much assistance is in the form of grants-in-aid for specific categories of activities—housing, police, fire, welfare, flood control, and education, for example. By offering monies (which communities must at times match) in specific areas and by giving local communities much control over how the monies are administered, the federal government has kept a low profile; hence, it has not been viewed as violating local control.

When intervention is direct, obligatory, and manifest, however, resistance is evident. For example, many suburban communities have fought and stopped the building of public housing projects. Or, the resistance to the busing of school children to achieve equal educational opportunity arises, in part, from people's perception that they have lost control of their community (of course, bigotry and racism are also factors).

It would be difficult to understand the dilemmas of America's urban areas without appreciating the extent to which people in America believe in local autonomy. The belief defines for many what is "wrong" with the cities, while being intimately connected to the substance of their social problems. For indeed, the structure of community problems has been, as we will come to see, heavily influenced by this dominant belief system.

Political Organization in the Metropolitan Region
One of the major consequences of the growth of metropolitan areas and the resulting incorporation of separate and autonomous suburban communities has been the political decentralization of decision-making in urban America. In the old big cities, political machines represented a highly centralized form of decision-making, with the result that policies—both good and bad—could be easily implemented across the whole city. In contrast, the multiple communities in a modern metropolitan area now make unified and concerted political action difficult. Each separate community has its own local officials and city government, which, on the one hand, represents a traditional American ideal of a decentralized and democratic polis, but also, on the other hand, makes planning across an entire metropolitan region difficult. While local governments act autonomously, they are in reality part of a larger urban system that, as we will argue later, probably needs to engage in metropolitan planning. From this perspective, American metropolitan areas can be seen as having built into their structure the incapacity to respond politically to many of their most critical problems, such as housing, crime, traffic, pollution, sanitation, and police and fire protection.

Besides dispersing political power, suburban incorporation and the persistence of local autonomy beliefs have resulted in the duplication of many public services. Such duplication often represents an enormous waste of the financial resources of a metropolitan region, since vital services can be financed less expensively and administered more efficiently at the metropolitanwide than at the local level. Resources that could be used for attacking many problems, such as pollution, congestion, poor housing in the cities, and crime in the streets, are spent in duplication of services. Thus, resources necessary for resolving problems are sometimes unavailable for either the large core cities or their suburbs.

Political fragmentation is a continual dilemma facing a federalist political system. Decentralization of political power has many advantages, the most notable of which is to minimize the gap between political leaders and the citizenry. Centralization has many disadvantages, the most prominent of which is to create a wasteful bureaucracy that is out of touch with those it is supposed to serve. The dilemma facing America's metropolitan areas, then, is how to restructure government so that the benefits of decentralization can be realized, while at the same time maintaining some degree of administrative centralization to deal with metropolitan problems. Such a formula calls for a delicate balance that is difficult to effect in the first place, and even more difficult to maintain. Establishing this balance in dealing with urban problems will remain an enduring dilemma, especially since there are contradictory cultural beliefs encouraging and discouraging federal involvement in urban politics.

Economic Organization in America's Urban Areas

The white, middle-class exodus to the suburbs has created an economic imbalance within America's urban areas. First, the movement of industries, businesses, and commerce to the suburbs has frequently led to the decline of the central business district in many large cities. In turn, the decline of this area has undermined the tax base which the central city needs to survive and prosper. Second, the high-income resident, in moving to the suburbs, no longer spends money in or pays taxes to the city, resulting in an even greater erosion of the revenue necessary to maintain a large city. Third, state and federal tax formulas typically create a situation whereby the city pays more in taxes than it receives in services. The overall result of these three forces is to make it increasingly difficult for cities to finance necessary services, especially at a time in the 1980s when federal budgetary cutbacks in the domestic side of the budget are evident.

These cutbacks have created fiscal problems for all communities in America's metropolitan areas, but the problems are particularly severe for the large central city that typifies most metropolitan regions. The central city is an integral part of a metropolitan area; yet, it has a decreasing base of property tax revenue and less claim on the federal government's resources. Given the fact that public services cost more than ever, an economic crisis of severe proportions has emerged for the large city in America. In addition, the residents of contemporary cities—the poor, the minorities, and the aged, not to mention the more affluent city-dwellers who can exercise greater control over their place of residence—are requiring an increasing number of services in the form of housing, welfare, police protection, and health care. Under current conditions, the central city is decreasingly able to pay the rising costs of these necessary services. In 1932 municipalities were collecting more taxes than the federal and state governments combined. Of all tax monies received, cities received 52 percent; today the intake of cities is less than 10 percent of the total. With rising costs and increasing demand for services in the burdened cities, finding new fiscal formulas for core cities represents a real dilemma for American society.

This dilemma is aggravated by the fact that much of the work force in the central city does not live in the city. Indeed, the large city has increasingly become solely a workplace for the suburbanite, with the result that the commuter derives a livelihood from the city, uses many of its facilities (police, transportation, sanitation), and yet in most cases pays no personal taxes to it. The city may well become, as it already has in many instances, a service area for the affluent middle-class suburbanites who return home to their suburban community, where they deposit their money, buy their wares, and pay their taxes. Since this trend is likely to continue, despite some recent trends for a few to migrate back into the core city, the dilemmas of finding new sources of tax revenue and city financing will increase.

The Political Economy of Urban Blight

The movement of industry, commerce, and middle-class residents out of the city has been paralleled by a substantial migration of the poor into the city. While some descendants of early immigrants have vacated their ethnic enclaves for residence in suburbia, or in more prosperous areas of the large city, the rapid influx of blacks and other impoverished minority groups into the city's tenements has perpetuated the urban slum. To illustrate how rapid migrations of blacks into the cities have been, it can be noted that in 1910, 73 percent of the black population lived in the rural South, whereas by 1960, 73 percent resided in urban areas.[14] Similar migrations of Hispanics and Asians have occurred in more recent decades.

The massive influx of the poor into the cities has created extensive demand for low-cost housing, which is available only in the decaying tenements that were constructed around the turn of the century. Since the demand has been great and the supply low (especially for blacks, who have been openly discriminated against), landlords have maintained the tradition, begun in the last century, of charging comparatively high rents and providing little property maintenance and few improvements. While in absolute terms the quality of ghetto housing is now superior to that at the turn of the century, the standards of decent housing have risen as the level of affluence in the broader society has grown. Thus, housing is still a major problem for urban minorities forced to live in substandard dwellings.

While the persistence of substandard housing at the city's core is often the result of personal greed by landlords and of the inability of the poor to afford better living conditions, the urban housing blight has other sources—many of them built into the structure of American institutions and communities. Inhibited by beliefs in local control, the federal government has never really (until very recently) approached the question of housing on a national level. For example, in a society with a federally conceived and financed highway system and with a national farm policy, there is currently no national urban policy, though American society has been urbanized for half a century. Traditionally there has been no national research—until the last few years—on how to deal with the construction and distribution of housing. Research on housing financed by the federal government lags by billions of dollars behind that financed by the government for agriculture, manufacturing, medicine, and other areas of applied technology. Even massive federal programs such as urban renewal, public housing, and Model Cities have had little impact on housing blight. In many cases, as with the FHA and VA housing mortgage insurance programs, the federal government has encouraged urban blight by stimulating the building of new houses in the suburbs rather than in the central cities.

The structure of the housing industry also helps to account for the blight in the cities. The building industry, naturally, seeks to make a profit. Contractors are therefore likely to build in middle- and high-income areas in the suburbs, where profits are greatest. Housing is also a local industry, with few national corporations of the magnitude of the Ford Company or General Motors. Yet the housing industry provides one of the most important commodities, does an annual business of close to $30 billion, employs over 5 million workers, and creates a vast market for other industries. However, because the housing industry is so decentralized, it goes comparatively unregulated by the federal government, so that clear national housing policies—should they ever be initiated—would be difficult to implement, as has been the case with the urban renewal program, Model Cities, and other federal programs.

The American Dilemma:
Racial and Ethnic Segregation
in American Communities

As the affluent whites moved out, the poor, especially blacks, migrated into the cities. Because they had few industrial skills and because of racial discrimination, blacks were confined to the worst jobs in the most dilapidated parts of the city. Currently other minorities are also locked into the decaying city core surrounded by the more affluent whites in the suburbs, but not to the same degree as blacks. Furthermore, within the core cities segregation of the racial and ethnic minorities into ghettos, like those of their immigrant predecessors, remains extremely high. The explosiveness of "urban apartheid" is all too apparent—urban violence and instability. For the present, it can be noted that residential segregation of blacks continues to be high within cities and between the city and suburbs. Segregation results from more than racial bigotry; it has been built into federal policies and into the demographic forces accompanying urbanization.

Blacks migrated to America's core cities at the very time that industry and commerce were moving to the suburbs. Similarly, present-day ethnic migrants to the cities—the various subpopulations of Hispanics and to lesser extent, Asians—are entering the urban core more than its more affluent suburbs. Such demographic patterns reflect political processes. For black Americans, the federal government would not insure the financing of integrated neighborhoods through FHA or VA programs. Thus, in essence, during the 1940s and 1950s blacks were locked out of the suburbs, and hence, of the economic and educational opportunities available there. For present-day migrants, the pattern of racial and ethnic segregation is so well established that there is little choice but to move into the decaying urban core. For there is little low-cost housing available in the suburbs, and local suburban governments have exerted strict zoning controls to inhibit efforts by the federal government in recent years to make suburban housing available to the poor and to disenfranchised ethnic populations.

Prospects for America's Urban Future

Certain problems became well entrenched during the period of initial urbanization that created the large city, and then during the more recent decades of suburbanization that spawned the giant metropolitan region. These problems are not easily resolved because their solutions involve the generation of new formulas for financing communities, the creation of alternative forms of community governance, the movement of large numbers of people, and the redirection of dominant and pervasive beliefs. Yet, without fundamental changes, the governance of cities and the metropolitan region will remain fragmented and wasteful; the serious pollution of the environment will persist; the fiscal crises of not just the core city but also the newer suburban communities will escalate; the deterioration of housing will continue; and the potentially volatile effects of racial and ethnic segregation will increase.

At present, government "solutions" to the problems of metropolitan areas are, in a sense, part of the problem. They have been underfunded, piecemeal, sporadic, inequitable, and for the most part, ineffective. Most programs have involved a grant-in-aid system in which the federal government pays some, most, and on occasion, all the costs of specific programs introduced by local communities. Urban renewal and later Model Cities were typical programs that sought to maintain local control of federal monies designated for slum clearance, business district revitalization, and housing construction. More recently, as specific programs fell out of favor, general revenue sharing has been a more typical policy in which each community is given federal tax monies for various budget categories which, to varying degrees, must be matched by local tax revenues. Over the years, the matching requirements for many budget categories have declined, creating a simple grant system for communities. In addition, a wide variety of aid programs, such as rent subsidies, mortgage subsidies, low-cost housing incentives, come and go depending upon political and ideological trends in Washington.

The basic problem with all such efforts is that they have been seriously underfunded in the first place; and since there has been a real concern to maintain some local control, meager federal funds have often disappeared into the quicksand of local politics. But much more fundamentally, federal programs have sought to assist, for the most part, *individual* citizens and *individual* communities, whereas many of the problems of urban America affect the whole metropolitan region. Revenue sharing or grants to individuals or to each separate community will not resolve such problems. Rather, they will contribute to, and aggravate, the problems of governing and financing the operation of the giant metropolis.

The basic dilemma confronting America's urban regions is balancing the efficiencies and equities of metropolitan programs with people's desire to maintain a sense of local community and to control services such as fire, police, schools, and zoning policies. This dilemma is compounded in most regions by the juxtaposition of county government, state agencies, federal bureaus, and local city governments. And over the years, new metropolitan districts—regulating, for example, water, sewage, air quality—have been added to the governmental mix. These diverse bodies cut across many urban regions, have different sources of funding, often duplicate services, and are almost always protective of their jurisdiction.

Thus, a critical shift in public and political thinking must occur, for the metropolis must now be considered a governmental unit in and of itself. Other governmental bodies will, for many purposes, need to be subordinate to metropolitan government. In particular, tax revenues need to be collected at the metropolitan level and then redistributed to local governmental bodies for developing their specific budgets. Much of the revenue would be retained at the metropolitan level, where certain services would be funded and administered. In particular, it is more efficient and politically expedient to administer traffic, pollution control, sewage, health and welfare services at the metropolitan level. More problematic are schools, police, and fire protection, since people tend to want these services controlled by the community. Probably the most equitable procedure would be to fund schools, fire, and police at the metropolitan level, and then redistribute the tax revenues to local governments where they would be free, within general administrative guidelines, to spend the monies as local elected officials determine.

Such a proposal presents severe problems, of course. Counties, cities, the state, and the federal government are not likely to subordinate their prerogatives to a metropolitan authority. There is also the problem of creating a metropolitan taxation system that replaces existing mixes of income, sales, and property taxes that are collected and administered by a confusing array of federal, state, county, and city governments. And most difficult to effect would be community representation in a metropolitan government. For example, how would unincorporated areas be represented, or what could be done if communities wanted to secede, or refused to join, a metropolitan government?

The very fact that the above proposal seems utopian signals, we feel, the depth of problems in America's urban regions. And to the extent that the present system of funding and governance persists, "urban blight" will remain one of America's most enduring dilemmas.

Chapter 11

America in the World System

$\mathbf{V}$irtually all aspects of American society are influenced by its involvement in a world system. The term "system" connotes an interconnectedness among nations; and the goal of world-system analysis is understanding the nature, pattern, and forms of relations among different societies. Such analysis can obviously be very encompassing, since there are manifold types of connections that could be explored. Yet, most world-system analyses focus on political and economic relations, because these circumscribe other types of relations among nations.[1] Our goal in this chapter, therefore, is to examine the dilemmas that result from American society's involvement in political and economic ties to other nations.

The Dynamics of the World System

While the concept of "political economy"[2] connotes the interconnectedness of political and economic processes, it is also important to recognize economic and political processes operate separately from each other. Indeed, they often contradict one another, creating problems and dilemmas for individual nation-states as well as for relations among nations. For this reason, we will divide our analysis of world-system dynamics into an initial discussion of the world economy, and then, a review of the world political order.

The World Economy

Over the last few hundred years, capitalism has dominated the world economic order.[3] Even nations such as the USSR and China, which to some degree have sought to isolate themselves from world capitalism, have, in the end, participated as "capitalists" in the world economic system. Their participation underscores a basic contradiction, which we will explore in more detail later, between the internal political processes of a nation and its economic involvement in the world capitalist order. As domestic political processes have become more centralized and socialist within most nations and as internal economic processes have become politically regulated, often the opposite has been occurring at the world-system level. No nation can politically dominate the world, especially in a nuclear age; and as a result, economic processes have gone relatively unregulated. That is, the inherent dynamics of capitalism have been allowed to operate more freely in the world system than they have within any particular nation where political power is used to intervene in the economic order. Yet, ironically, the impact of unfettered capitalism has generated highly volatile political processes which can disrupt, if not destroy, the current economic system.[4]

The Dynamics of Capitalism. In examining the unfolding dynamics of world capitalism, we should review from chapter 2 the key elements of capitalist economic systems and some inherent contradictions of capitalist economies. In a system of relatively free markets for goods and services where economic units are driven by a desire for profits, several transformations inevitably occur. First, some economic units come to dominate markets, as monopolies or oligopolies, and to dictate prices for labor, raw materials, and finished goods. Second, market systems, where the "laws" of supply and demand for goods and services operate, experience periodic recessions and depressions as a result of overproduction and/or decreases in demand. Third, as capitalists seek to reduce costs for materials and labor, they create resentments and resistance among their workers and suppliers. Fourth, capitalist units must constantly expand and grow in order to sustain the interest of investors; as a result, severe problems of coordination, control, and regulation within and between corporate units emerge.

As we noted in chapter 2, these transformations create pressure within a society for government regulation of markets, of corporate units in those markets, of relations among corporations, of relations between labor and management, and of liaisons between the private interests of corporations and the public interests of democratic governments. World capitalism, however, generates these same pressures for central authority but without the corresponding capacity to mobilize a world government to regulate, coordinate, and control economic processes. Thus, the dynamics of world capitalism revolve around the inherently self-transforming nature of capitalism and the inability to create centralized regulatory agencies at a world level. It is in this contradictory dynamic that the basic economic dilemma of the world order resides.

At the world level, we must view nation-states and large corporations as the relevant economic units. While governments and corporations within a society often clash, there is considerable cooperation between government and capital in world markets and in relations with other nations.[5] Hence, economic conflicts among corporations of different nations often become a political conflict among governments, and vice versa. Yet, whether private corporation, government, or a combination of the two is defined as the key unit for analysis, the dynamics are much the same because they inhere in capitalism as a *system of relationships*. While the units do make some difference, far more fundamental is the nature of their relationship.

The World System Oligopoly: Core and Periphery. If we visualize world capitalism as profit-seeking activity among corporate units—whether allied with government or not—in a relatively unregulated market, then the first transforming dynamic is the domination of markets by oligopolies. Such was clearly the case historically, since a few nations initiated industrial production and came to constitute the "core" nations of early world capitalism.[6] Other, more "peripheral" nations became suppliers of inexpensive resources—both labor and materials—and ready markets for many finished goods. The Western nations of Europe, North America, and subsequently Japan, constituted a core oligopoly in world capitalism; and while considerable rivalry and economic competition among them existed, they all shared in common the domination of world markets in the undeveloped world. As a consequence, they could dictate to nations the price that they would pay for resources and the nature of their own capital investment in foreign lands. To a lesser degree, they could set the costs of goods sold to other nations, although competition among core capitalists gave some price relief to peripheral nations.

Without a world government to create the functional equivalent of antitrust laws, the core nations were left relatively free—save for their own competition and warfare—to exploit other nations. Nevertheless, other nations have developed productive capacities and expanded the number of core nations; and early peripheral nations, such as India, China, and states in the Middle East, have been able to transform technological and capital investments from the core into viable industries that allow them to compete in world markets. Moreover, the dependence of a larger number of industrial nations on others for basic resources—oil, minerals, gas, for example—and their growing reliance on these and other nations as export markets have created some counterpower to offset domination by core nations. OPEC in the 1970s is the most effective illustration of this change. But, the world economy is still dominated by the West and Japan, with China and Russia remaining marginal economic participants.

Economic Cycles in the World System.[7] All capitalist market systems reveal cycles of over- and undersupply of goods and services relative to market demand. When there is demand and when the supply is low, then more corporate units will begin production. As they do so, the supply eventually begins to pass demand, creating an oversupply of the goods or services. This process is accelerated with large-scale production in highly competitive markets, for as all corporate units seek to realize the economies of mass production, they simply glut a market more rapidly. Oversupply can be further accelerated by political processes in nation-states, for through tariffs, mandatory conservation, fiscal policies, and other political acts, the demand for a good or service can be decreased—hastening oversupply relative to demand.

When supply begins to exceed demand, capitalists must respond to their slackening profits. One response is to cut production; which, if widespread across many economic sectors, starts a world recession. Another response is to cut costs, and thereby to maintain profits. This second response can involve such strategies as (1) expanding production to reduce the cost per unit in hopes of gaining a price advantage against competitors, (2) closing outmoded production facilities, and (3) moving production to countries with more favorable labor costs or tax benefits. These stategies can be implemented even in good economic times, for unregulated capitalism always involves efforts to increase profits. But in recessionary periods, these strategies are even more likely.

In economically stagnant times, when supply equals or exceeds demand and when capitalists employ various strategies to maintain profitability, political processes are likely to become paramount as each nation-state attempts to protect its industries. In domestic economies, political processes operate to stimulate demand, but in the world economy the response to stagnation often does just the opposite: reduces demand. For example, tariffs and quotas on some imported goods might be imposed—a tactic which invites reprisals that further reduce aggregate demand. Moreover, stagnating economic conditions invite political turmoil—riots, revolutions, liberation movements, and even wars—which, in turn, reduces demand for many goods on the world market. If such political turmoil escalates, production can be disrupted.

Thus, unlike a domestic economy, where political intervention in economic processes can occur, political responses in the world system often tend to aggravate the business cycle. Responses can only occur within national boundaries, or among allied nations; they cannot regulate the dynamics of the overall world market. Indeed, they are likely to accelerate a recession, to exacerbate international political tensions, or to initiate military misadventures and warfare.

Resistance and Resentment in the World System. Within any capitalist society, workers organize in an effort to protect themselves from exploitation—low wages, dangerous working conditions, injury, and other potential abuses—by cost-conscious, profit-seeking corporate units. In this effort, they usually enlist the aid of government, and over time, the battle between labor and management is mitigated by a variety of regulatory agencies. At the world-system level, where the actors are nations, resistance to exploitation by core nations is more complex and difficult. Such resistance is likely to increase as the economic gap between developed and developing widens, as is illustrated by the fact that between 1960 and 1980, the per capital GNP gap widened by almost 70.9 percent.[8]

One strategy to combat the gap, and resulting tensions, is for dependent nations to organize resistance to domination by core nations and to force them to trade under more favorable conditions. This approach can only succeed if an alliance among nations can hold, if they possess something of value which core nations cannot get elsewhere, and if they are invulnerable to coercion by core nations. OPEC showed how this strategy can be employed successfully, but it can also create problems for those employing it. One problem is that core nations could find new sources of oil, implement conservation measures, and develop alternative energy sources—all of which in the early 1980s disrupted the OPEC cartel for a period.

Another strategy has been outright revolt against core nations and the subsequent nationalization of foreign capital. Cuba and much of the old British Empire employed such a strategy, but it too creates dangers. One is military reprisal by a colonial power; another is economic sanctions; yet another is support for guerrilla insurgents. Unless nations employing this strategy have an economic and military ally (as was the case with Cuba) or the tacit assent of the core nation (as was evident in the latter days of the British Empire), this strategy is likely to produce economic and political chaos within the nation that seeks to mitigate its domination by another.

The further danger of economic revolt is that it can trigger political responses by core nations which are disproportionate to the situation. Vietnam, the Cuban missile crisis, and the Soviet invasion of Afghanistan are conspicuous examples of situations where economic issues became symbolic political questions that triggered a military response. Such responses may or may not be successful, but they tend to disrupt economic processes, and in the end, increase economic and political dependency on more powerful nations, since to lose a military encounter invites occupation or to win one usually requires powerful allies who rarely depart at the termination of the conflict.

Problems of Coordination and Control of World Capitalism. Within all capitalist societies, the long-term trend has been toward increasing government regulation of economic processes. While short-term policies may shift from a conservative to liberal profile, the trend is toward increasing regulation. The reasons for this trend are, as we stressed earlier, varied, including: the inevitable growth of capitalist economies, creating severe problems of coordination; the need to resolve tensions between capital and labor; the desire to bend economic processes toward political goals, such as war, full employment, preservation of resources, profits for capitalists, and other socially defined ends.

At the world-system level, many of these same pressures exist.[9] Corporations grow and expand into ever more diverse markets; the exchange of resources, raw materials, finished goods, services, and currencies becomes incredibly complex, necessitating monitoring and regulation at the world level; the tension between core and peripheral nations results in international efforts to promote harmony among nations and to prevent domestic insurgency. Aggravating these regulatory problems is the inherent competitiveness of capitalism driven by a combination of short-term interests of corporations and the ever-shifting political goals of governments. Yet, as we have seen, there is no political authority to implement policies that coordinate, control, or regulate large-scale multinational corporations and nation-states; and as a result, problems of coordination are greater in the world system.

A variety of "solutions" have evolved or have been imposed by core nations, but many of them have simply worsened the situation. The most evident "solution" to the existence of an active world economy is the growth of multinational corporations[10] which, because of their high levels of capital, can penetrate markets in all parts of the world and which are increasingly free from political regulation. Such corporations are, in a sense, world actors. They must abide by the laws of nations in which they make investments and to which they sell goods and services, but they are relatively free to move capital and facilities anywhere in the world. Their size and dispersion makes them a force that can coordinate large amounts of capital, technology, and labor; but their competitiveness on world markets and their varying degrees of affiliation with, and sponsorship by, competitive national governments also make them a disruptive force, likely to increase economic and political instability. At present, it is difficult to assess which outcome is more likely, since multinationals are in a state of change.

Another solution to the increasing volume, rate, and

diversity of economic exchanges among nations has been to create new or expand old markets. For example, with the abandonment of the old gold standard for determining the value of a nation's currency, the creation of free-floating currencies and the extension of the system of currency-exchange markets created many problems of coordination. As technical markets, these monetary exchanges provide an essential service, but in capitalism virtually all markets become arenas of short-term speculative investment and profit-taking. Thus, the technical functions of money exchanges—exchanging currencies and payments for imported/exported goods—have, to some extent, been compromised by speculation involving efforts to buy currencies that are cheap and sell them when they rise. Such speculation can often have severe consequences for a national economy, compelling governments to take political actions (devaluation, restriction of money supplies, import quotas, international borrowing) which, in the end, only fuel speculation in the market. Thus, as key market mechanisms for facilitating exchanges in the world economy also become arenas for short-term speculation, new economic and political problems of coordination and control evolve.

Yet another strategy for coordinating world economic activities has been to create specialized organizations, such as the International Monetary Fund (IMF), General Agreement on Tariffs and Trade (GATT), International Energy Authority (IEA), the European Economic Community (EEC), and the World Bank. Some of these, such as the IEA, are purely defensive responses by nations—in this case, Europe—to particular threats—the oil crisis of 1973–74. Others do represent efforts to regularize international exchanges and prevent major economic dislocations (e.g., the IMF and GATT), but in the end "regulatory" bodies can only do what their most powerful core-nation members dictate. Still other organizations, such as the EEC, are both political and economic bodies which function best when confining their activities to technical issues—rates of currency exchange, trade agreements, and the like—and which become ineffective when attempting to act as political bodies, since such actions immediately bring into the debate the different political interests of member nations. Thus, while various ad hoc organizations can facilitate the flows of goods, services, and capital in the world system, their more technical functions can be easily upset by political policies of their most powerful members.

Another incipient strategy for regularizing economic relations in the world system is the development of an international body of law. Such efforts have been thwarted by several basic constraints. First, without an overall political authority, the laws are unenforceable. As has become evident, bodies such as the United Nations are often ineffective as law-enacting and law-enforcing agents. Second, because there is no standard of "justice" at the world level, there are no moral criteria for developing laws that address the rights, claims, and obligations of both poor and rich actors. Third, multinational corporations are not defined as legal entities at the world level, despite their increasing rates of investment and marketing in increasing numbers of countries. Rather, *portions* of such corporations are subject to the laws of only those nations in which they do business; these laws vary and do not extend beyond sovereign boundaries. Moreover, unlike nation-states which can enter political alliances, multinationals are, in their present state of evolution, less likely to formulate, much less agree to, laws in an open and competitive international market where there is no regulatory authority and where competition is intense. In its present form, international law is relatively ineffective at coordinating or controlling the activities of corporate actors. Only when political treaties and alliances are created among smaller groups of nations is there some capacity to regulate multinationals, but the political nature of these treaties can also create other kinds of problems, such as war, increased polarization between core and peripheral nations, political instability in those excluded by treaties or adversely affected by them, and so on.

A final strategy, which is more a consequence of profit-seeking on a world scale than a conscious strategy, is the pattern of mutual investment of multinational corporations in diverse nation-states. Such investment creates economic interdependencies which, some have argued, are the forerunners of political alliances and other integrating processes. Economic interdependencies take a number of forms, including: construction of joint production and marketing facilities by multinationals, the loaning of capital by nationally chartered banks to other governments, and the investment of large sums of money by governments and wealthy individuals in one government into the productive activities of another (e.g., OPEC's "petro dollars" in the United States). Depending on the nature of these links, economic and political stability is increased or decreased. For example, if foreign investment in production facilities is exploitive of labor and resources, if loans by banks are at exorbitant interest rates, and if foreign cash investments are used as tool for narrow political leverage, interdependencies are likely to promote both economic and political instability. Conversely, if production facilities provide employment and marketable goods for the world system, if loans stimulate economic growth and the creation of jobs and viable markets in the world economy, and if cash investments do the same, then interdependencies are more likely to promote world integration. At present, both extremes can be observed; and problems of integration are still greatly exacerbated by developing patterns of mutual investment in the world economic system.

In looking at the dynamics of the world economy, then, it is evident that the basic dilemma revolves around the ability to develop political authority, or its functional equivalent, to deal with the inherent problems and contradictions of capitalism. The world economy is, today, in the midst of major changes in the relations between core and periphery, in the adjustments made to inevitable world economic cycles, in ways of coping with the consequences of exploitation of the poor by wealthy nations, and in ways of dealing with the problems of regulation among corporate and sovereign actors. As we have emphasized, each of these changes poses problems and dilemmas that resist resolution. And this fact alone ensures that their persistence will increase both accommodative and antagonistic political processes.

The World Political Order

General Conditions of Political Centralization. There are several general conditions in all societies wherein political centralization and consolidation of power occur.[11] First, as we have already noted, increasing productivity in a society creates problems of coordination which can only be resolved by the expansion of government and the centralization of power. For this reason all capitalist societies, over the last 100 years, have become more centralized politically. Second, populations in all societies exert pressure on government to meet social needs—medical care, full employment, redistribution of wealth, education, human and civil rights—and these pressures require centralization to mobilize and coordinate necessary resources, or as is more often the case, to repress a population whose expectations cannot, or will not, be fulfilled. Third, a society whose leaders and members perceive external threats to their economic well-being, to their military security, or to their way of life tends to mobilize resources and to centralize power in order to deal with the threat.[12] Fourth, once political consolidation occurs, the concentration of power in a system of bureaucratic structures becomes, itself, a force for further consolidation and centralization of power.[13] Regulatory agencies typically seek to protect themselves by expanding their authority and functions; social agencies do the same; and the military bureaucracy typically finds, and even creates by its actions, new threats from inside or outside the society to justify its growth.

Political Centralization in the World Economy. Processes at the world level intensify political dilemmas. Involvement in the world economy aggravates problems of coordination, regulation, and control of corporations; import-export balances, fluctuations in currencies; resource and materials distribution; and other economic processes. Governments inevitably centralize to deal with the problems. Moreover, as tentative efforts to develop international agencies to cope with world economic (and political) problems expand, governments must develop ever more explicit policies toward, and administrative articulation with, these agencies—thereby furthering political centralization.

As indigenous populations of the world's nations become exposed to, interdependent with, or exploited by corporate, political, and social agencies of other nations, then traditions and ways of life are changed. And people become more cosmopolitan and begin to expect more from government.[14] Pressures mount on government to meet this "revolution of rising expectations"; and if government cannot do so, then insurgency and civil war often ensue—all of which force further political consolidation, usually in the military.

World economic competition and exploitation, fueled by historical animosities and the growing militarization of many governments, exacerbates leaders' and a population's sense of threat. Indeed, threats of external enemies are often magnified by leaders in an effort to divert the public's attention away from the failings of government. But the result is further political control and militarization.

Militarization in the World Political Economy. In the absence of effective world political authority, economic processes force political centralization of nation-states to "protect their interests" in a world economy typified by competition, scarce resources, outright exploitation of poor by rich nations, and the domestic ravages of world economic cycles. Political centralization for self-protection is, to a great extent, a circular process. For as nations become politically organized to deal with their world-system problems—whether as individual nations or as members of alliances such as NATO or the Eastern Bloc—solutions to problems are increasingly defined in political and often military terms. When historical animosities among populations are added to this volatile mix, it is not surprising that the world political system is dominated by growing militarism, tempered by mediation agencies such as the United Nations and by the potential for a nuclear holocaust.

Two trends in militarization are evident. The old core

nations of the West and those that have developed industrially in the last fifty years have, as a result of two world wars and several "limited" engagements involving large-scale mobilization, developed high technology and nuclear arsensals for mutual protection. Increasingly, higher proportions of total GNP are devoted in these nations toward military-related activities. Moreover, twenty-five of these nations have developed active military export industries which have helped arm the rest of the world's restive populations and their oppressors.[15] Yet, despite the growing militarism of these countries, political democracy is prominent in most, and increasingly, protest against the dangers of nuclear weapons is evident.

In contrast, the Third and Fourth worlds of developing or peripheral nations are increasingly run by the military, with severe abuse of human rights and with active insurgency movements within their borders. In 1981, fifty countries were run by the armed forces; and most of these had to engage in repression of, if not military action against, revolutionary elements within the society. Such nations have inevitably become active buyers on the world arms market; and they have become symbolic pawns in the larger political and military strategies of the Soviet bloc and the United States (and only occasionally its reluctant allies in NATO).

These two trends help account for the $550 billion spent on arms in 1982, the $1.6 trillion for arms and standing military operations (including 25 million soldiers and another 45 million reservists), and the $100 billion to stockpile nuclear weapons. Indeed, over the last decade, the rate of arms imports to developing nations has kept pace with economic aid; and thus, although many of the world's economic problems require political solutions (agreements and treaties of nation-states), the world political system is far more capable of propagating war. Such is inevitably the case in a world system which cannot generate political authority; which is economically dominated by self-interested and profit-seeking multinationals; which is typified by a highly competitive and speculative system of international markets; and which reveals nation-states, with their own traditions, history of dominance or subordination, and present domestic problems, as prominent economic actors. In some respects, it is surprising that, in light of these conditions, there is not more warfare in the world.

The most prominent political and economic actor in the world system is, of course, the United States. The dynamics of the world system are profoundly influenced by the actions of the United States, but equally important, especially for our purposes in this chapter, the operation of the world system greatly circumscribes the internal structure, culture, and operation of American society.

American Society and the World Political Economy

The Culture of Domination

Basic American values of activism, achievement, progress, and humanitarianism have, over the last six decades, been translated into a series of beliefs about the United States' role in world affairs. From an initial belief in "helping our allies" in World War I, and later, in World War II, beliefs became more assertive, if not grandiose.[16] For example, beliefs range from such matters as "making the world safe for democracy," "protecting American interests," "fighting the specter of world Communism" to "America is the greatest nation on earth."

These beliefs reflect, and at the same time legitimate, America's economic and political dominance of the world over the last five decades, especially between 1945 and 1965. They have legitimated military interventionism—Korea, Vietnam, Cuba, Central America—and they have been used to make it seem proper that the United States should shoulder the major military burden and nuclear deterrent capability for the Western democracies and Japan. The humanitarian value component in these beliefs has been used to legitimate the rebuilding of the ravaged European economies, the assistance program for Japan, the funding in large part of the United Nations, and the giving of economic aid to much of the underdeveloped world.

More recently, as American economic dominance has declined in the face of the resurgence in Japan and Western Europe, these beliefs, or the culture of American domination, have begun to shift in ways that are difficult to predict. For now, there is insecurity about the inevitability of personal and national "progress" and about our capacity as individuals and a nation in the world system to "actively" control events. New, challenging beliefs in the more "limited role" of America in the world political economy are now evident, as are beliefs about the need to "retool" and "reindustrialize" in the face of world economic competition. At the same time, there is a defensive quality to beliefs about "protecting American workers' jobs" and "limiting imports of foreign goods."

These new beliefs still reveal an implicit culture of domination, *as if* America could actively choose how it would participate in the world system, whether by reducing its presence, by retooling, or by protectionism. The world economic and political dynamics discussed earlier make such beliefs, we argue, unrealistic and non-isomorphic with the realities of the world system. Yet, the cultural ambivalence created by beliefs in our world dominance and the changing political economy of a world where America can no longer dominate so completely will remain one of the more interesting dynamics of the 1980s and 1990s. Just how this cultural conflict will resolve itself remains to be seen. It will, in the end, reflect the political and economic realities of America's new place in the world's political economy in the next decades.

America's Changing Place in the World Economy

Ascendance of the American Economy. There is, of course, little doubt that the United States still dominates the world economy as both the largest market and the largest producer of goods by volume. Yet, productivity per capita has declined; and over the long run, this decline will translate into less buying power and less volume of production in relation to other nations. But the decline is slow, primarily because the U.S. economy has so dominated world markets in the post–World War II period and because the United States is so large in comparison to its Western competitors. It is still a huge, affluent market for foreign goods.

Several factors account for America's economic dominance of the world, especially from 1940 to 1970. First, America's industrialization initially lagged somewhat behind Europe's; thus, its production facilities were somewhat newer. Second, America imported a large hard-working labor force which was willing to work for low wages, increasing profits for capitalists who could reinvest some of these profits in other enterprises. Third, innovators in the United States made a number of production breakthroughs, such as assembly-line production and mechanized agricultural machinery, that greatly escalated production in comparison with Europe. Fourth, unlike European nations, the United States was able to avoid the ravages of military invasion on its soil and the consequent destruction of property, life patterns, people, and industry. When the U.S. did become involved in wars, such as its own Civil War and World Wars I and II, the expanded production allowed for the refinement of manufacturing techniques and the creation of new capital for investment in industrial production. Fifth, since America was a land full of immigrants who needed to be assimilated, the public school system—from elementary schools in ethnic ghettos to the system of land grant colleges—was dramatically and democratically expanded, creating a less elitist system than its European counterparts. As such, the system created real opportunities for the talented, while providing congeries of research-oriented, technology-producing universities. Sixth, the United States has been a land of abundant natural resources for agricultural and industrial production—giving it a clear advantage over the Old World and Japan. Seventh, the United States, relative to its counterparts in Europe, was under-populated with room to expand to new geographical regions and grow numerically in ways that stimulated rather than shackled production. As the population moved westward, for example, new industries such as the railroads, shipping, mass-production agriculture, and herding were stimulated; and new markets for finished goods were created. Or, as the population grew in numbers and became urbanized and then suburbanized, additional new industries, such as housing and automobiles, were stimulated, while aggregate demand for consumer goods and services increased and stimulated production.

As a result of these forces, American production was more technologically advanced and was greater in volume and varieties of goods than the rest of the world's. And, given the ascendance of the American military and its brief nuclear monopoly, American corporations could extract resources from other nations and create markets for their goods. And with the ravaged economies of Japan, Europe, and Russia, along with the internal disruption created by the Chinese Revolution in the late 1940s, the United States had few competitors; hence, it could control the world's markets and could easily be the dominant economic power. Yet, the confluence and convergence of events could not possibly be sustained, despite the illusions created by America's culture of domination. Inevitably, a period of decline would set in as other industrial nations rebuilt thir economies and as the United States lost its nuclear monopoly.

Readjustment of the American Economy. While America buys and produces more goods and services than any other nation, it ranks seventh in most economic-social indexes.[17] That is, productivity as it affects people's affluence and lifestyle has, relative to other industrial nations, declined over the last three decades. While this decline is viewed with great alarm, particularly within both domestic and world markets, problems for many U.S. industries—cars, small electronics, steel, heavy equipment, farm machinery—some of the change in relative position was inevitable, for a number of reasons.

First, with the Marshall Plan and other aid programs to Europe and Japan, these countries could rebuild with newer, more technically advanced plants which would eventually outproduce the aging American facilities in many basic industries—steel, clothing, heavy equipment, shoes, consumer electronics. Second, and compounding the situation, many American corporations did not reinvest profits into modernization of aging plant. Instead, profits were used to diversify into new industries and to increase short-term profitability by merger and/or conglomeration.[18] That is, it is more profitable in the short term to buy or merge with another concern and extract its profits than it is to tear down and rebuild old production facilities. This trend continues to the present day and signals a fundamental flaw in the American management system: excessive concern with, and too high a reward for, short-term as opposed to long-term profits.

Third, American corporations have often had an adversarial relationship with government, resisting regulation and demanding low taxation. As a consequence, well-articulated liaisons for a "partnership" between government and industry do not exist, often putting U.S. corporations at a disadvantage in world markets with corporations that do have closer ties to government.

Fourth, many basic industrial corporations have also had adversarial relations with labor. As a result, labor has sought large pay-benefits packages to compensate for the often unresponsive, if not abusive, policies of management. This antagonism has created severe quality control problems in industry and has made American products less attractive domestically and on the world market. Moreover, American labor has simply priced itself out of a job, especially since corporations feel little loyalty to their workers and will simply move production facilities to foreign areas where less expensive labor can be found. Such acts do little to reduce labor-management conflict, increasing long-standing tensions.

Fifth, as other nations rebuilt their industries and as the Third World began to develop, the United States lost its easy access to many resources which it had been able to extract cheaply. Moreover, because of the often exploitive actions of U.S. corporations and the government in foreign countries, intense resentments accumulated, and the resulting anti-American movements closed many markets for raw materials or created pressures for cartels, such as OPEC, which worked to raise the costs to the United States and other industrial nations of basic resources. Since the U.S. had always had abundant resources, or easy access to those of other nations, profit-seeking corporations had been extremely wasteful in their use; and as shortages developed, industries had not developed conservation systems comparable to those in Japan and Europe, where many resources had always been scarce.

Sixth, the culture of domination may have blinded leaders in both industry and government to the realities of the world system. It may have been presumed that U.S. industry could always outcompete its counterparts in other nations and that it could always get resources, or have markets, through a combination of economic and political pressure, cooptation, and intervention. The realities of a modernizing industrial base in other nations and the depth of anti-American sentiment in those nations where the United States had intervened were simply ignored through unreflective acceptance of cultural beliefs.

Seventh, successful industrial systems generate affluence which, in turn, creates demands for tertiary services and products—recreation, fast foods, counseling services, vacation resorts, etc. These become "growth" industries which attract capital, thereby decreasing the capital available for reinvestment in basic industries. This deflection of investment is aggravated by conglomeration and diversification, as old-line basic industries invest in this new area of profit-making. While new service industries create jobs, they do so at the expense of older industries that need retooling; as a consequence, older industries lose their capacity to compete in world markets where tertiary industries are not so well developed.

Finally, and perhaps most important, American production, especially that portion subsidized by tax revenues, has increasingly been devoted to military procurement.[19] The creation of the military-industrial complex has decreased the technical personnel, the tax revenues, and the basic research facilities available to nonmilitary production. Since military products are kept secret, stockpiled, and discarded, they do not expand the economy in the same way as equivalent investments in nonmilitary production. For example, making a better tank does not have the same impact on the general economy as producing a better tractor or truck. While production of the tank and the tractor both create jobs for those who make either product, much of the technology that goes into the tank is kept secret and soon becomes obsolete in the arms race. Moreover, the tractor will be used in other productive activities (farming), whereas the tank will not; as a consequence overall productivity declines. Thus, as the United States has assumed a large portion of the defense and deterrent burden for the "free world," its productive process has been skewed—particularly the vital research, development, and advanced technology sector—away from domestic production, giving those nations that America "protects" a decided economic advantage in world markets. For example, there is an inverse relationship between military expenditures as a proportion of GNP and both the annual rate of capital investment and the rate of growth in manufacturing productivity. That is, the more money devoted to military production, the less domestic productivity is in the nonmilitary sector.[20]

For this long list of reasons, then, it should not be surprising that America's once unassailed economic position in the world is less commanding than in the decades between World War II and the end of the Vietnam War in the 1970s. The very presence of this decline is a cause for potential political action; and thus, it is important to examine the shifting political presence of America in the world system.

America's Changing Place in World Politics

The Growth of the Military-Industrial Complex. In the first half of this century, the United States entered the two world wars initially as an arms supplier, and only after the war was well in progress, as an explicit combatant. This somewhat unique role certainly contributed to those tenets in the culture of domination emphasizing America's obligation to make the world safe for democracy. Yet, after each war, there was rapid demobilization[21] and a consequent return to domestic economic priorities.

In the aftermath of the Korean War, there was demobilization, but with an important difference: the persistence of Cold War and beliefs in the imminent threat of world Communism. Under such conditions of threat, the United States began to develop a peacetime weapons arsenal to combat the threat wherever it might appear. As America's nuclear monopoly was also lost, the sense of threat increased, and a race began to stockpile nuclear weapons. The magnitude of the change is best illustrated by the fact that, in a noninflationary time, the military budget went from 13.3 billion in 1950 (it had been 80.5 billion in the last year of World War II) to 45 billion in 1960.[22]

This change had been anticipated by Presidents Truman and Eisenhower. Truman warned against the bill which allowed for changes in military procurement procedures that, for all practical purposes, suspended competitive bidding for military hardware and NASA contracts:

> This bill grants unprecedented freedom from specific procurement restrictions during peacetime. . . . There is a danger that the natural desire for flexibility and speed in procurement will lead to excessive placement of contracts by negotiation and undue reliance upon large concerns.[23]

Truman's concern over a complex of formal and informal liaisons between administrative branches of the Pentagon, large corporations, and influential members of Congress whose states and districts were heavily involved with defense contractors was given formal expression by President Eisenhower before he left office. Eisenhower labeled this set of liaisons "the military industrial complex"—a label which has persisted to this day.[24]

The growth of the military-industrial complex was fed by the Cold War, by the panic created by the launching of Sputnik, and by the political rhetoric of the presidential campaign in 1960 in which candidate John Kennedy criticized the Republicans for creating a "missile gap" between the U.S. and the USSR. The postulation of such a "gap" was, over the next decades, to become a standard tactic in justifying expenditures for high-technology nuclear warheads, missiles, ships, airplanes, submarines, guidance systems, and anything else needed to close the reported gap.

The noncompetitive system of military procurement, as legitimated by Cold War and later "postulated gap" beliefs, was streamlined under the Kennedy Administration. Liaisons between the Pentagon and defense contractors were rationalized; and the Pentagon itself was structurally reorganized as a quasiprivate corporation that "did business" with other private corporations. The result was a structure much more capable of exerting influence on Congress, the public, and the federal budget.

The significance of the military-industrial complex for both the domestic and the world system is difficult to underestimate. Moreover, its effects on domestic processes have consequences for world system processes, and vice versa.

Militarization and Domestic Processes. There are a number of major domestic consequences of militarization. First, defense spending has contributed to the large budget deficits, the cumulative impact of which affects basic economic processes.[25] Budget deficits do, in the end, cause inflation. More recently, the impact of deficits on monetary stability and interest rates has become evident. And, as has been evident between 1975 and 1984, inflation eventually creates a severe economic recession, especially if efforts to deal with it involve dramatic intervention by the Federal Reserve Board to raise interest rates and control the money supply. An economic recession in America has consequences throughout the world capitalist system. For, since America is the world's largest market, a decrease in demand here adversely affects production in nations which supply the American market. And, as production declines in other nations, they too enter a recession, and demand for American goods in their domestic markets declines, aggravating the recession in America.

A second consequence of large-scale defense spending is that it limits overall productivity. As we noted earlier, the production of military hardware creates jobs, for defense workers; and it generates capital for defense contractors. As these workers spend their money and as capital is reinvested, new jobs are created. Such multiplier effects should not be underestimated, but they are not so great as they could be for nonmilitary production. Nuclear warheads, missiles, sophisticated airplanes, aircraft carriers, and other military hardware are not *used* to create *further productivity* as are a truck, a piece of farm equipment, a machine for a factory, a transportation corridor, a shopping center, etc. That is, besides the multiplier effects of salaries and capital being spent to create jobs for others who, in turn, do the same, there is a multiplier effect created by products that can be used again and again in the processes of an economy. This last kind of multiplier effect is virtually nonexistent in stockpiled military hardware.

A third, and related consequence of heavy military procurement is the diversion of research and development monies, brainpower, and facilities away from the domestic economy. Much military hardware is now extremely sophisticated and requires the development of new technologies and the application of complex engineering and production techniques. However, often these technologies and techniques, besides being kept secret, simply do not have application for nonmilitary production. Thus, as the U.S. and USSR remain in a nuclear arms race, and as efforts are made to develop ever more sophisticated conventional weapons, the government has increasingly subsidized military more than civilian research. For example, between 1970 and 1980, the federal government spent $117 billion on military research, $36 billion on space-related technologies, $79 billion on civilian research.[26] Such disproportionate spending cuts domestic production because military technologies can rarely be used to bolster civilian productivity. But equally important, the spending imbalance places American industry at a disadvantage in the world system. For instance, Japan's government spends virtually no money on military research, and in the last decade, the nations of the European Common Market spent $115 billion for civilian research, only $7 billion for space technologies, and only $36 million on military research.[27] At these rates of relative spending, the great technological advantage that the United States once enjoyed in the world system will decline.

In sum, then, it is clear that military spending has, in net consequences, had adverse affects on domestic economic productivity. This conclusion is supported by the fact that the United States, which is first in military spending, has sunk to seventh in economic-social rank and that the USSR, which is second in military spending, is twenty-third in economic-social rank.[28]

Militarization and World System Processes. Aside from the economic consequences, there are political consequences to militarization. One is that, if a strong military exists, world political problems are likely to be viewed in military terms. Intervention, as opposed to negotiation, becomes more likely, as the recent decades of American interventionism have shown. Such intervention is typically done so that large sectors of the indigenous population are harmed and develop strong resentment toward the United States.

A second consequence is that insurgency movements in developing countries become arenas for the U.S. and the USSR to compete for political gains and, equally often, for their respective "honor." In a nuclear arms race, where by its nature the weaponry is impossible to use, limited wars become arenas to act out mutual hostilities, to test conventional equipment, and to gain at the other's expense.

A third outcome is that, once a military-industrial system exists, it begins to market its products also to other governments. The instruments of war—airplanes, tanks, guns, missiles—are placed in the hands of all governments, which, once they have the weaponry, are also likely to define their problems with neighbors or internal insurgents in military terms. As a result, war and insurgency are constant conditions in most of the world.

A fourth consequence is that as various military powers arm the world, terrorist groups have access to weapons that can disrupt societies to a sufficient degree to create instability, or to the point where governments are forced to step up their repression of citizens. For in the world today, an extremist group, driven by an ideology and a belief in its moral right, can obtain sophisticated weapons and create domestic turmoil far in excess of its popular support. Such groups increasingly make negotiated political solutions impossible, and throw regions of the world into perpetual conflict. Regional battles further polarize the superpowers, who frequently take sides and put their weaponry and prestige on the line.

Finally, as the major nuclear powers build up their arsenals, their sense of threat increases. As their insecurity about "gaps" and "vulnerability" increases, the arms race escalates further. And, while efforts to control nuclear weapons have been made,[29] these have yet to control the stockpiling, much less the proliferation, of nuclear arms. The ultimate consequence of these events could be nuclear annihilation of the planet. Other consequences pale in significance against this prospect. Just how to stop the race and the proliferation remains one of America's, and the world's, most pressing dilemmas.

Chapter 12

Ecological Processes
and Survival

The Dynamics of Ecosystems

Patterns of Interconnection in Ecosystems

Ecosystems involve the relationships among life forms and the inorganic dimensions of the environment.[1] Understanding these relationships is a crucial scientific activity, since the survival of life on earth, including human life, is dependent upon the relations among a large number and variety of plant and animal organisms as well as between these life forms and basic inorganic materials and processes. The nature of these relationships can be conceptualized in terms of three basic kinds of relations: chains, cycles, and flows.

A chain is a sequence of links among life forms. One crucial set of links is the "food chain," in which one species is a food source for another which, in turn, becomes food for yet another species, and so on. Such chains are extensive; in fact, the entire phylogenetic universe can be visualized as a complex series of food chains. When such chains are disrupted, the consequences reverberate up and down the links.

A cycle is a series of interdependencies among organic and inorganic materials that folds back on itself. Some of the most critical cycles revolve around the processes of plant photosynthesis, in which the conversion of the sun's radiant energy into biomass sets in motion a series of cycles that operate to sustain the plants that perform photosynthesis. For example, plants become food for herbivores which, in turn, become food for carnivores, both of which emit the carbon dioxide crucial to plant photosynthesis. Or, the waste residues produced by herbivores and carnivores become food and are essential nutrients for microorganisms, called decomposers, that convert wastes into nutrients for plants engaged in photosynthesis. Thus, the ecosystem can also be visualized as a series of cycles that sustain the circulation of organic and inorganic materials.

A flow is a movement through the ecosystem. The sun's energy flows through the ecosystem in the photosynthetic cycle, but much of this energy is lost as heat, since both plant and animal forms generate heat as they act on inorganic and organic materials. Forces that cause further loss of energy either by cutting off the sun's light or by disrupting the cycles revolving around photosynthesis will also cause great disruption to natural flows in the ecosystem. Other flows revolve around wind and tidal energy, around the passing of minerals through geological processes, and around chains of linkage among organisms. Hence, as with chains and cycles, the ecosystem can be conceptualized as a series of flows as organic and inorganic materials and energy pass through the system.

Of course, chains, cycles, and flows are highly interrelated. Often, the distinction among them depends upon one's focus and purpose. For example, plant photosynthesis as it becomes implicated in a food chain among herbivores and carnivores can be analyzed as a cycle of processes sustaining plant life or as a flow of energy from the sun to the planet and out from the planet as heat. The crucial point in analysis is that each process points to the interrelatedness among species and between species and the inorganic materials of the universe. The complexity of these interdependencies makes the detailed analysis of even a portion of the world's ecosystem difficult. And this fact of interdependence, as sustained by various chains, cycles, and flows, signals the importance of understanding the place of humans and their patterns of sociocultural organization in the web of ecosystem interconnections.

Patterns of Human Organization and the Ecosystem
   One way to simplify the analysis of the relationship between human society and the ecosystem is to focus on the consequences of humans for the capacity of resources to renew themselves. Air, soil, and water are sustained by a variety of chains, cycles, and flows whose detailed operation is beyond the scope of our analysis. But, in a general way we can assess the extent to which human patterns of sociocultural organization disrupt them. To the extent that the rejuvenation of these resources is disrupted, the capacity to sustain human and many other forms of life is correspondingly reduced.
   Figure 12.1 shows the basic dynamics of the relationship between human society and the ecosystem.[2] As is diagramed in the figure, the degree of disruption to renewable resources is tied to the level of waste residues discharged into the environment. In turn, such discharge is a function of the levels and the forms of consumption, economic production, and energy conversion as these are encouraged by patterns of social organization and cultural symbols. Thus, the disruption of renewable resources is connected to sociocultural patterns. If a society's values and beliefs do not emphasize consumption, if patterns of social organization do not require high levels of consumption, then economic production and energy conversion are reduced, the total volume of wastes discharged into the environment is not likely to be harmful, and the depletion of minerals, living resources, and fossil fuels is not likely to be extensive.
   For most of human history, local ecosystems often be-

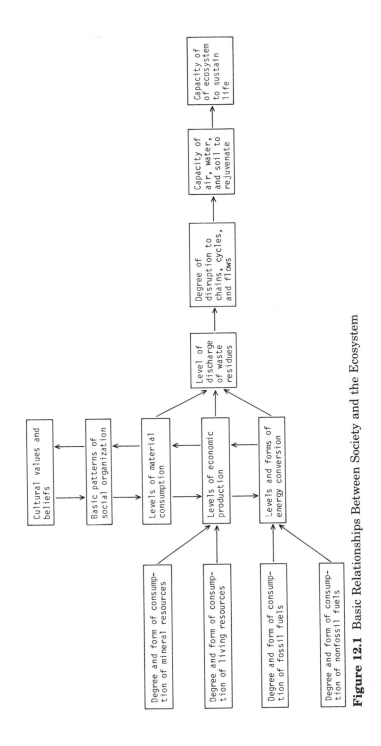

Figure 12.1 Basic Relationships Between Society and the Ecosystem

324 ECOLOGICAL PROCESSES AND SURVIVAL

came depleted, forcing migration and resettlement. But on a larger scale, the world ecosystem was not dramatically altered by wastes. It is only in the last 150 years that cultural beliefs and their attendant patterns of institutional, community, and class organization have changed so as to introduce modes of economic production and energy conversion that discharge high enough volumes of toxic residues to threaten the rejuvenatory capacity of the air, water, and soil.

These changes obviously accompanied the industrial revolution, as new technologies allowed for the harnessing of energy from fossil fuels to machines in order to produce large numbers of goods and commodities. Such changes reflected transformations in the old agrarian social and cultural order in Europe and later elsewhere; but they also accelerated the transformations and shaped the profile of cultural values as well as demographic, institutional, community, and stratification patterns.[3] These changes are represented in figure 12.2.

Industrial societies are guided by beliefs and cultural symbols stressing acquisition, consumption, and materialism. Whether such beliefs ultimately cause or reflect industrial patterns of organization is less important than the recognition that once such symbols and patterns exist they are mutually reinforcing. Social organization into urban communities, stratification systems based upon material displays, and a political economy dependent upon a high GNP all require extensive productive, marketing, and energy-conversion processes. These processes are also mutually reinforcing for each other and for the patterns of social organization and cultural symbols. The result of high levels of gathering, producing, marketing, and energy conversion is the discharge of high levels of waste into the environment.

This discharge disrupts basic food chains by killing off various species; it interrupts critical cycles by altering the flow of radiant energy by polluting the air, disturbing the actions of microorganisms that provide nutrients for the soil, and killing off plant and animal forms necessary for the conversion of carbon dioxide into oxygen. It dramatically alters natural flows of water, air, sediment, and heat through the eco-

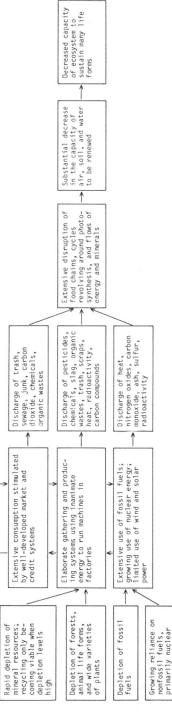

Figure 12.2 American Society and the Ecosystem

The flowchart contains the following boxes and connections:

Cultural values and beliefs emphasizing materialism, acquisition, consumption

→ Social organization into urban communities, stratification systems revolving around displays of material goods and lifestyles, and political economy dependent upon high GNP

→ Extensive consumption stimulated by well-developed market and credit systems

→ Elaborate gathering and producing systems using inanimate energy to run machines in factories

→ Extensive use of fossil fuels; growing use of nuclear energy; limited use of wind and solar power

Rapid depletion of mineral resources; recycling only becoming viable when depletion levels high

Depletion of forests, animal life forms, and wide varieties of plants

Depletion of fossil fuels

Growing reliance on nonfossil fuels, primarily nuclear

Discharge of trash, sewage, junk, carbon dioxide, chemicals, organic wastes

Discharge of pesticides, chemicals, slag, organic wastes, trash, scraps, heat, radioactivity, carbon compounds

Discharge of heat, nitrogen oxides, carbon monoxide, ash, sulfur, radioactivity

→ Extensive disruption of food chains, cycles revolving around photosynthesis, and flows of energy and minerals

→ Substantial decrease in the capacity of air, soil, and water to be renewed

→ Decreased capacity of ecosystem to sustain many life forms

system. The result is for the soil, air, and water to have a lessened capacity to renew themselves.

With respect to air rejuvenation, as toxic chemicals and wastes dumped into lakes and streams find their way to the oceans, there is some degree of disruption to the ocean's phytoplankton, which is responsible for 80 percent of the oxygen that many life forms require. If such disruption reached an unknown threshold point where the microcellular forms comprising the phytoplankton were suddenly destroyed, then we would have a world that would literally choke to death over a twenty-year period. While direct air pollution represents a serious health threat, it is far less critical ecologically than the run-offs of residues from the land and waterways that can potentially destroy the life forms involved in the cycles revolving around the reproduction of air.

In regard to the soil, dumped wastes and extensively used pesticides and chemical fertilizers not only flow into waterways and eventually the ocean; they also kill off microorganisms responsible for aerating and refertilizing the soil. Moreover, pesticides kill off many of the life forms—birds and other insects—that can control the pests which do damage to crops. Currently, there is very little soil in the United States (and increasingly in the world) which is not heavily saturated with pesticides. Since pesticides do not break down for a long period of time, their level of concentration in the soil constantly increases. At some unknown point, it is conceivable that many of the microorganisms critical to the life-sustaining capacity of the soil could be destroyed to such a degree that agricultural production, itself, would be threatened.

With respect to water, the discharge of wastes—from community sewage to industrial sludge—directly contaminates the water and requires the use of ever greater quantities of chlorine to make it safe for human consumption. These toxic wastes also percolate through the soil into the subterranean water table, thereby polluting the sources of well water. As natural flows of water are disrupted by dams and flood projects as well as by the extensive pumping of water up from the ground table for irrigation in chemical-intensive agriculture, the natural cleansing of the water as it flows over and under the ground is disrupted. Moreover, the flow of wastes, chemicals, and sewage into the water kills off many of the microorganisms essential to maintaining the water as a habitat for other life forms. The result, in extreme cases, has been "dead lakes" such as Lake Erie in the United States, where the water can sustain only a limited range of life forms, or highly polluted lakes and waterways that pose a health hazard. Thus, as industrial systems dump large quantities of residues into the water, and at the same time, disrupt the flows and food chains that can clean and sustain the life-supporting capacities of the water, they decrease dramatically the ability of the water to renew itself.

Problems in Assessing Ecological Damage

Because ecosystems are complex webs of interconnection, it is difficult to assess the damage to renewable resources. Such "damage" must be assessed in light of three simple principles.[4]

1. Simplified ecosystems are subject to more rapid change than highly differentiated systems of diverse relations among a wide variety of species. The simplification of ecosystems will thus increase their instability.

2. Alterations in relations of ecosystems will be amplified over time and space, with relatively small changes potentially being amplified into large-scale ecological disruption.

3. The ultimate outcome of changes introduced into ecosystems is difficult to determine owing to time lags. The point of no return in the destruction of an ecosystem can be passed before it is recognized that a destructive and irreversible chain of events has been initiated.

Thus it is difficult to assess just how severe current ecological problems are. It is not presently known how simplified the world's ecosystem has become with the extensive use of single-crop agriculture and chemical pesticides. Nor can the amplified effect of currently observable changes in the quality of water, air, and soil be accurately assessed.

Determination of the lag effects, to say nothing of determining a point of no return, is presently impossible. But sufficient alteration and clear disruption of the ecosystem have occurred to warrant investigation as a basic problem of survival for the human species. And since the United States is the world's most extensive consumer, its largest producer, and its greatest consumer of energy, it should not be surprising that America is also the world's biggest polluter. Indeed, the U.S. has less than 6 percent of the world's population but consumes 35 percent of the world's mineral and energy and is responsible for one-half of the pollutants emitted into the world's ecosystem. To a great extent, then, the problems of the world's ecosystem are tied to the dynamics of American society.

American Society and Ecological Disruption

Cultural Beliefs and Pollution

Because the discharge of wastes is so intimately connected with patterns of consumption and production, ecological disruption is legitimated by a series of beliefs. These beliefs, in turn, reflect on values deeply held by most Americans. We can group these beliefs into four general complexes: (1) beliefs in economic growth and expansion, (2) beliefs in consumption, (3) beliefs in technological progress, and (4) beliefs in the rejuvenative capacity of nature.

1. *Economic growth.* During initial industrialization in America, a belief in growth was perhaps necessary to encourage heavy investment of capital in the productive apparatus. Indeed, such basic values as activism, materialism, and progress provided the moral impetus for such a belief; as a result, the economy became structured around the presumption, "the more the better." This belief was consonant with an underpopulated, early industrial society where renewable resources were plentiful in relation to the total volume of waste. Moreover, a capitalist economy (see chapter 2) cannot be sus-

tained without growth, since the promise of growth and higher profits is what encourages capital investment.

The dilemma posed by this "growth ethic" is severe. On the one hand, it sustains the economic system, while on the other, it legitimates processes that disrupt the ecological system. The dilemma is typically resolved in favor of expanded economic activity, because economic interests, including labor, have more political influence than conservation groups; and because the relative impacts of stalled economic growth are far more immediately evident than ecological disruption (especially in light of the lag and amplification effects which hide the full impact of ecological disruption in the short run).

Yet, the exposure of 2,200 high-priority toxic dump sites in recent years[5] has heightened public awareness of the effects of unrestrained economic activity. Even these debates do not directly address the problem, since it is the "health issue" that is defined as "problematic." In many ways, the health question diverts attention away from the more fundamental issue: disruption of the basic cycles and flows upon which life depends. Thus, the growth ethic is not likely to be seriously challenged as long as concern focuses on health problems of selected populations, since "solutions" will tend to revolve around "clean-ups" and "treatments" as opposed to a more fundamental alteration in the growth premises of the American economy.

2. *Consumption.* Americans value the consumption of ever-increasing quantities and varieties of commodities. Such consumption is considered to generate both progress and prosperity, while being an indicator of people's realization of such values as activism and achievement. The coalescence of these values into a consumption ethic—the belief that increasing consumption is good and proper—was an important force behind America's economic growth. And once a large productive apparatus exists, it has a vested interest in manipulating the value of materialism by stimulating needs for consumption. In turn, such stimulation generates greater economic demand, leading to increased production, and so on, in a consumption-production cycle.

Once begun, the production-consumption cycle is difficult to alter. People come to define their self-worth and station in life in terms of consumption patterns. Economic interests stimulate economic growth by the extension of credit and by advertising that encourages people to structure their psychological and social worlds around consumption. Alternative beliefs that encourage "cutting back" on consumption will, under these circumstances, be viewed with suspicion because they challenge the core of people's day-to-day functioning.

3. *Technological progress.* Traditionally in the American experience, a wide number of problems has had an easy solution: more technology. There is strong belief that the application of more scientific knowledge can meet any challenge. Such a belief reflects basic values of activism in which people are to rationally and efficiently use knowledge to master the environment. The faith in technology is now more problematic than in the past, for it can delay immediate action on ecological problems in the name of "more research" while they intensify to a point where endeavor will be less effective than would be the case if one presumed that no technological solution could be found.

Even today, in the midst of widespread concern over pollution, science is at times seen as the ultimate cure. For example, the problem of generating enough food to feed the world's population has been turned over to the agricultural experts, who, through the selective breeding of grains and intensive use of fertilizers and pesticides, have succeeded in feeding the world *in the short run.* But many have argued that this is being done at a long-range cost of simplifying ecosystems, and hence, creating new problems while forestalling an international program of population control.

At present, there are technological solutions to most pollution problems, but they are costly. And in a capitalist system, there is little incentive to incur increased costs unless government intervenes. But such intervention arouses an ideological debate of its own between private and public interests (see table 2.1). As a consequence, it is often easier to wait for "more advanced technology" and delay use of present technologies.

4. *Rejuvenating nature.* Historically, the capacity of the air, soil, and water to rejuvenate themselves has been impressive. Even in cases where serious pollution has occurred, once environmental control policies are in place, waterways and lakes have made remarkable recoveries. The problem is that such events encourage a belief in "nature's plenty" which can "come back" if given the slightest chance. Such beliefs result from short-term events in microsystems and ignore the long-term consequences of pollution in the macro, world system. They also ignore the lag and amplification effects of micro alterations to the larger ecosystem.

The basic dilemma for the United States is that all over the world, and particularly in the United States, nature has been considered a "free good." No charge has been levied on the use of renewable resources such as air and water to dump refuse. The use of nature as a free good represents a pioneer conception of unbounded, inexhaustible resources that can be used to realize such values as progress. Moreover, in a competitive capitalist system, or in a state-managed system where government is under pressure to increase consumer activities, there are clear incentives to free use of nature.

Beliefs that challenge these practices and argue that renewable resources are a "common good," increasingly in short supply, are likely to go unheeded. Even with increased ecological consciousness, changing beliefs may not be easy. It will cost the public money to visualize nature as a common good: industries will have to pay for their pollution, which in turn will mean that they will raise prices; the federal government will have to engage in expensive monitoring and control of pollution emitted by industries, with the result that federal taxes will be raised; and local communities will have to increase taxes to pay for their pollution and to expand their sewage and garbage treatment facilities. These facts can rather easily be mobilized to counter efforts to alter beliefs toward a conception of nature as a common good whose preservation is in the public interest.

These four belief complexes currently dominate American culture. They shape social action and at the same time are supported by current structural arrangements in the society. This reciprocity between culture and structure makes both highly resistant to change. For as long as beliefs legitimate arrangements that allow Americans to enjoy the good life, change in either the beliefs or the established modes of conduct which they legitimate will be resisted. It is in this sense that disruption of the ecology is a dilemma of structure and culture in America.

Social Structure and Pollution

In analyzing the structure of pollution in America, our attention should focus on the basic social structures which have served as a frame of reference in previous chapters: (1) communities, (2) institutions, and (3) stratification. The ways in which these structures shape human affairs are the ultimate reasons that problems of pollution arise.

Community Structure and Pollution. Urbanization involves the increasing concentration of a population into a relatively small geographical area. In the United States the current population of over 225 million is settled on a little over 1 percent of the land area. Such a high degree of urbanism necessarily causes pollution, for the wastes of millions of people and a large industrial complex are being discharged into a very small ecological space. It is therefore likely that the air, water, and land within any large urban area will be polluted and that ecosystem disruption will be high, perhaps setting off chains of events extending considerably beyond the urban area. Were the American population more geographically dispersed, the degree of *noticeable* air and water pollution would be considerably less. As necessary as geographical dispersion may be for avoiding further ecological damage, however, the current *pattern* of urban organization in America, regardless of population dispersion, will continue to cause ecological problems. It now appears that ways of treating sewage, disposing of wastes, transporting people, supplying energy, raising revenue, and governing urban areas pose serious ecological problems.

The pattern of industrialization within urban areas is one source of ecological problems. During the last century, the first industries tended to settle along major lakes, rivers, and bays. This pattern provided needed power, sources of transportation for materials and goods, and most important, a free dump for wastes, since water was believed to be a plentiful free good. A pattern of urban industrial organization which, with the expansion of industry, was most likely to cause ecological problems was thus established 120 years ago. Just as water was considered a free good, so was the air into which wastes could be ejected in an effort to realize basic values of progress.

Because of this long tradition of using the environment as a refuse dump, solving ecological problems will be difficult. However, a number of alternatives are currently available: (1) closed cycle operations, in which water is treated and recycled through industrial plants; (2) export of wastes to an environment more capable of absorbing them; (3) treatment of effluents, or liquid wastes; and (4) plant abatement, by which manufacturing processes are changed so that no dangerous effluents are emitted into the water and air. The technology for all of these solutions exists and could be used, but it is expensive. And it is this fact which poses a dilemma. To use existing technologies will raise both taxes and prices; but to wait for new technologies or to ignore the problem will cost more in the long run, and potentially, create an ecological crisis which no amount of money can resolve.

The *rate* of urbanization in America has exacerbated ecological problems. As we noted in chapter 10, the United States moved from a rural to urban profile between 1800 and 1860. New York, Philadelphia, Boston, Chicago, St. Louis, and other large cities went from small towns to massive urban complexes in only half a century. Such a rapid rate of urbanization severely burdened the sewage facilities of these urban areas, and they simply dumped untreated organic wastes into adjacent waterways. Even with the adoption of sophisticated treatment methods, many large cities continue to be major sources of water pollution because their drainage systems have been jury-rigged for 100 years. For example, in New

York, Chicago, Cleveland, and many older cities, treatment of wastes is accomplished by interceptor sewers that have been built to catch wastes from the original sewer system and carry it to treatment plants. But during rainy seasons or excessively heavy use, the interceptor sewers are overwhelmed by the water coming from the older system, with the result that untreated sewage overflows into the waterways. Technologically, these problems can be overcome, but the costs to the taxpayer make any change in sewage treatment fiscally and politically difficult.

Initial urbanization in America was accomplished without the automobile, but suburbanization and the creation of the large metropolitan area were, to a great extent, the product of the car. Although the automobile gave people more flexibility in where they could live, its emissions now seriously pollute the urban air. For example, it has been estimated that 75 percent of all carbon monoxide and 50 percent of the sulfur oxides, hydrocarbons, and nitrogen oxides—the ingredients of smog—are emitted by automobiles. As urban areas have been restructured around the car, the implementation of alternative, nonpolluting modes of urban transportation has been made economically infeasible. In Los Angeles, for example, the entire metropolitan area is almost completely dependent on automobile transportation, creating a severe smog problem and making alternative forms of transportation economically difficult. Other large cities are not so dependent on cars, but most urban transportation still revolves around their extensive use.

To attack the pollution generated by the urban structure will require comprehensive political decisions extending across entire metropolitan areas and into rural areas. Unfortunately, as we noted in chapter 10, a pattern of community political decision-making has been established that presently precludes this possibility. American metropolitan areas grew during a period when laissez-faire, states' rights, decentralization of government, and local control were dominant beliefs, with the result that unified political decision-making is most difficult over a large urban region. As long as political power in metropolitan areas remains fragmented among suburban communities surrounding the central city, there will be a lessened political capacity to deal with urban pollution. It will be difficult to have planning, waste standards, industrial waste monitoring and enforcement procedures, land use controls, effluent- and sewage-treatment facilities, and alternatives to automobile transportation systems on a regional level.

Should the federal government, through additional revenue sharing or grants-in-aid, assist this political system in an effort to abate pollution, much of the aid could be lost in duplication of effort and financial squabbles among competing municipalities. To avoid this, it may prove necessary to abandon traditional concepts of urban government, for pollution problems do not end at a community's border. Rather, they extend throughout an urban region and well into its rural fringe. Governmental boundaries may thus have to be established with respect to ecological regions, rather than political units. The fact that such governmental reorganization would violate strong beliefs in local control, as well as established political and economic arrangements, indicates the extent to which pollution problems are built into the culture and structure of community government in America.

In addition to these political dilemmas, American urban communities have what may now be an antiquated revenue-raising system—a system that makes financing pollution control at the metropolitan level impossible. Property taxes are probably not a viable way to generate the massive amounts of capital needed to address pollution problems. Financial solutions will require more than just new sources of revenue; an entirely new system of deriving revenue to finance cities may be required. To use forms of revenue sharing from the federal government to supplement this system will probably be ineffective within the context of the fragmented political structure of urban areas. But to rely on taxes from assessed property is likely to prove inadequate for already burdened cities. As the present financial problems of cities reveal, the entire tax structure in cities will probably have to be revised. Property taxes may have to be supplemented by commuter taxes on those coming into the central city from the suburbs; pollution taxes may have to be assessed on older cars and on industries that produce wastes; tax incentives and rebates may have to be created to encourage industries to move out of urban areas and cut down on their pollutants; sewage treatment costs to the public will probably have to be raised to support research and investment in new sewage systems and treatment facilities; a better formula for sharing state and federal income tax revenues will have to be devised; and most important, all these tax reforms will probably have to be metropolitan instead of confined to local municipalities. Again, while one or two of these reforms are being tried in some urban areas, such an approach is piecemeal and not comprehensive. Without a comprehensive implementation of many reforms, ecological disruption will continue, if not intensify.

In sum, we can see that ecological problems in the United States are intimately connected to current patterns of urban organization. Urbanism per se creates pollution problems, since it concentrates the wastes of large numbers of people and industrial complexes into a small ecological space. Equally significant, however, are the existing forms of urban industrialism, the modes of sewage treatment, the basis of transportation, political organization, the system for raising revenues, and the cultural beliefs legitimating these patterns of organization. Until these features are changed, it is most likely that pollution and ecological disruption will continue to be built into the American community structure.

Pollution and the Stratification System. In absolute terms, the lowest income and poverty groups have a better standard of living than ever. The increase in the standard of living, however, has not been accomplished through a redistribution of the wealth; on the contrary, the poor of today receive no greater a share of the total wealth than they did previously (chapter 7). Their demands for more affluence have, therefore, been met by increased economic output that trickles down the stratification ladder and in the process causes increased industrial pollution. Were the wealth to be redistributed, such increased output and the resulting pollution would not be necessary to meet the demands of the poor to share in American affluence. The United States has thus made the poor more affluent without making the rich poorer.[6]

Respective amounts of pollution vary by social class in American society. The greatest polluters are the affluent, who generate the greatest economic demand (and, hence, stimulate industrial pollution), consume the most polluting goods, and dispose of the majority of nondegradable or nonrecyclable wastes. Yet it is the poor who are most likely to live where land, water, and air have been polluted. Another inequity stems from the fact that programs to eliminate pollution will weigh most heavily on the poor, not the affluent. The affluent are in the vanguard of the ecology movement not only because they are sincerely concerned and mobilized by new beliefs but also because they can afford to be. It is the poor who are likely to have to pay a greater *proportion* of their limited income in the higher prices and taxes that will inevitably result from an attack on America's ecological problems. Furthermore, since it is likely that much of the money to fight pollution will be taken out of the domestic rather than the military budget, the poor will see many of the programs that directly benefit them cut back under future efforts to clean up the environment. As one ghetto resident cynically observed, "friends of the earth are not the friends of the poor." It is therefore not surprising that the poor have been slow to climb on the ecology bandwagon; they have much to lose. The poor also have much to gain from a serious attack on pollution problems, since it is they who tend to live in the most ecologically disrupted areas. But unless the poor are exempted from the costs of such an attack, the fight against pollution could increase inequality in the United States.

Present ecological problems, and their solutions, are thus connected with the stratification system. The affluent are the big polluters, and it is they who can make the sacrifice in income and standard of living that a cleaner environment may require. Until the poor and disfranchised minorities can be assured that monies directed toward the environment are not coming out of domestic programs, they will resist federal and state environmental legislation; and while their power is not great, it is added to other structural roadblocks to pollution control in America.

Pollution and the Institutional Structure. Economic processes in any industrial society have three principle consequences for the environment: (1) they deplete *stock* resources, such as oil, coal, gas, and various metals and minerals; (2) they consume renewable resources, such as air, water, soil, and plant life; and (3) often, as a result of depletion of renewable resources, they disrupt necessary cycles, flows, and energy chains within the ecosystem. While the depletion of stock resources presents short-run economic problems, they are not so serious as is the exhaustion of renewable resources and disruption of the ecosystem. In the long run, substitutes can probably be found for various stock resources, but there is no substitute for life-sustaining resources like air and water, or for those ecological processes upon which human health and food supplies depend.

The exhaustion of renewable resources and ecosystem disruption can be intentional, such as when massive doses of pesticides are dumped onto crops or when the by-products of industries and consumers are emitted as pollutants into the soil, air, and water. Some of this "economic fallout" directly disrupts the environment and then dissipates; but much of it accumulates in the environment, as was the case with DDT and other chlorinated hydrocarbons, so that their impact increases over time. In either instance, it now appears that considerable damage is being done to vital resources and ecological processes.

In accordance with basic values, the American economy is structured around growth and continual expansion, as is revealed by the fact that economic health is now defined as an annual increase in the gross national product. More substantively, full employment, monetary stability, and political processes are intimately connected with continued growth of the economy. Therefore, as we noted earlier, economic enterprises frequently engage in extensive advertising to stimulate desires in the public for more and more goods. Moreover, many industries continually bring out new models of products to instill a sense of psychological obsolescence in the consumer; products are constantly being packaged in "new, more convenient," and often nondegradable ways to stimulate additional consumer demand; manufacturers sometimes build in obsolescence so that goods will self-destruct at a rate compatible with continued economic growth; consumers have been cajoled into thinking that for each task they must perform, from opening a can to making an ice cube, they need a special gadget; an enormous credit industry has emerged to stimulate purchases beyond the immediate capability of consumers; and if such artificially stimulated demand is insufficient to assure growth, appeals are sometimes made to the government to provide a subsidy, impose a protective tariff, or buy surplus goods. All such technqiues for ensuring growth have generated economic prosperity for most Americans, but they have also caused economic fallout. Economic growth means increased energy conversion and hence greater quantities of carbon dioxide, ash, sulfur dioxide, nitrogen oxides, heat, and carbon monoxide. More production creates greater residues of pesticides, fertilizers, slag, chemicals, scrap, and junk. And more consumption will generate increased levels of trash, sewage, and carbon monoxide. At the same time, however, economic growth increases employment; and as recent recessions have disclosed, a drop in the rate of growth, or even an actual decrease in growth, produces severe unemployment and other economic dislocations. Thus, the stability of the present structure of the American economy, and the fate of many workers, now depends upon growth, setting into bold relief one of America's most difficult dilemmas: environmental stability versus economic stability. At present, it appears that, in the absence of visible ecological catastrophies, economic stability is preferred over ecological stability by both the public and political decision-makers. Many times, of course, the two issues may not come into conflict, but more often than not, there is a clear conflict between these two desirable goals.

Government efforts to control pollution must be viewed as being between the horns of this dilemma. While stricter governmental controls could probably cut down dramatically on the amount of economic fallout, more extreme measures may be necessary to stop agricultural and industrial pollution. Economic growth would probably have to be drastically slowed down, since it is likely that with continued economic expansion the benefits of increased government regulation of pollutants would be negated by increased energy conversion, production, and consumption. To slow the rate of growth would require some far-reaching adjustments within the economy. For example, in the face of population growth, full employment within the structure of the existing economy may be impossible, and as a consequence, new ways, from outright welfare to governmental subsidies and "make work" projects, might have to be devised to get income to people so that they could buy products and hence maintain the economy. A new system of corporate taxation would probably be necessary to derive the revenue required by the nonworking populace. America's habits of consumption would also have to change: people would have to get used to recyclable and degradable packaging, planned resistance to obsolescence, and fewer gadgets. To effect these changes in consumption habits would, in turn, require more government control of the market to regulate demand and supply of only those goods that would improve the quality of life and the environment. Yet, the very fact that these solutions to economic pollution would probably cause severe short-term, perhaps even long-term, economic and perhaps political disruption emphasizes the built-in roadblocks to easy ecological solutions. Further, such changes would go against deep-seated beliefs of many Americans in growth and consumption.

The existence of such roadblocks would thus require more "practical" but probably less effective solutions to ecological problems. While only a stopgap measure, one short-term approach would be for the government to subsidize (as it has done for many industries, such as the railroads and airlines) a waste recovery industry that could recycle many of the current residues back into the economy. However, recycling should not be viewed as a cure-all for problems of industrial pollution. From figures 12.1 and 12.2, it should be clear that the wastes generated in energy conversion and in many productive processes are not recyclable. Federal standards limiting emissions of nonrecyclable wastes would certainly improve the pollution picture. But it is improbable that all these wastes could be eliminated; and with rapid economic growth, the impact of federal regulation could prove minimal. Government subsidy of pollution-fighting industries and the strict regulation of emissions may not be the panacea that many experts believe them to be. The government may have to limit economic growth, and at the same time, cope with the economic and social problems stemming from such a radical alteration of the economy.

To change the economy, however, will require that the public find ways to overcome the power of economic interests and/or build its own base of power. The largest and most powerful corporations in America emit the most wastes and produce the most polluting products, such as cars and gasoline. Given the current structure of the American government, these corporations are able to press their interests more effectively than the public or environmental groups. Despite the impressive proecology advertising campaigns mounted by industrial corporations (another indicator of their power to shape public opinion), they will quite naturally continue to lobby against any pollution legislation that would threaten their profits. Thus, the narrow interests but enormous political power of America's corporations represent yet another major obstacle to pollution control.

Ultimately, control of pollutants will be done by administrative agencies operating under regulatory laws. The laws presently on the books are only partially effective, and formulating future pollution control laws will present problems.

One difficulty lies in the lack of a legal tradition supporting environmental law. It was well into the twentieth century before serious conservation laws were enacted in America. The Bureau of Reclamation was established at about the turn of the century, and the National Park Service was expanded, stimulating the passage of limited numbers of conservation laws by state and federal governments. It was not until the Dust Bowl of the 1930s, however, that legislators began to realize the dangers of unregulated use of renewable resources; with this realization came the enactment of the Soil Conservation Act. After this promising beginning, however, the thousands of conservation laws enacted over the last forty years have proved, by and large, ineffective in dramatically abating ecological disruption. Even a cursory review of the federal codes and statutes reveals that most "conservation" laws are an "administrative handbook" telling corporations and individuals how to apply for permission to extract resources. With some noticeable exceptions, the laws do not prevent harmful extraction.

With this short and largely ineffective legal tradition, it is not surprising that recent laws have suffered from defects.

1. Traditional conservation laws and more recent antipollution laws are often phrased in ambiguous language. Given the court system's traditional favoritism toward economic interests, state and federal agencies charged with enforcing vague laws are naturally reluctant to press charges or take violators to court for fear that even these weak laws, and perhaps the agency's very function, will be invalidated.

2. Existing antipollution laws typically mandate weak civil penalties and hardly ever carry criminal sanctions. Companies faced with relatively minor fines tend to view pollution penalties as just another cost to be absorbed and passed on to the consumer in the form of higher prices. It may be that, until companies are confronted with criminal penalties and heavy civil damages, antipollution laws will not be effective in preventing ecological disruption. The most comprehensive, unambiguous federal antipollution law ever en-

acted, the Clean Air Act of 1970, carries no criminal penalties. As recent events have underscored, even this clearly written law can be weakened as corporations exert pressure upon legislators. If the Clean Air Act can be circumvented, then weaker pieces of federal legislation will probably prove even less effective, especially when the government is subjected to pressure by corporations seeking to avoid higher costs and a public reluctant to pay higher prices and taxes.

3. The vast majority of laws do not address the sources of pollution; they require treatment of pollutants *after* they have been created. For example, because there are few state laws prohibiting the use of phosphates and other chemicals in consumer products, the burden of cleaning the water into which these chemicals are dumped must fall upon sewage treatment facilities. To take a further example, the Clean Air Act did not specify that the internal combustion engine must be replaced but only that the emissions from this engine must be reduced.

4. Finally, many state antipollution laws are enacted with "grandfather clauses" which allow established industries to continue their harmful activities. One result is to encourage outmoded and highly polluting industries to stay in an area, while discouraging the new industries which must utilize expensive antipollution equipment from becoming established. In the end, such laws often perpetuate the very industrial processes that they were designed to discourage.

This ineffectiveness of antipollution laws is compounded by inducements to polluting found in other types of legal statutes. Present tax codes, for example, sometimes encourage unnecessary pollution; traditional depletion allowances, which allow corporations extracting resources to deduct from their taxes the "depletions" of these resources, encourage rapid and sometimes wasteful resource extraction to obtain the highest depletion allowance. Property tax laws also support depletion allowances by allowing lower assessed evaluations for land as resources are extracted, once again providing a potential inducement to careless and rapid extraction. Even when corporations are found liable for their pollutants, they are, under some circumstances, allowed to deduct as a business expense the cost of cleaning up their effluents; and under some state statutes, even legally imposed fines for pollution can be deducted as a business expense. These laws encourage pollution by offering incentives for wasteful resource extraction and by mitigating the costs incurred by companies that disrupt the environment.

In sum, then, it must be reluctantly concluded that the present legal structure in America cannot control the pollution of the environment. The many state and federal conservation codes often facilitate as much as inhibit harmful resource extraction; tax laws sometimes provide incentives for pollution, rather than the reverse; and explicit antipollution codes are sometimes circumvented by political pressures from the polluters and an economically squeezed public. To overcome these problems, a comprehensive national body of laws carrying severe criminal and civil penalties will probably be necessary. This new federal body of law will have to involve piecemeal legislative acts, for a writing and rewriting of pollution, conservation, and tax laws will probably prove necessary. If present trends continue, there may come a time when the environment cannot be protected through the current maze of state and federal codes whose ambiguities, conflicts, and overlaps have made legal solutions to ecological problems problematic.

What may be needed from federal legislators is a set of clear *national* quality standards for the air, soil, and water, with no region in America being allowed to tolerate pollution levels exceeding these standards. Aside from the reluctance of federal legislators to enact such bold legislation, however, there are fundamental problems with setting such standards. What level of pollution is tolerable? At what point does pollution begin to harm the ecosystem? What are the short-run versus the long-run consequences of various pollutants? These are difficult questions to answer, for despite the heightened scientific concern with ecological problems, there is much ignorance with respect to the impact of pollutants on the environment. This lack of knowledge places legislators in the position of setting standards without clear scientific guidelines.

In such a state of ignorance, legislators will tend to avoid enacting wide-ranging laws, or if they do enact laws, they will write ambiguities into them. For example, the Water Quality Act of 1965 established rather vague water quality standards that could be voided upon "due consideration to the practicability and to the physical and economic feasibility of complying with such standards . . . as the public interest and equities of the case may require." Given many courts' sympathetic attitude toward communities and industries, the Water Quality Act has proven difficult to enforce. Arguments are rather easily made that pollutants serve the public interest by keeping taxes low or providing jobs for workers in polluting industries.

The only significant piece of legislation which explicitly sought to redress these deficiencies was the Clean Air Act of 1970. In this act, tolerable emissions were specified, and explicit deadlines were set for compliance with these standards. The auto makers have been granted several extensions, and currently, with the fear that more economic dislocation will result from enforcement of the standards, there is considerable pressure to suspend or weaken the law. If unambiguous standards for clean air cannot be enforced, similar standards probably cannot be set for emissions into the soil and water which, in both the short and the long run, pose a more serious threat to the ecosystem than air pollution. But pollution of the soil and water is not so observable as air pollution, and thus, not so disturbing to the public. Equally significant, the interaction of pollutants with the water and soil is more complex than with the air, so that legislators will not know just what standards to establish.

If we nevertheless assume that minimal quality standards for the air, water, and soil could be enacted, the next legislative problem is how to induce communities and industries to pay for *all* remaining pollutants that they discharge into the environment. Laws in this area provide that the more pollutants emitted in excess of minimum standards, the more offenders must pay in penalties; and when offenders are corporations, the more they must pay in fines which cannot be passed on to consumers. Such laws might serve as incentives for industries to clean up the last of their harmful effluents. Before this kind of law can be enacted, however, legislators must determine how to create the formulas for assigning these costs. As we have already noted, there is considerable ignorance as to how pollutants interact with each other in different environments over varying lengths of time to cause varying degrees of harm to different ecosystems. How, then, are costs for emissions into the air, water, and soil to be assessed? Yet, unless tentative legislative efforts are made to construct these formulas, industries and communities will have few incentives to restrict effluents.

To further remove current inducements for pollution, broad programs of laws may be necessary. It would seem necessary that depletion allowances and lowered tax assessments for harmful resource extraction be stricken from federal and state laws. Accompanying the elimination of these incentives to pollute should come laws encouraging research on pollution control and installation of emission control devices. One approach would involve high tax write-offs for antipollution activities, although any such law would have to be monitored carefully by the Internal Revenue Service to prevent industries from simply renaming research in unrelated areas, "antipollution development." Another strategy might create laws requiring polluting companies to reinvest a certain percentage of their profits into effluent control, while at the same time, preventing these corporations from passing their increased costs on to consumers. However, all such approaches would further complicate the tax system, which, as we saw in chapter 7, has created other problems of inequality.

To add weight to such laws, and to aid in their enactment where legislative bodies hesitate, some have proposed a constitutional amendment containing an Environmental Bill of Rights. Bringing industrywide and class action suits against polluters is presently most difficult because there are few unambiguous legal doctrines that can provide the necessary precedents. In this relative legal vacuum, the doctrine of "balance of equities" now guides many pollution suits. This doctrine charges the courts to consider the "good" consequences (a clean environment) against the "bad" effects (higher taxes and unemployment, for example) of rules favoring environmentalists. Often the courts rule that the economic benefits of pollution outweigh the alleged costs to personal health and the ecology. A constitutional amendment could rebalance legal precedent in favor of the environment.

The law, therefore, can be both a tool to deal with pollution problems and a roadblock to resolving them. We have emphasized the obstacles in order to highlight the extent to which pollution is built into the present legal system in America. Such need not necessarily be the case, of course, but calculating ecological damage and writing pollution control formulas present formidable obstacles to those who seek to write effective laws. Coupled with the economic, social, and political dislocations that the enforcement of such laws would have, the problems of using law as a tool for pollution control become even more acute. These problems may indeed be surmountable; but to prevent ecological disruption they will need to be attacked with political resolve. Such resolve will reflect the priorities, decision-making processes, and administrative capacities of the federal government.

To seriously address environmental problems will probably require a reordering of national priorities. The costs of a comprehensive environmental program will be enormous, perhaps as much as $50 billion per year for a decade just to reverse present environment disruptions, and close to that amount thereafter to maintain restored ecological balances in the face of an expanding economy. The sources of expense are many: tax incentives for polluters will be expensive and inevitably raise federal, state, and local taxes; revenue sharing and grants-in-aid to cities attempting to revamp sewage systems will cost a great deal; and the large federal bureaucracy needed to implement, monitor, and enforce antipollution codes will also be expensive.

Conflicting with these needs are the ever-increasing revenue demands in the domestic sphere. For example, welfare costs will continue to rise; proposed national health care systems will be expensive; education costs are likely to continue to increase; law enforcement costs will not remain stable; perpetuation of agricultural and industrial subsidies will continue to drain federal revenues; foreign aid will remain high; and the total revenue needs of the executive departments will expand. While considerable revenue can be raised from closing tax loopholes, raising corporate and individual taxes, and expanding the economy, and hence, tax revenues, it appears that it will still be necessary to reorder national priorities to generate the large sums needed to preserve the ecology.

If the nation is to maintain current standards of living *and* address pollution problems, the only available source of revenue is the Pentagon's budget. Currently, the military and related agencies receive at least 35 percent (probably closer to 50 percent in indirect subsidies) of all federal tax revenues, making them the largest single source of nondomestic funds. To maintain the present military budget *and* address pollution problems would require drastic increases in taxes; or, to maintain the military budget, keep taxes down, and still attack pollution problems would probably involve, for example, poorer schools, expensive private health care, less police protection, widespread poverty, continued urban decay, and inadequate transport systems. The political influence of the Pentagon, and the corporations and labor organizations receiving its contract dollars, is great. This situation underscores the dilemma of addressing ecological problems, for unless the military budget can be tapped, Americans will have higher taxes and lessened social services. The public is not likely to accept these, while the military is not likely to accept drastic budget cuts. When these political problems are compounded by the economic consequences of reordered priorities—short-term unemployment for workers and falling stock prices for the owners of corporations doing business with the Pentagon—then the difficulties of changing priorities to maintain the ecology become even more pronounced.

Even if Congress could change priorities and enact comprehensive quality standards for the air, water, and soil, a new set of political obstacles would probably emerge, given the present pattern of government administration in America. As was emphasized in chapter 3, the United States is a federalist political system with considerable power residing in city, county, and state governments. While there are many advantages to such a system, a problem with all types of national legislation is the coordination of city, county, and state governments with the federal agencies that administer national legislation. It is perhaps inevitable, in a federalist system, and perhaps desirable from one viewpoint, that state and local governments have conflicting interests, but one less positive result is to make implementation of national legislation difficult. In order to avoid conflicts among and between various levels of government, it may be necessary for anti-pollution agencies to have considerable power over local governments. However, existing government agencies, state and local government, well-organized interests, and the public are likely to resist the allocation of such power. There are many sound reasons for resisting the concentration of power in administrative agencies, but without this power, it is more difficult to cut through the rivalries of diverse bodies and effectively implement national pollution control.

Another problem with the current pattern of administration in America is that, even when they have considerable power, agencies frequently fail to enforce regulatory laws. One type of misregulation involves failure to maintain quality standards. For example, the U.S. Department of Agriculture has, on numerous occasions, not enforced bans and limitations on the use of certain dangerous pesticides. A second source of misregulation is the undue influence on federal agencies by those very industries they are established to regulate. For instance, the Department of Agriculture is frequently an advocate of the chemical pesticide industry. The public record reveals quite clearly that it has consistently encouraged the use of pesticides, while underemphasizing research on and use of alternative forms of pest control. A third source of administrative incompetence can be seen in the reluctance of agencies to argue for tougher standards where the standards are weak or ambiguous. Sometimes the reason for this reluctance is that if agencies pushed for tougher standards, they could expose their previous laxity in enforcement. A final administrative obstacle to implementation of regulatory law can be seen in the reluctance of existing agencies to use even the limited sanctions at their disposal. Should an agency finally take action against an offending industry or community, it usually secures a cease-and-desist order which requires the violator to stop its illegal activities. Most typically, only after such an order has been ignored will minimal (rarely maximum) civil penalties be sought by regulatory agencies.

This pattern of administration now appears to be well institutionalized, with the result that its failings will likely continue even if antipollution laws are enacted. The current Environmental Protection Agency will probably be less successful than anticipated in avoiding such administrative problems. A "supra-agency" with power over all other agencies in the federal government might well be necessary for effective enforcement of antipollution laws. Establishing an agency with such wide authority, however, will create many problems. One of them will be opening and maintaining lines of authority to other executive departments in the federal government, as well as to state and local governments. For at a minimum, a supra-agency will probably require authority over the departments of Health, Education, Commerce, Interior, Agriculture, Transportation, and Housing and Urban Development. In light of the history of rivalry, duplication of effort, and jealousy among these agencies, it will be difficult to create a new agency with authority over all of them. Various departments would probably oppose the creation of this supra-agency in the first place, and undermine its effectiveness should it be created. In July 1970, President Nixon formed the Environmental Protection Agency to consolidate pollution control policy and activity, but the record of the last 15 years on enforcement of the unambiguous Clean Air Act, and more recently, the toxic waste "superfund," reveals that it has had a difficult time asserting authority over other executive departments, to say nothing of private interests. If this situation is to prove typical, then the difficulties in the administration of environmental law will be compounded.

The prognosis, then, for an effective administration of antipollution laws reveals many problems, most of which inhere in the current structure of government in America. These problems are exacerbated by the complexities of the task with which an environmental agency would be charged. Laws cannot simply prohibit the emission of all pollutants, for such a prohibition is not economically, politically, or socially possible. A more reasonable approach is that a way must be devised to induce polluters to cut back their harmful activities even when they do not exceed minimum standards. This inducement can come only by requiring polluters to pay for all their emissions within the tolerable limits of national quality standards. As was emphasized earlier, there are problems with writing legal formulas for determining what the costs should be, since understanding of the short- and long-run consequences of pollutants to the ecosystem is far from complete. The administrative problems involved in just creating the accounting system represents a roadblock to monitoring and controlling pollution in America. Moreover, the governmental agency charged with enforcing what initially—in light of current ignorance—would be somewhat arbitrary cost formulas will quite naturally be resisted by industry and communities. One result could be endless legal battles as polluters seek to document that their pollutants should not cost so much as existing formulas claim.

In evaluating the political capacity of the United States to regulate its emissions into the ecosystem, then, it is clear that there are a number of structural obstacles. The reordering of national priorities in the direction of environmental protection will be difficult owing to the Pentagon's power. And even should these obstacles be surmounted, the pattern of government administration in America reveals another set of problems that could reduce effective environmental protection. While these same conditions may have positive outcomes for some sectors of the society, they represent a severe dilemma in how to begin resolving the problem of ecological disruption.

Survival of the Species: The Ultimate Dilemma

Humans are multiplying at an increasing rate. From 1850 to 1930, the world population doubled, from one to two billion. Currently the world's population is estimated at 4.6 billion and by the year 2020 will double again. A rapidly expanding population poses a problem for ecological balances, since it creates ever-increasing demands for industrial and agricultural goods. In the agricultural sector of the economy, the demand for food causes the use of the pesticides and chemical fertilizers that kill many organisms necessary for life-sustaining energy flows and mineral cycles. Moreover, in order to keep abreast of growing demand, single-crop or a limited-rotation agriculture becomes necessary. Such agricultural techniques strip the ecosystem of the natural stability arising from diversity, while at the same time making crops extremely vulnerable to pests and disease. In turn, this susceptibility intensifies reliance upon pesticides and various chemical killers. Thus, the short-run demands for agricultural products created by an expanding population can force a pattern of agricultural production that could decrease the soil's capacity to feed the human species in the long run.

In the industrial sector of the economy, population growth escalates demand for consumer goods, which increases the discharge of pollutants into the air, soil, and water. This demand is likely to be particularly severe as the "revolution of rising expectations" among populations of Third World nations stimulates the production of increased numbers and varieties of industrial goods. And, since such societies are often politically unstable, it is unlikely that their governments can divert resources to pollution control.

Thus, the world is faced with the specter of an expanding and expectant population. For as more mature industrial systems seek solutions to pollution problems, the Third and Fourth World will demand the consumer goods which will dramatically increase the discharge of waste residues that are, to an unknown degree, disrupting the ecosystem. While America and other industrial societies are largely responsible for the world's pollution today, they will be joined by the industrializing world of tomorrow. If the nations of the world do not destroy the species through nuclear war, then ecological disruption, and the slow death to the species that this would entail, will become our greatest problem of survival. And it will pose a dilemma not only for America but for all humans as well.

Notes

1. The Cultural and Organizational Basis of Human Dilemmas

1. See Jonathan H. Turner and Leonard Beeghley, *The Emergence of Sociological Theory* (Homewood, Ill.: Dorsey Press, 1982).

2. Max Weber, *Economy and Society,* ed. Guenther Roth and Claus Wittich (Berkeley: University of California Press, 1978).

3. Karl Marx and Friedrich Engels, *The Communist Manifesto* (1848; New York: International Publishers, 1971).

4. Emile Durkheim, *The Division of Labor in Society* (1893; New York: Free Press, 1947), esp. the "Preface to the Second Edition" (1904 edition).

5. Karl Marx. *Capital: A Critical Analysis of Capitalist Production* (1867; New York: Random House, 1978).

6. Talcott Parsons, *The Social System* (New York: Free Press, 1951).

7. See, for useful discussions, Sheldon Stryker, *Symbolic Interactionism* (Menlo Park, Calif.: Cummings, 1980); Erving Goffman, *Interaction Ritual: Essays in Face to Face Behavior* (New York: Anchor, 1967).

8. Robin M. Williams, Jr., *American Society: A Sociological Interpretation,* 2d ed. (New York: Knopf, 1970), pp. 438–500.

9. Jonathan H. Turner and Charles Starnes, *Inequality: Privilege and Poverty in America* (Santa Monica: Goodyear, 1976), pp. 66–68.

10. This was, of course, the dilemma posed by Adam Smith in *An Inquiry into the Nature and Causes of the Wealth of Nations* (1776; New York: Random House, 1937). And this dilemma formed the basis for Emile Durkheim's sociology.

11. For an in-depth analysis, see Jonathan H. Turner, *Patterns of Social Organization* (New York: McGraw-Hill, 1972).

12. Amos Hawley, *Human Ecology* (New York: Ronald Press, 1950).

13. See Jonathan H. Turner, *Societal Stratification: A Theoretical Analysis* (New York: Columbia University Press, 1984).

14. For a useful analysis of sex and age conflicts, see Randall Collins, *Conflict Sociology* (New York: Academic Press, 1976), pp. 225–84.

15. For a more detailed discussion, see Jonathan H. Turner, "The Eco-system: The Relationship Between Nature and Society," in D. Zimmerman, L. Weider, S. Zimmerman, eds., *Understanding Social Problems* (New York: Praeger, 1976).

16. This discussion borrows from Williams, *American Society*.

17. And that is all we can do: guess and estimate. There are no hard data on the issue.

2. The Contradictions of Capitalism

1. Jonathan H. Turner, *Patterns of Social Organization* (New York: McGraw-Hill, 1972), pp. 17–80.

2. Ibid.; see also Jonathan H. Turner, "A Cybernetic Model of Economic Development," *Sociological Quarterly* (Spring 1971), 12:191–203.

3. Karl Marx, *Capital* (1867; New York: Random House, 1978).

4. Karl Marx and Friedrich Engels, *The Communist Manifesto* (1848; New York: International Publishers, 1971).

5. Marx and Engels, *Communist Manifesto*.

6. Bruno Ramirez, *When Workers Fight* (Westport,. Conn.: Greenwood Press, 1978); P. Taft and P. Rose, "American Labor Violence: Its Causes, Character, and Outcome," in H. O. Graham and T. R. Gurr, eds., *Violence in America* (New York: Bantam Books, 1969), pp. 380–82.

7. Adapted from Jonathan H. Turner, *American Society: Problems of Structure* (New York: Harper and Row, 1976) and *Social Problems in America* (New York: Harper and Row, 1976).

8. Work on the "military-industrial complex" has declined in recent years—an interesting fact in itself. But some of the original analyses are still relevant. For example, see Seymour Melman, *Pentagon Capitalism: The Political Economy of War* (New York: McGraw-Hill, 1970); A. Yarmolinsky, *The Military Establishment* (New York: Harper and Row, 1971). Also see special supplement, "Servants or Masters: Revisiting the Military Industrial Complex," *Los Angeles Times,* July 10, 1983, 6:1–15.

9. Employment Research Associates, Lansing, Michigan, 1982. This study used Defense Department procurement figures and Bureau of Labor Statistics impact figures for 156 industries.

10. Robert W. DeGrasse, Jr., *Military Expansion, Economic Decline* (New York: Council on Economic Priorities, 1983).

11. For examples and analyses of these processes, see Jules Abels, *The Rockerfeller Billions* (New York: Macmillan, 1965); Morton Grad, *How Rockerfeller Built the Standard Oil Company* (Girard, Kan.: Haldeman-Julius, 1931); Mathew Josephson, *The Robber Barons* (New York: Harcourt Brace Jovanovich, 1962); E. K. Hunt and Howard J. Sherman, *Economics,* 3d ed. (New York: Harper and Row, 1978), pp. 85–87; M. Green, B. C. Moore, and B. Wasserstein, *The Closed Enterprise System* (New York: Bantam, 1972); Paul Sweezy and Paul Boman, *Monopoly Capital* (New York: Monthly Review Press, 1966).

12. See note 6.

13. Marx and Engels, *Communist Manifesto;* Marx, *Capital*.

14. For illustrative data see Studs Terkel, *Working* (New York: Pantheon, 1974); U.S. Congress, Senate, Committee on Labor and Public Welfare, *Worker Alienation* (Washington, D.C.: Government Printing Office, 1972). For an extreme critique, see Harry Braverman, *Labor and Monopoly Capital: The Degradation of Work in the Twentieth Century* (New York: Monthly Review Press, 1974). For a more bal-

anced view, see Irving Howe, ed., *The World of the Blue-Collar Worker* (New York: Quadrangle, 1972).

15. Membership in labor unions increased dramatically during the first half of this century, peaked in the mid 1950s, and has declined somewhat in recent decades to about 20 percent of the total work force. See U.S. Department of Labor, *Handbook of Labor Statistics* (Washington, D.C.: Government Printing Office, 1980).

16. For some basic references on inflation and its causes, see John Blair, ed., *The Roots of Inflation* (New York: Franklin, 1975). For a more radical perspective, see Howard J. Sherman, *Stagflation: A Radical Theory of Unemployment and Inflation* (New York: Harper and Row, 1976).

17. Blair, *Roots of Inflation;* see also John A. Garraty, *Unemployment in History* (New York: Harper and Row, 1978); Dixon Wecter, *The Age of the Great Depression: 1929–1941* (Chicago: Quadrangle Books, 1971); Howard H. Sherman, *Radical Political Economy* (New York: Basic Books, 1972) and *Profits in the United States: An Introduction to a Study of Economic Concentration and Business Cycles* (Ithaca, N.Y.: Cornell University Press, 1968).

3. The Dialectic Between Democracy and Governance

1. Jonathan H. Turner, *Patterns of Social Organization* (New York: McGraw-Hill, 1972).

2. For representative samples, see Charles H. Anderson, *The Political Economy of Social Class* (Englewood Cliffs, N.J.: Prentice-Hall, 1974); Peter Berger, ed., *Marxism and Sociology: Views from Eastern Europe* (New York: Appleton-Century, 1969); Lewis A. Coser, ed., *Political Sociology: Selected Essays* (Evanston, Ill.: Harper and Row, 1967); Randall Collins, *Conflict Sociology* (New York: Academic Press, 1975); Peter M. Blau, "Critical Remarks on Weber's Theory of Authority," *American Political Science Review* (June 1963), 57:305–16; C. Wright Mills, *The Power Elite* (New York: Oxford University Press, 1950); Scott Greer and Peter Orleans, "Political Sociology," in E. L. Faris, ed., *Handbook of Modern Sociology* (Chicago: Rand McNally, 1964); Seymour M. Lipset, "Political Sociology," in R. K. Merton, L. Brown, and L. S. Cottrell, eds., *Sociology Today* (New York: Basic Books, 1959); Morris Janowitz, "Political Sociology," in *International Encyclopedia of the Social Sciences* (New York: Macmillan, 1968); Robert Dahl, "Power," in *International Encyclopedia of the Social Sciences.*

3. This definition is closest to Max Weber's definition in *Economy and Society,* ed. G. Roth and C. Wittich (Berkeley: University of California Press, 1978), pp. 212–99.

4. Herbert Spencer, *The Principles of Sociology* (1874; New York: D. Appleton, 1885); Peter M. Blau, "A Formal Theory of Differentiation in Organizations," *American Sociological Review* (April 1970), 35:201–18.

5. Spencer, *Principles;* Georg Simmel, "The Sociology of Conflict," *American Journal of Sociology* (1903–4), 9:490–525; "Conflict" in K. Wolff, ed., *Conflict and the Web of Group Affiliations* (New York: Free Press, 1955).

6. Gerhard Lenski, *Power and Privilege: A Theory of Stratification* (New York: McGraw-Hill, 1966).

7. Simmel, "Sociology of Conflict."

8. This was, of course, Karl Marx's great contribution to sociological analysis.

9. Weber, *Economy and Society.*

10. Emphasis is on the *relative centralization* of power.

11. General commentaries on the political process in America tend to overemphasize its lack of representativeness and responsiveness. Such views are more ideological than real, since compared with most political systems, the American is amazingly open to input from public opinion, local constituencies, and vested interests.

12. Jonathan H. Turner, *Social Problems in America* (New York: Harper and Row, 1976), pp. 124–30.

13. Consult the Congressional Budget Office's annual report on the budget for the years 1940, 1950, 1960, 1970, and 1980 for relevant comparisons (Washington, D. C.: Government Printing Office).

14. Quincy Wright, *A Study of War* (Chicago: University of Chicago Press, 1942).

4. Control in a Free Society

1. George B. Vold and Thomas J. Bernard, *Theoretical Criminology,* 2d ed. (New York: Oxford University Press, 1979), pp. 381–84.

2. Harry Elmer Barnes and Negley K. Teeters, *New Horizons in Criminology,* 3d ed. (Englewood Cliffs, N.J.: Prentice-Hall, 1959), pp. 38–49; Edwin H. Sutherland, *White Collar Crime* (New York: Dryden, 1949); "Corporate Crime: The Untold Story," *U.S. News and World Report* (September 6, 1982), pp. 25–30; Daniel R. Fusfeld, "The Rise of the Corporate State in America," *Journal of Economic Issues* (March 1972), 6:1–23; and David R. Simon and D. Stanley Eitzen, *Elite Deviance* (Boston: Allyn and Bacon, 1982).

3. See, for example, *Uniform Crime Reports, 1983* (Washington, D.C.: Government Printing Office, 1984).

4. See, for example, Edward C. Banfield, *The Unheavenly City Revisited* (Boston: Little, Brown, 1974), pp. 183–85; and James O. Wilson, *Thinking About Crime* (New York: Basic Books, 1975).

5. Leonard Savitz, *Dilemmas in Criminology* (New York: McGraw-Hill, 1967), p. 68; Gresham M. Sykes, *Criminology* (New York: Harcourt, Brace Jovanovich, 1978), pp. 366–79.

6. E. Cumming, I. Cumming and L. Edell, "Polceman as Philosopher, Guide, and Friend," *Social Problems* (Winter 1965).

7. Jerome Skolnick, *The Politics of Protest* (New York: Simon and Schuster, 1969).

8. See J. H. McNamara, "Uncertainties in Police Work: The Relevance of Police Recruits' Background Training," in David Bordua, ed., *The Police: Six Sociological Essays* (New York: Wiley, 1967); and A. Niederhoffer, *Behind the Shield in Urban Society* (Garden City, N.Y.: Doubleday, 1968).

9. Jerome Skolnick, *Justice Without Trial* (New York: Wiley, 1966), pp. 238–39.

10. See Edwin Sutherland and Donald R. Cressey, *Criminology,* 10th ed. (Philadelphia: Lippincott, 1982), for data on plea bargaining here and in the following paragraph.

11. Lewis Katz, Lawrence Litwin, and Richard Bamberger, eds., *Justice is the Crime: Pretrial Delay in Felony Cases* (Cleveland, Ohio: Case Western Reserve University Press, 1972).

12. Peter Greenwood et al., *Prosecution of Adult Felony Defendants in Los Angeles County—A Policy Perspective* (Washington, D.C.: Government Printing Office, 1973).

13. A. Blumberg, *Criminal Justice* (Chicago: Quadrangle Books, 1970), pp. 56–57.

14. Ibid., pp. 122–23.

15. S. Swank, "Home Supervision: Probation Really Works," *Federal Probation,* (December 1979), 43:50–53.

16. H. Sacks and C. Logan, *Does Parole Make a Difference?* (Hartford, Conn.: Connecticut School of Law Press, 1979) and M. Sigler, "Abolish Parole?" *Federal Probation* (June 1975), 34:42–48.

5. Dilemmas of Kinship

1. For a further discussion, see Jonathan H. Turner, *Patterns of Social Organization: A Survey of Social Institutions* (New York: McGraw-Hill, 1972); Randall Collins, *Family Sociology: Gender, Love, and Property* (Chicago: Nelson-Hall, 1985).

2. William J. Goode, *World Revolution and Family Patterns* (New York: Free Press, 1963).

3. Ruth S. Caven, *The American Family* (New York: Crowell, 1969).

4. Robin M. Williams, Jr., *American Society,* 3d ed. (New York: Knopf, 1970), pp. 69–74; Turner, *Patterns,* pp. 97–98.

5. Turner, *Patterns,* p. 99.

6. Andrew Cherlin, *Marriage, Divorce, and Remarriage* (Cambridge, Mass.: Harvard University Press, 1981).

7. Ibid.

8. Kingsley Davis, "The American Family in Relation to Demographic Change," in C. F. Westoff and R. Parke, eds., *Demographic and Social Aspects of Population Growth* (Washington, D.C.: Government Printing Office, 1972).

9. Cherlin, *Marriage;* Randall Collins, *Family Sociology.*

10. Collins, *Family Sociology.*

11. Ibid.

6. Problems of Education in the Technocratic Society

1. For a more detailed analysis, see Jonathan H. Turner, *Patterns of Social Organization* (New York: McGraw-Hill, 1976); Gerhard Lenski and Jean Lenski, *Societies* (New York: McGraw-Hill, 1982).

2. Talcott Parsons, "Family Structure and the Socialization of the Child," in T. Parsons and R. F. Bales, eds., *Family, Socialization, and Interaction Process* (New York: Free Press, 1955).

3. A. H. Halsey, "The Sociology of Education," in N. J. Smelser, ed., *Sociology* (New York: Wiley, 1976).

4. Burton R. Clark, *Educating the Expert Society* (San Francisco: Chandler, 1962); and Halsey, "Sociology of Education."

5. Randall Collins, *The Credential Society: A Historical Sociology of Education and Stratification* (New York: Academic Press, 1979).

6. W. V. Grant and L. J. Eiden, *Digest of Education Statistics, 1982* (Washington, D.C.: Government Printing Office, 1983), pp. 1–2.

7. Robin M. Williams, Jr., *American Society: A Sociological Interpretation*, 3d ed. (New York: Knopf, 1970), pp. 433–39. See also chapter 1 in this book.

8. John Holt, *The Underachieving School* (New York: Dell, 1972); and R. Peters, *Authority, Responsibility, and Education* (New York: Paul S. Eriksson, 1973), pp. 140–56.

9. Charles E. Silberman, *Crisis in the Classroom* (New York: Random House, 1970), pp. 113–57; E. Z. Friedenberg, *Coming of Age in America* (New York: Random House, 1963), pp. 155–88.

10. John I. Goodlad, "The Schools vs. Education," *Saturday Review,* April 19, 1969.

11. Jonathan H. Turner, *American Society: Problems of Structure* (New York: Harper and Row, 1972), pp. 196–204.

12. Collins, *Credential Society.*

13. Grant and Eiden, *Digest,* p. 66.

14. Silberman, *Crisis in the Classroom,* p. 60; also see S. Bowles, "Unequal Education and the Reproduction of the Social Division of Labor," in E. and M. Useem, *The Education Establishment* (Englewood Cliffs, N.J.: Prentice-Hall, 1974), pp. 17–43.

15. Silberman, *Crisis in the Classroom,* pp. 98–112.

16. National Commission on Excellence in Education, *A Nation at Risk* (Washington, D.C.: Government Printing Office, 1983).

17. These data are taken from Grant and Eiden, *Digest.*

18. John Kenneth Galbraith, *The New Industrial State* (Boston: Houghton Mifflin, 1971).

19. Collins, *Credential Society.*

20. Grant and Eiden, *Digest,* pp. 1, 92.

7. Wealth and Poverty in America

1. There are, of course, exceptions. For example, see William Domhoff, *Who Rules America?* (Englewood Cliffs, N.J.: Prentice-Hall, 1967) and *Who Really Governs?* (Santa Monica: Goodyear, 1978).

2. Jonathan H. Turner, *Societal Stratification: A Theoretical Analysis* (New York: Columbia University Press, 1984).

3. Gerhard Lenski, *Power and Privilege: A Theory of Stratification* (New York: McGraw-Hill, 1966).

4. As Lenski documents, and as I also analyze in *Societal Stratification,* inequality in some resources, particularly material wealth, and power, is curvilinear; it increases with initial increases in productivity in human societies and declines slightly with industrial and postindustrial production.

5. In fact, prestige is often given as a way to compensate those without power and material wealth.

6. Turner, *Societal Stratification*.

7. For a summary of these, see Robin M. Williams, Jr., *American Society: A Sociological Interpretation*, 3d ed. (New York: Knopf, 1970), pp. 452–53. See also Jonathan H. Turner and Charles Starnes, *Inequality: Privilege and Poverty in America* (Santa Monica: Goodyear, 1976).

8. For a more recent effort to understand wealth issues historically, see Jeffrey Williamson and Peter Lindert, *American Inequality: A Macro-Economic History* (New York: Academic Press, 1980). See also Jonathan H. Turner's review essay on this work: "Trends in American Inequality: Economic vs. Sociological Models," *Contemporary Sociology* (September 1982), 11:528–32.

9. Jonathan H. Turner, *Social Problems in America* (New York: Harper and Row, 1976), p. 201. See also, Turner and Starnes, *Inequality*, pp. 82–87.

10. For a comparative analysis, see Donald Treiman, *Occupational Prestige in Comparative Perspective* (New York: Academic Press, 1977).

11. Robert K. Merton, *Social Theory and Social Structure* (New York: Free Press, 1968).

12. For a review of the literature on social class position and beliefs, see James Kluegel and Eliot Smith, "Beliefs About Stratification," in A. Inkeles, et al., eds., *Annual Reviews in Sociology, Volume 7* (Palo Plto: Annual Reviews, 1981), pp. 29–56.

13. This discussion is from Turner and Starnes, *Inequality*.

14. Ibid.

15. This discussion borrows from Leonard Beeghley's more extensive analysis in his *Living Poorly in America* (New York: Praeger, 1984). See also Joe R. Feagin, *Subordinating the Poor* (Englewood Cliffs, N.J.: Prentice-Hall, 1976); Herbert Gans, "The Positive Functions of Poverty," *American Journal of Sociology* (September 1972), 78:275–89; Joe Thomas, *Profiles of Families in Poverty* (Washington, D.C.: Center for Social Policy, 1982); Loretta Schwartz-Nobel, *Starving in the Shadow of Plenty* (New York: Putnam, 1981).

16. For example, in the late 1950s and early 1960s Michael Harrington's *The Other America* (1962; Baltimore: Penguin Books, 1971) galvanized public sentiment in favor of helping the poor. By 1970, the sentiment reversed itself; and in the early 1980s, in the midst of a severe recession, there was little sentiment to do something about poverty. See Hazel Erskine, "The Polls: Government Role in Welfare," *Public Opinion Quarterly* (Summer 1975), 39:257–74.

17. Mollie Orshansky, "How Poverty is Measured," *Monthly Labor Review* (February 1969), p. 38. See also her "Documentation of Background Information and Rationale for Current Poverty Matrix, Technical Paper no. 1 for *The Measure of Poverty* (Washington, D.C.: Department of Health, Education, and Welfare, 1976), pp. 233–36.

18. Joe R. Feagin, "Poverty: We Still Believe That God Helps Those Who Help Themselves," *Psychology Today* (November 1972), 6:101; Leonard Goodwin, *Do The Poor Want to Work?* (Washington, D.C.: Brookings Institution, 1972); Joan Huber and William H. Form, *Income and Ideology: An Analysis of the American Political Formula* (New York: Free Press, 1973); Joe R. Feagin, "America's Welfare Stereotypes," *Social Science Quarterly* (March 1972), 52:921–33.

19. No doubt, many poor do suffer psychological problems and motivational apathy. But we suspect these are the minority.

20. Jonathan H. Turner, *Patterns of Social Organization* (New York: McGraw-Hill, 1972).

21. For a summary, see Mary Bryna Sanger, *Welfare of the Poor* (New York: Academic Press, 1979).

22. For a summary of these programs, see Turner, *Social Problems in America.*

23. Daniel P. Moynihan, ed., *On Understanding Poverty* (New York: Basic Books, 1969).

24. Beeghley, *Living Poorly in America.*

25. Ibid.

26. The most recent budget is found in Congressional Budget Office, *Tax Expenditures: Current Issues and Five-Year Budget Projects for Fiscal Years 1981–1985* (Washington, D.C.: Government Printing Office, April 1980).

27. Turner, *Social Problems in America* and Jonathan H. Turner, *American Society: Problems of Structure* (New York: Harper and Row, 1977); Turner and Starnes, *Inequality.*

28. Milton Friedman, *Capitalism and Freedom* (Chicago: University of Chicago Press, 1962).

29. J. A. Pechman and P. M. Timpane, eds., *Work Incentives and Income Guarantees: The New Jersey Negative Income Tax Experiment* (Washington, D.C.: Brookings Institution, 1975); Peter N. Rossi and Katherine C. Lyall, *Reforming Public Welfare: A Critique of the Negative Income Tax Experiment* (New York: Russell Sage Foundation, 1976).

8. Racial and Ethnic Antagonism

1. For example, neuro-anatomy involves so many genes on different chromosomes that it is difficult to change. In contrast, skin and eye color, facial features, height are controlled by comparatively few genes, and hence, are more readily subject to change through mutation.

2. In constructing the model in figure 8.1, and in developing the description of the processes outlined, we have borrowed from the following theoretical discussions: Herbert M. Blalock, Jr., *Toward a Theory of Minority Group Relations* (New York: Wiley, 1967); Edna M. Bonacich, "Toward a Theory of Middleman Minorities," *American Sociological Review* (March 1973), 38:583–94 and "A Theory of Ethnic Antagonism: The Split Labor Market," *American Sociological Review* (March 1972), 37:547–49; Tamotsu Shibutani and K. M. Kwan, *Ethnic Stratification: A Comparative Approach* (New York: Macmillan, 1965); Jonathan H. Turner and Edna Bonacich, "Toward a Composite Theory of Middleman Minorities," *Ethnicity* (Fall 1980), 7:144–58; Jonathan H. Turner and Royce Singleton, "A Theory of Racial Oppression," *Social Forces* (March 1978), 56:203–20; and James W. Vander Zanden, *American Minority Relations: The Sociology of Racial and Ethnic Groups,* 3d ed. (New York: Ronald Press, 1972).

3. Bonacich, "A Theory of Ethnic Antagonism."

4. Bonacich, "Toward a Theory of Middleman Minorities." Turner and Bonacich, "Toward a Composite Theory."

5. Leon Festinger, *A Theory of Cognitive Dissonance* (Evanston: Row, Peterson, 1957) and *Conflict, Decision, and Dissonance* (Stanford: Stanford University Press, 1964).

6. For analysis of this, see Turner and Singleton, "A Theory of Racial Oppression"; and Jonathan H. Turner, Royce Singleton, and David Musick, *Oppression: A Socio-history of Black-White Relations in America* (Chicago: Nelson-Hall, 1984).

7. For a more detailed analysis of the dynamics of this process, see Turner and Singleton, "A Theory of Racial Oppression"; Turner, Singleton, and Musick, *Oppression.*

8. See Jonathan H. Turner, *Social Problems in America* (New York: Harper and Row, 1977), pp. 369–70.

9. For a summary, see Jonathan H. Turner, *Patterns of Social Organization* (New York: McGraw-Hill, 1972), chapter 2.

10. Robert K. Merton, *Social Theory and Social Structure* (New York: Free Press, 1968).

11. Peter M. Blau, *Inequality and Heterogeneity: A Primitive Theory of Social Structure* (New York: Free Press, 1977).

12. U.S. Bureau of the Census, "Consumer Income" *Current Population Reports* (Washington, D.C.: Government Printing Office, 1981).

13. Gunnar Mydral, *An American Dilemma: The Negro Problem and Modern Democracy* (New York: Harper and Row, 1944).

9 Sexual Inequality and Antagonism

1. Jonathan H. Turner, *Social Problems in America* (New York: Harper and Row, 1976), p. 315.

2. U.S. Department of Labor, *Women at Work: A Chartbook,* Bulletin no. 2168 (Washington, D.C.: Government Printing Office, April 1983), p. 4.

3. Ibid., p. 6.

4. Marie Richmond-Abbot, *Masculine and Feminine* (Reading, Mass.: Addison-Wesley, 1983), pp. 226–27.

5. R. Rapoport and R. N. Rapoport, *Dual Career Families* (Baltimore: Penguin Books, 1971).

6. M. Poloma, "Role Conflict and the Married Professional Woman," in C. Safilios-Rothschild, ed., *Toward a Sociology of Women* (Lexington, Mass.: Xerox Publishing, 1972); for nonprofessionals, see: Joanne Miller and Howard H. Garrison, "Sex Roles: The Division of Labor at Home and the Workplace," *Annual Review of Sociology* (1982), 8:237–62.

7. M. Poloma and T. N. Garland, "The Married Professional Woman: A Study in the Tolerance of Domestication," *Journal of Marriage and the Family* (Fall 1971), pp. 970–83.

8. L. L. Holmstrom, *The Two-Career Family* (Cambridge, Mass.: Schenkman, 1972).

9. C. Bird, *Born Female: The High Cost of Keeping Women Down* (New York: Pocket Books, 1971). For relevant data, see U.S. Bureau of the Census, *Statistical Abstracts of the United States, 1982–83* (Washington, D. C.: Government Printing Office, 1983); see also Joan Wallach Scott, "The Mechanization of Women's Work," *Scientific American* (September 1982), 247:170–78.

10. L. R. Walum, *The Dynamics of Sex and Gender: A Sociological Perspective* (Chicago: Rand McNally, 1977), pp. 54–56.

11. Carol Whitehurst, *Women in America: The Oppressed Majority* (Santa Monica: Goodyear, 1977).

12. B. Levy, "Do Teachers Sell Girls Short?" *National Education Association Journal* (December, 1972), pp. 780–90.

13. Whitehurst, *Women in America.*

14. Cynthia Fuchs-Epstein, *Women's Place: Options and Limits in Professional Careers* (Berkeley: University of California Press, 1971).

15. D. Donlon, "The Negative Image of Women in Children's Literature," *Elementary English* (April 1972), pp. 10–22.

16. F. Howe, "Sexual Stereotypes Start Early," *Saturday Review* (October 16, 1971).

17. Whitehurst, *Women in America.*

18. Walum, *Dynamics of Sex and Gender,* p. 55.

19. Pamela Roby, "Structural and Internalized Barriers to Women in Higher Education," in Safilios-Rothschild, *Toward a Sociology of Women;* Cynthia Fuchs Epstein, *Women in Law* (New York: Basic Books, 1981).

20. F. D. Blau, "Women in the Labor Force: An Overview," in J. Freeman, ed., *Women: A Feminist Perspective* (Palo Alto: Mayfield, 1975).

21. Department of Labor, *Women at Work,* pp. 14, 20.

22. Ibid., p. 10.

23. Ibid., p. 8.

24. R. E. Eckert and J. E. Stecklein, "Academic Women," in A. Theodore, ed., *The Professional Woman* (Cambridge, Mass.: Schenkman, 1971).

25. Fuchs-Epstein, *Women's Place;* and J. Kosa and R. E. Coker, Jr., "The Female Physician in Public Health: Conflict and Reconciliation of Sex and Professional Roles," *Sociology and Social Research* (Winter 1975), 49:205–17.

26. Fuchs-Epstein, *Women's Place,* p. 161, and *Women in Law.*

27. W. C. Blankenship, "Head Librarians: How Many Men? How Many Women?" in Theodore, *Professional Woman,* pp. 93–102.

28. Blau, "Women in the Labor Force."

29. Whitehurst, *Women in America.*

30. Ibid.

31. Ibid.

32. Safilios-Rothschild, *Toward a Sociology of Women.*

10. The Chaotic Metropolis

1. For basic descriptions of this form, see: Amos Hawley, *Urban Society* (New York: Ronald Press, 1971); Brian Berry and John D. Kasarda *Contemporary Urban Ecology* (New York: Macmillan, 1977); Kingsley Davis, *World Urbanization, 1950–1970* (Berkeley: Institute of International Studies, 1972); John Walton and Louis H. Masotti, eds., *The City in Comparative Perspective* (Beverly Hills: Sage, 1976); Gideon Sjoberg, *The Preindustrial City* (New York: Free Press, 1965); Scientific American, *Cities: Their Origin, Growth and Human Impact* (San Francisco: W. H. Freeman, 1973).

2. Today, about 70 percent of the population lives in a "metropolitan area," although many of these areas are not large. By comparison, only 31 percent of the population lived in a "metropolitan area" in 1900. See Harry Gold, *The Sociology of Urban Life* (Englewood Cliffs, N.J.: Prentice-Hall, 1982), p. 77.

3. This is only a rough estimate, since there is some disagreement over just when urbanization was initiated. For readable descriptions of early urban centers, see Lewis Mumford, *The City in History: Its Origins, Its Transformations, and Its Prospects* (New York: Harcourt, Brace, World, 1961); John Pfeiffer, *The Emergence of Society* (New York: McGraw-Hill, 1977); Jane Jacobs, *The Economy of Cities* (New York: Random House, 1969); Jane Dora Hamblin, *The First Cities* (New York: Time-Life, 1973).

4. For a more detailed analyses, see Jonathan H. Turner, *Patterns of Social Organization* (New York: McGraw-Hill, 1972) and "A Cybernetic Model of Economic Development," *Sociological Quarterly* (Spring 1971), 12:191–203.

5. For descriptions of these, see Pfeiffer, *Emergence of Society*.

6. Prominent examples include Los Angeles and Orange Counties in California.

7. Anselm L. Strauss, *Images of the American City* (New York: Free Press, 1961), p. 91.

8. Arthur Schlesinger, "The City in American History," in P. Hatt and A. Reiss, eds., *Reader in Urban Sociology* (New York: Free Press, 1951).

9. Strauss, *Images*.

10. R. F. Allen and C. H. Adair, *Violence and Riots in Urban America* (Worthington, Ohio: C. A. Jones, 1969), p. 31.

11. C. M. Green, *The Rise of Urban America* (New York: Harper and Row, 1965). For a shortened account, see J. L. Spates and J. J. Macionis, *The Sociology of Cities* (New York: St. Martin's Press, 1982), pp. 200–37.

12. Edward C. Banfield, *The Unheavenly City: The Nature and Future of Our Urban Crisis* (Boston: Little, Brown, 1970).

13. Scott Greer, *Urban Renewal and American Cities: The Dilemma of Democratic Intervention* (Indianapolis: Bobbs-Merrill, 1966).

14. Karl E. Taeber and Alma F. Taeber, *Negroes in Cities: Residential Segregation and Neighborhood Change* (Chicago: Aldine, 1965).

11. America in the World System

1. For major reference points in the study of the world system, see Immanuel Wallerstein, *The Modern World System: Capitalist Agriculture and the Origins of the European World Economy in the Sixteenth Century* (New York: Academic Press, 1974), "The Rise and Future Demise of the World Capitalist System: Concepts for Comparative Analysis," *Comparative Studies in History and Society* (September 1974), 16:387–415, "World-System Analysis: Theoretical and Interpretive Issues," in B. H. Kaplan, ed., *Social Change in the Capitalist World Economy* (Beverly Hills: Sage, 1978), pp. 219–35, and *The Capitalist World Economy* (Cambridge: Cambridge University Press, 1979); Walter C. Goldfrank, ed., *The World System of Capitalism: Past and Present* (Beverly Hills: Sage, 1979); Terence K. Hopkins and Immanuel Wallerstein, eds., *Processes of the World System* (Beverly Hills: Sage, 1980).

2. Much of the study of political economy has been usurped by Marxian thinkers and involves an explicit and implicit critique of capitalism as a form of social organization. Our use of these terms is intended to be more neutral, since no one has ever accused the authors of being Marxists.

3. See Wallerstein, *The Modern World System.*

4. Of course, many critics would not view this as cause for great alarm. However, volatile political processes could indeed involve nuclear weapons, which is, to understate the matter, cause for concern.

5. In state-capitalist systems such as the Soviet Union, such is formally and assuredly the case, since most capital is owned and managed by government. But less centralized governments also act in ways to protect the interests of their multinationals overseas.

6. The origin of this concept and the related notion of periphery is found in the U.N. Economic Commission on Latin America in the late 1940s and 1950s. It was Wallerstein's *The Modern World System,* that brought it into more general usage and, we might add, gave Marxist analysis of capitalism new life. See also the discussion by Terence K. Hopkins, "The Study of the Capitalist World-Economy," in Goldfrank, *The World System of Capitalism.* For other basic works on the dynamics of core capital, see P. Baran and P. Sweezy, *Monopoly Capital* (New York: Monthly Review Press, 1968); R. J. Barrett and R. E. Muller, *Global Reach* (New York: Simon and Schuster, 1974); M. Barret-Brown, *The Economics of Imperialism* (Harmondsworth, Eng.: Penguin, 1974); A. G. Frank, *Dependent Accumulation and Underdevelopment* (New York: Monthly Review Press, 1979).

7. For interesting articles on these processes see Part 1 of "The World Social Economy: Cycles and Trends," in Hopkins and Wallerstein, *Processes of the World System,* pp. 9–126.

8. Ruth Leger Sivard, *World Military and Social Expenditures, 1981* (Leesberg, Va.: World Priorities, 1981), p. 17.

9. See, for analysis, S. Amin, *Unequal Development* (New York: Monthly Review Press, 1970); Barret-Brown, *Economics of Imperialism; Marxist Theories of Imperialism* (London: Routledge and Kegan Paul, 1980); A. G. Frank, *Dependent Accumulation.*

10. See, for analysis and commentary, Raymond Vernon, *Storm over the Multinationals: The Real Issue* (Cambridge, Mass.: Harvard University Press, 1977) and *Sovereignty at Bay: The Multinational Spread of U.S. Enterprises* (Harmondsworth, Eng.: Penguin, 1971); Michael Taylor and Nigel Thrift, eds., *The Geography of Multinationals* (New York: St. Martin's Press, 1982); Don Wallace, Jr., *International Regulation of Multinational Corporations* (New York: Praeger, 1976); M. Tharakan, *The New International Division of Labour and Multinational Companies* (Farnborough, Eng.: Saxon House, 1980); J. H. Dunning and K. O. Haberich, *The World Directory of Multinational Enterprises* (The Hague: Sijthoff and Noordhoff, 1980).

11. See Jonathan H. Turner, *Societal Stratification: A Theoretical Analysis* (New York: Columbia University Press, 1984), chs. 4–6.

12. Spencer and Simmel were probably the earliest sociological thinkers to give formal expression to this idea. See Herbert Spencer, *Principles of Sociology* (1874–96; New York: D. Appleton, 1892–98), and Georg Simmel, "Conflict" in K. Wolff, ed., *Conflict and the Web of Group Affiliations* (1908; New York: Free Press, 1955).

13. W. Richard Scott, *Organizations: Rational, Natural, and Open Systems* (Englewood Cliffs, N.J.: Prentice-Hall, 1981), pp. 313–15.

14. Indeed, they too become aware of, and increasingly committed to, Western values of "activism," "achievement," and "progress," creating a culture of "rising expectations."

15. Ruth Leger Sivard, *World Military and Social Expenditures, 1981* (Leesburg, Va.: World Priorities, 1981). See also R. L. Sivard, *Military Budgets and Social Needs: Setting World Priorities* (New York: Public Affairs Committee, 1977). Statements and data in the next two paragraphs are extracted from these reports.

16. Grandiose proclamations have, of course, typified the American experience—from the Declaration of Independence to the Monroe Doctrine. And American "gunboat diplomacy" was well known in the nineteenth and early twentieth centuries.

17. See, for example, Sivard, *World Military and Social Expenditures*, p. 17.

18. See chapter 2 for a fuller discussion.

19. Seymour Melman, *Pentagon Capitalism: The Political Economy of War* (New York: McGraw-Hill, 1970).

20. Sivard, *World Military and Social Expenditures*, p. 19.

21. Stanley Lieberson, "An Empirical Study of Military-Industrial Linkages," *The American Journal of Sociology* (November 1971), pp. 718–30; Melman, *Pentagon Capitalism*.

22. Jonathan H. Turner, *American Society: Problems of Structure* (New York: Harper and Row, 1972), pp. 168–70.

23. Ibid., p. 169; see also R. Kauffman, "The Military Industrial Complex," *The New York Times Magazine* (April 9, 1969).

24. Turner, *American Society*, p. 169; see also "Servants or Masters," *Los Angeles Times,* July 10, 1983.

25. In 1984 budget, the increase in defense spending, coupled with a tax cut and lowered tax revenues from a deep recession, created a deficit of over $200 billion—the largest in American history.

26. Sivard, *World Military and Social Expenditures*, p. 17.

27. Ibid.

28. Ibid.

29. The following is a partial listing of the general world treaties that have been signed by more than 20 nations to control nuclear weapons: Antarctic Treaty (1959); Outer Space Treaty (1967), Latin American Nuclear-Free Zone Treaty (1967), Non-Proliferation Treaty (1971), Seabed Treaty (1971). The following are agreements between the U.S. and USSR: the Hot Line Agreement (1963), Accidents Measures Agreement (1971), Prevention of Nuclear War Agreement (1973), Partial Test Ban Treaty (1963), Threshold Test Ban Treaty (1974), Peaceful Nuclear Expositions Treaty (1976), ABM (SALT I) and Protocol (1972), Salt I Interior Agreement (1972), SALT II (1979, but never ratified by the U.S.).

12. Ecological Processes and Survival of the Species

1. For basic references, see Paul Ehrlich, J. P. Holdren, and Richard W. Holm, *Man and the Ecosphere* (San Francisco: Freeman, 1971); E. J. Kormondy, *Concepts of Ecology* (Englewood Cliffs, N.J.: Prentice-Hall, 1969); Otis D. Duncan and A. Schnore, "The Eco-system," in R. A. Faris, ed., *Handbook of Sociology* (Chicago: Rand

McNally, 1964); Paul Ehrlich, Richard W. Holm, and Irene C. Brow, *Biology and Society* (New York: McGraw-Hill, 1976).

2. Adapted from Jonathan H. Turner, "The Eco-system: The Interrelationship of Society and Nature," in D. H. Zimmerman, D. L. Wieder, and S. Zimmerman, eds., *Understanding Social Problems* (New York: Praeger, 1976), pp. 292–321.

3. Ibid.; see also Jonathan H. Turner, *Social Problems in America* (New York: Harper and Row, 1970) and *American Society: Problems of Structure* (New York: Harper and Row, 1976).

4. Turner, "The Eco-system."

5. See "EPA Says 2,200 Sites May Vie in Superfund," Denver *Rocky Mountain News,* May 22, 1984, p. 22.

6. Kenneth Boulding, "No Second Chance for Man," in *The Crisis of Survival* (Glencoe, Ill.: Scott, Foresman, 1970).

Index